The
RISK
THEATRE
MODEL
of
TRAGEDY

Gambling, Drama, and the Unexpected

EDWIN WONG

◆ FriesenPress

Suite 300 - 990 Fort St
Victoria, BC, V8V 3K2
Canada

www.friesenpress.com

ISBN
978-1-5255-3755-4 (Hardcover)
978-1-5255-3756-1 (Paperback)
978-1-5255-3757-8 (eBook)

1. DRAMA
2. LITERARY CRITICISM / SEMIOTICS & THEORY
3. PERFORMING ARTS / THEATER-PLAYWRITING

Distributed to the trade by The Ingram Book Company

Printed in Canada

For Melpomene, that Muse the Muses among

Contents

PART III
A POETICS OF TRAGEDY

ACKNOWLEDGMENTS

W hat should have been ostensibly the easiest part of the book to write, for one reason or another, seemed the most difficult to the point where I was hoping this page would write itself, or, worse yet, that this page was unwanted and unnecessary because the people to whom I was most indebted would not want to be associated with this questionable book. But, we know that the labours involved in producing a book, even if credited to a single author, is never the product of one individual, but rather is the culmination of many conversations spoken in many places over many years. The role of the author is perhaps to interpret and record these conversations, subordinating some of them, while augmenting, highlighting, developing, and idealizing others. The result is that a book is not the work of one hand, but rather, of many hands.

In this light, a book without an acknowledgement page would be as curious a thing as a book without footnotes, and footnotes have always been an author's prerogative, a way not only for the author to give thanks to the community of other authors, but also to show the reader something of the work's intellectual etymology. But not all debts are strictly intellectual debts. Even if the author's undertaking has been to record, interpret, and build on conversations—whether spoken or in print—it is still a hair-pulling process full of wrong turns and dead ends. To finish a book really requires a bit of luck and much friendly encouragement.

My first two attempts to write a theory of tragedy were failures. In the first two attempts, I had tried to create a model of tragedy based on the antagonism between the protagonist, who, with his suffering, wants to be the king of pain to spite the world, and the consoler, who, in telling the protagonist that all sorts of other people suffer, invites the sufferer to rejoin the community at large. This approach to tragedy is based on the Middle Comic poet Timocles' view that tragedy helps us bear our trials more easily by showing us the suffering of others. While I agree with this view, it felt strained to base an entire theory of tragedy around the antagonism between sufferers and consolers. The skeletal frame of the idea worked, but there wasn't quite enough meat on the bones.

It wasn't until the winter of 2006 that the lucky break-through happened. I was finishing my master's thesis at Brown University. At that time, I loved wandering around the big Borders bookstore in Providence Place Mall. And it was there in the finance and economics section that Nassim Taleb's *Fooled by Randomness: The Hidden Role of Chance in Life and in the Markets* jumped out at me. Its message was that, when you least expect, highly improbable events could ruin you. And immediately, I realized two things: first, that tragedy could be looked at as a theatre of risk, and second, that after I finished writing my thesis, I would need to start building a new theory from the ground up, one based on uncertainty and chance.

Now, fortunately one of my elementary school teachers had put it into my brain in grade 7 that I would write a book one day. That teacher was Mr. Durrance. And it is very likely that it was because the idea of writing a book had been in my head for such a long time that I persevered. So, it is fitting to begin by acknowledging Doug Durrance. Of course, at that time, I had no idea what kind of book I would write. That would come later.

The idea of writing a theory of tragedy came four years later when I read Nietzsche's *The Birth of Tragedy*. For various reasons, he appealed to me. He was an existentialist. He had gone mad. His philosophy was dangerous. Although I had never read an ancient Greek tragedy, and knew nothing about tragic choruses and dancing satyrs, the book had me in its grip. It was his style. His style is like the style of no other. He wrote as if the fate of modernity and culture depended on how tragedy was interpreted. Aesthetic phenomena were all-important. At that moment, I knew what kind of book I would write. Nietzsche may not be the most persuasive writer. But he is, bar none, the most convinced writer.

Nietzsche, before he became a philosopher, was a classicist, or, in those days, a philologist. He studied Greek and Latin. To follow his footsteps, I would have to learn Greek and Latin (and perhaps German) as well. In the fall of 2000, I quit my job plumbing and enrolled in the Department of Greek and Roman Studies at the University of Victoria. Here, many friends and mentors helped me along, and it brings warm memories to thank Debbie Almisurati, Katey

Boal, Peter Gölz, Ingrid Holmberg, Gregory Rowe, Terry Scarborough, Leslie Shumka, and Denise Wadsworth. My greatest debt of gratitude during these happy years belongs to Laurel Bowman. I learned of the art of tragedy from her, and, not only that, by working as her research assistant, I learned of the rigours of conducting true academic research.

The next stop was Brown University, which was made possible by a generous Joukowsky Fellowship. I would like to thank David Konstan for showing me the wonders than a searching and inquisitive mind can achieve. I would also like to thank Charles Fornara, who supervised my thesis. To this day, the sharpness of his analytic mind holds me in awe. Next, it is a pleasure to thank Adam Bravo and Peter Lech for their friendship. And, it always brings a smile to my face to recall Asya Chernyak (now Sigelman) and our conversations on art, music, literature, and theology. Sometimes I wonder, if people still talk with that degree of conviction we once held.

After eight fairy-tale years in academia, it became time to become a civilian again. I'm indebted to Roni Kratzmann for getting me an interview at Bayside Mechanical. At Bayside, I'd like to thank Peter Desaulniers, Tor Hansen, and Ray Draper for sharing their insights on project management, estimating, and business. After leaving Bayside to finish this book, a few years later, I was hired by PML Professional Mechanical. At PML, thanks to Gord McLaren, I work a flexible schedule, and this freedom has been invaluable. My time at Bayside and PML has helped fund the book and the theatre competition. Without the opportunities there, this project would have been impossible.

In the last year, I've had the opportunity to take risk theatre on the road. Audiences at the University of Calgary, the University of Massachusetts, Boston, the University of Victoria, and at the Society for Classical Studies AGM have provided valuable feedback. I'm deeply indebted to both the attendees for their suggestions and to the organizers for inviting me to share this exciting new vision of theatre.

Next, it gives me great pleasure to thank my friends for their advice and the intrepid readers who read and commented on the text at various stages of development. Input from Emily Armstrong, Farideh Borgi, Natalia Cherepneva, Elaine Davies, Carla DeSantis, Mark Grill, Lyn Hewett, Jenny Hildebrand, Emma Kelly, Chad MacKay, Michael Routliffe, and Damian Tarnopolsky have dramatically benefitted the book. I would also like to say thank you to Kim Schacht and Sarah Mitchell at Friesen Press for guiding me through the publishing process.

In October 2017, while I was thinking of ways of putting risk theatre on a practical footing, I had the good fortune of meeting Michelle Buck, the general manager of Langham Court Theatre. She introduced me to Keith Digby, who, in turn, brought Michael Armstrong onto the team. A short seven months later in June 2018, the Risk Theatre Modern Tragedy Competition was inaugurated. Its purpose is to promote the writing and production of risk theatre plays. Seven months from conception to inauguration for a major new playwright competition was an exceptionally aggressive target and it is a testimony to the time and effort put in by Michelle, Keith, and Michael that everything came together. I would like to thank Langham Court Theatre for hosting the competition and the team for their hard work. Thanks to them, risk theatre has achieved that elusive goal of combining theory with practice.

In closing, I would to thank my son, Erik Kratzmann-Wong and my parents, Yan-Ting and Grace Wong for their unflagging encouragement and support. It has been a great pleasure to remember you all here, because this book stands as a tribute to all the goodness you have shown me.

PREFACE

Tragedy today is a tired art. It no longer earns the attention and publicity that it did in previous ages. It used to be held in the highest regard. Milton considered it "the gravest, moralest, and most profitable" of poems.[1] No longer. The spectators queuing for the tragic theatre are few and far between and the dramatists working on tragedy even fewer. Eugene O'Neill, the last of the true tragedians—the ones descended from Aeschylus who were big, bold, and perhaps a little wooden in their delivery—perished in 1953.[2] The last great tragic epoch dates further back to the late eighteenth and early nineteenth century Germany, the Germany of Lessing, Schiller, and Goethe. That was long ago. To find an age when tragedy was the greatest show on earth, we have to go back even further, back to Marlowe and Shakespeare's England, back to the late sixteenth and early seventeenth century, back to the glory that was *Dr. Faustus* and *Macbeth*. What has happened between now and then?

---

1   Milton, preface to *Samson Agonistes*, p. 1.

2   O'Neill's ties with the ancients included writing trilogies (e.g., *Mourning Becomes Electra*) and staging mask plays (e.g., *The Great God Brown*).

THE WORKING MODEL

Then, dramatists laboured, apprenticed, and worked in the way carpenters, plumbers, and other tradespeople do now. Just as carpenters today build houses by reading blueprints, dramatists then would construct tragedies by reading and interpreting a template of tragedy, otherwise known as a working model. A blueprint of a single-family dwelling not only reflects the idea or theory of a house (it sits on a foundation, trusses support the roof, it has plumbing and electrical components, etc.), but it also specifies how a house is put together (wood framing or steel stud, plastic or copper water pipes, etc.). Like a set of blueprints, a working model of tragedy combines the theory, or philosophy, of tragedy with real-world considerations of how tragedy is written. The ultimate aim of a working model is to furnish the builders of tragedy with a template.

Working models come in many forms. A working model can be a play itself. Just as it is possible to learn house building by taking apart an existing house, when Roman tragedies were rediscovered at the turn of the fourteenth century, the Italian Latinists were able to write tragedies by imitating Seneca.[3] A working model can also be a guidebook, otherwise known as a how-to guide. Aristotle's *Poetics*, the most famous working model of tragedy, is a guidebook.

In the *Poetics*, Aristotle lays down tragedy's specifications. For evidence of his influence, look to the prefaces of *Samson Agonistes* and *Phaedra*, or to the *Three Discourses on Dramatic*

---

3   On the influence of Senecan tragedy on Mussato, Loschi, Dati, and others, see the discussion in Kelly, *Ideas and Forms of Tragedy from Aristotle to the Middle Ages*, 185-93.

Poetry where Milton, Racine, and Corneille pay him homage.[4] The *Poetics* gave them the stricture of the unities; it advised them of the sort of characters audiences clamoured after; it directed them to write plots arousing pity and fear to bring about the catharsis of pity and fear. A working model acts like an engine: pour into its motor words, verbs, and adjectives, and it fabricates plays that move the soul. *Then*, dramatists such as Milton, Racine, and Corneille had a working model. *Now*, modern dramatists lack one. "There was no model I could adapt for this play," writes Miller in the preface to *Death of a Salesman*, "no past history for the kind of work I felt it could become."[5] To have, or not to have a blueprint or a working model: that is the difference between now and then.

If the tragedians had a working model in the *Poetics*, what happened? There may be one, or a multitude of reasons for its decline. Perhaps its tale had gone stale. Or it could be that modern dramatists wanted change, wanted to speak with their own voice. Or perhaps serious playwrights shunned it because screenwriters subsequently claimed it for themselves. As titles such as *Aristotle's Poetics for Screenwriters* attest, Hollywood usurped its potential for use on the silver

---

4   Milton, preface to *Samson Agonistes*, pp. 1-2; Racine, preface to *Phaedra*, trans. John Cairncross, pp. 145-7; Corneille, "On the Uses and Elements of Dramatic Poetry," trans. Beatrice Stewart MacClintock, in *European Theories of the Drama*, 100-10; Corneille, "Discourse on Tragedy and of the Methods of Treating It, According to Probability and Necessity," in *Dramatic Essays of the Neoclassic Age*, 2-34; Corneille, "Of the Three Unities of Action, Time, and Place," trans. Donald Schier, in *The Continental Model: Selected French Critical Essays of the Seventeenth Century*, 101-15.

5   Miller, preface to *Death of a Salesman*, xi.

screen.[6] Whatever the case, independent dramatists searching for a unique voice had to look elsewhere. For their purposes, the *Poetics* had been exhausted.

But what happens in the absence of a working model? If we look at Germany in the sixteenth and seventeenth century, when the spirit of tragedy descended on the likes of Gryphius, Lohenstein, and Hallmann, the best they could produce was the *Trauerspiel* or "mourning play"—a distant second cousin to tragedy: the *Poetics*, at that time, was unavailable in Germany.[7] Likewise, the Roman novelist Apuleius recounted the caricature of itself that tragedy had become in the second century AD after provincial theories had displaced the classical model of tragedy:

"What's this?" I asked. "What kind of a woman is this redoubtable Queen of a tavernkeeper?"
"She is a witch," he said. "She is superhuman, able to drag down the heavens or lift up the earth, to harden running water or to dissolve mountains, to raise the dead or to tumble down the gods, to poke out the stars or to light up the darkness of hell."
"Now, now," said I, "please draw the tragic curtain, and dispense with the drop-scene, and speak plainly."[8]

---

6   Tierno, *Aristotle's Poetics for Screenwriters*.

7   On the insignificance of the influence of Aristotle on the *Trauerspiel*, see Benjamin, *Origin of German Tragic Drama*, trans. John Osborne, 60–2.

8   Apuleius, *The Golden Ass*, trans. Jack Lindsay, 37.

It is clear that, in the absence of an appropriate working model, there is a danger of the spectacle overtaking the art: in Apuleius' time, "tragedy" had become a byword for extravagant excess.[9]

Compared with the fame of Milton's *Samson Agonistes* and the enduring bright-lights, big-city productions of Corneille's *The Cid* and Racine's *Phaedra*, the relative obscurity of the *Trauerspiel* and the complete obscurity of second century Roman tragedy testify to the powerlessness of tragic drama in the absence of a working model. As a result, modern tragedians have had two choices, both unhappy: either make up for the lack of direction by increasing the spectacle (at the expense of art), or assume the dual role of writer and theorizer (thus increasing their labour). The writers of *Trauerspiele* chose the former. Miller chose the latter and succeeded. But how many others could rise to the occasion?

To fill the void left by the rejection of the *Poetics*, a proliferation of anti-Aristotelian models arose in the twentieth century: metatheatre, the Theatre of the Absurd, epic theatre, and the tragedy of the common man.[10] If Aristotle said that drama should do something, modern plays would do nothing. If Aristotle said that heroes should be noble, modern heroes would be proles. If Aristotle said that there should be an

---

9   On the evolution of tragic theory in late Roman Antiquity, see Kelly, *Ideas and Forms of Tragedy from Aristotle to the Middle Ages*, 16-35.

10   Abel, *Metatheatre: A New View of Dramatic Form*; Esslin, *The Theatre of the Absurd*; on epic theatre see Brecht, "A Short Organum for the Theatre," in *Brecht on Theatre*, trans. John Willett, 179-205; Miller, "Tragedy and the Common Man," in *The Theater Essays of Arthur Miller*, 3-7.

emotional bond between protagonist and audience, these modern writers would alienate audiences. These models found their voice by turning the *Poetics* upside down and inside out in an act of deliberate sabotage. The writers of anti-Aristotelian working models wanted change and effected change. But, as they sought change by banging on drums and hurling horses off cliffs, they paid a price.

In turning the *Poetics* on its head, the new working models turned their backs on tradition. As a result, modern theatre resembles the music of the *ars nova* in the fourteenth century or the *nuove musiche* of the early seventeenth century, when musicians dislocated the tonal centre and practiced avant-garde trips in rhythmic modes. But the novelty that such musicians gained by turning away from the tonalities, rhythms, and forms of tradition made it difficult for audiences to appreciate their strange sounds. For this reason, their new art forms were unsustainable; their compositions lacked the endurance of musical structures rooted in tradition such as the Gregorian chant, the fugue, and the sonata-allegro form. Novelty came at the price of intransience. Like these fleeting musical forms, twentieth century tragedy has also become unstable and experimental. Instead of conforming to audience expectations, it provokes audiences to riot.[11]

---

11   As was the case on the July 28, 1929 premiere of Brecht's *The Baden-Baden Lesson on Consent*. See Esslin, *Brecht: The Man and His Work*, 47:

> In the course of an interlude, designed to demonstrate man's inhumanity to man, a huge figure on stilts has his arms and legs sawed off by two clowns. During the first performance of the *Badener Lehrstueck* members of the audience fainted during the course of this gruesome scene with

Though bold and brash, it fails to endure because, in its defiance, it goes against the grain. For tragedy to rise again, what is needed is a working model that is both original *and* rooted in tradition.

RISK THEATRE

And that is precisely what I intend to do in this volume—propose a new working model of tragedy—*risk theatre*. As a neoclassical model of tragedy, risk theatre revives the best ages of the art: fifth century Athens, the English Renaissance, and the German Romantics. My theory of risk theatre draws its inspiration from the tragic corpus, since tragedy—from Oedipus and the plague to Hamlet and the ghost of his father—concerns itself with the management and mitigation of risk. By consulting the oracle and verifying the ghost's claims, for example, Oedipus and Hamlet both attempt to control risk; their failure is what makes tragedy tragic. Strategy leads to tragedy.

My term *risk theatre* derives from the notion that risk is central to the idea of tragedy. Risk theatre posits that each dramatic act is also a gambling act. Thus, the tragic occurs

---

its reminiscence of Brecht's experiences in the Augsburg military hospital. The then grand old man of the German theatre, Gerhart Hauptmann, left in disgust.

See also, Hayman, *Brecht: A Biography*, 143, quoting Theo Lingen, who played the role of Smith, the clown on stilts:

For the audience that was really too much. And as they sawed my head off . . . it started the biggest riot I've ever seen in a theatre. Everything that wasn't nailed to the walls flew to the stage. My fellow-actors fled . . .

when risk runs awry, and risk theatre entertains by dramatizing this risk. But, if tragedy had dramatized risk from the
beginning, and had continued to do so ever since, why did
this theory of risk theatre take so long to arrive? Theories
are products of their age, and nothing can stop a theory
whose time has come. But theories are also timely creations,
and cannot come before their time. Like other theories, risk
theatre had to bide its time. Take, for example, the theory of
thermodynamics and the theory of probability. The underlying principle of thermodynamics, that friction produces heat,
has been known since prehistoric times when cave dwellers
started fires by rubbing sticks together. But the theory of
thermodynamics only arose in the 1800s. Why? The answer
is twofold. First, there had been no use for it before that
time. Second, the advent of the Industrial Revolution with
its steam engines and miles of metal tracks made a theory
of thermodynamics indispensable: that theory arose in the
1800s because its time had come.

Like thermodynamics, an intuitive understanding of probability has been around for a long time. "To succeed in many
things, or many times, is difficult," says Aristotle, "for instance,
to repeat the same throw ten thousand times with the dice
would be impossible, whereas to make it once or twice is
comparatively easy."[12] Aristotle knows what every gambler
knows: the longer the streak, the more improbable the streak.
The realization of this fact, however, did not culminate in
a theory of probability until the 1600s. The reason? The
1600s saw the birth of an empirical spirit when the scientific

12   Aristotle, *On the Heavens*, trans. W. K. C. Guthrie, 292a29-31.

method began to displace the role of fate and fortune. It was a time of observation, measurement, and analysis, a time when Cardano and Tartaglia could lay down a mathematical basis of probability by recording the results of many dice throws. Probability theory arose in the 1600s not because probability was unknown before, but because its time had come.[13]

Risk theatre—the theory that each dramatic act in tragedy is a gambling act—arises today because our present age is one of risk. It is an age of calculated risks, an age when superdrugs spawn superbugs, the reactors at Chernobyl melted down, Long-Term Capital Management rocked the global financial system, and Deepwater Horizon drilled past the point of no return. It is an age when Leviathan hid in Madoff's spreadsheets and Behemoth lurked in Monsanto's patents. It is an atom-splitting age, an age of financial and genetic engineering, and an age when low-probability, high-consequence events lie in wait.

In the past, knowledge seekers would ask the oracle what would happen in the future. Now when I look around I see that the powerful and the influential have replaced the oracle. I see how, flush with technology and brimming with confidence, they gamble with the fate of the world as they

---

13   Sambursky, "On the Possible and the Probable in Ancient Greece," 48, a historian of science, finds that the theory of probability eluded the ancient Greeks in part because they lacked the technique of the scientific method:

> It was not chance that the beginnings of systematic experimentation coincided with the inception of the theory of probability in the 16th and 17th centuries. Both have their origins in the new approach of Man to Nature which developed after the Renaissance.

manufacture the future. They know, or think they know, what will happen. Then it occurred to me that they are like the heroes of tragedy who, having surmounted great risks, also know, or think they know, what will happen. Because today's masters of the universe—like the heroes of tragedy—face the consequences of low-probability, high-consequence scenarios, I wrote this theory of risk theatre. It may be that tragedy, as ancient an art as it is, still has an important lesson to offer moderns: things may not go as planned. By seeing the paths to failure on the stage, we will do better off the stage.

The rise of risk theatre is not unlike the rise of competing theories of tragedy. Consider Nietzsche's theory of tragedy and ask yourself whether the conflict between the Apollinian and the Dionysian was not, in a way, a reflection of a burgeoning awareness of the subconscious mind. Around the same time, was Dostoyevsky not introducing the world to the concept of the irrational in novels such as *The Double?* Or consider Hegel's theory of tragedy, which saw the tragic as a collision of moral forces. Can you see in Hegel's theory a dim but sure reflection of Newton's cosmos, a cosmos full of equal and opposite reactions, full of masses colliding and forces reacting? In the same way as Hegel and Nietzsche's theories embodied the most exciting developments of their time, risk theatre is my attempt to put a modern face on an ancient art. It is because today is an age of risk that I give you the theatre of risk, the theatre where unintended consequences play out.

HEROES AS GAMBLERS

In viewing tragedy—past and present—as risk theatre, I observed that the thrill of gambling is what drives tragic heroes to hazard higher enterprise. The greater the hazard heroes take on, the more they expose themselves to the unexpected. Such tragic heroes share common ground with notorious gamblers who go too far, such as "Wild Bill" Hickok, a real-life character from the American Wild West, or Hermann, Pushkin's fictional character in his short story *The Queen of Spades*.[14] Emboldened by fortuitous beginnings, their mania rises. Laughing exuberantly, they ante up and go all-in. These characters are the gamesters; caution is reserved for losers. Like gamblers, they lay down bankrolls, challenge the unknown, throw caution to the wind, and tempt destiny. Against all odds, they hold the Fates in thrall. Seventeen times in roulette they bet red; seventeen times the ball lands on the red slot. In craps, they roll one hundred numbers and no sevens. They roll with a hot hand.

These masters of the universe scorn chance and lord it over the die; they bid the sun stand still to prolong victory day. Spectators crowd around them, some in awe and others in horror at what must happen. Then it happens. It always

---

14   "Wild Bill" Hickok was a storied gunslinger and gambler of the Wild West. In 1876, his luck caught up to him and he was shot in the back of the head while playing poker. The poker hand he was holding at the time of death, a pair of black aces on eights, is known as the "dead man's hand" and it has come to signify the impact of low-probability, high-consequence events. Hermann, in Pushkin's *Queen of Spades*, finds and tests a foolproof way to win the game of faro. But, as he goes all-in, he confronts the unexpected and goes mad. See Pushkin, *The Queen of Spades*, trans. Ethel O. Bronstein.

does: they confront the unexpected. Like "Wild Bill" in Deadwood drawing black aces on eights, one day they too draw the dead man's hand. Or, like Hermann in Moscow, the day comes for them to draw madness in three, seven, and the queen of spades. Risk theatre is where heroes go to bump heads with low-probability, high-consequence events.

In the waiting wildness of tragedy lurks the unexpected. The dead man's hand is normally harmless, lying dormant, dreaming, buried under a million combinations, forgetful of humankind. But it awakens when heroes get greedy at the no-limit table. They do not know when to quit. They *cannot* quit, urged on by the gambling spirits. They ramble, and they gamble, tempting destiny, calling out the Fates, and making a loud din.

Disturbed from its rest, the unexpected awakens, waits, bides its time, and steals up on the ones drunk on victory. Then it strikes. It can take many forms. It could be the dead man's hand, or it could be the queen of spades. Sometimes it is Birnam Wood coming to high Dunsinane Hill.[15] But whatever form it takes, the unexpected takes heroes to a place from which there is no coming back.

THE WAGER

By dramatizing the gambling act, risk theatre entertains. But it does more than simply entertain: it educates. A gallon of milk costs $4.99. But how much is the "milk of human

---

15   Shakespeare, *Macbeth*. 5.5.31-4. All references to Shakespeare's individual plays are from Shakespeare, *The Riverside Shakespeare*.

kindness" worth?[16] As a valuing mechanism, risk theatre comes up with an answer. Just as a pair of scales is a weighing mechanism, tragedy is a valuing mechanism. Scales measure weight by balancing two quantities on opposing pans, while tragedy determines value by balancing the two sides of the hero's wager. By determining the value of the all-too-human, tragedy educates.

The tragic heroes of risk theatre gamble and make wagers. Each wager has two sides: *what is staked* is put up against *what is at stake.* The hero stakes life itself to play the game, stakes intangible and all-too-human things, such as the soul, the milk of human kindness, happiness, honour, love, family, friendship, faith, reputation, and duty. What is staked has *value*, has a personal or social significance. However, its true value is unknown, just like an x in an equation: it is difficult to determine the value of life from within life. What is at stake on the other side of the wager are things external to life—what the hero desires to have but does not have. What is at stake are objects of ambition, whether tangible (such as a crown, a precious artefact, a trophy husband, a trophy wife, or a kingdom) or notional (such as power, fame, fortune, and glory). Sometimes the object comprises an action, such as

---

16   The milk of human kindness is one of Macbeth's assets which he
      lays on the line to be king:

         LADY MACBETH. Glamis thou art, and Cawdor, and shalt be
         What thou art promis'd. Yet do I fear thy nature,
         It is too full o' th' milk of human kindness
         To catch the nearest way. Thou wouldst be great,
         Art not without ambition, but without
         The illness should attend it. (Ibid., 1.5.15-20)

revenge. But whether a crown, a kingdom, or an opportunity for retaliation, objects of ambition have a known value.

When the hero makes the wager, what is staked is balanced against what is at stake. When Macbeth stakes the milk of human kindness on the crown, he brings the milk and the crown to an equilibrium. When Marlowe's Faustus stakes his immortal soul on world dominion, he balances his soul against world dominion. When Solness in Ibsen's *The Master Builder* stakes happiness on becoming the master builder, he draws an equal sign between happiness and the title of master builder. The wager represents an equal sign in the human equation.

When the hero brings to an equilibrium what is staked and what is at stake, a form of *price discovery* happens. When, Macbeth, for example, counterbalances the milk of human kindness and the crown, x is solved. When Faustus sets his soul and world dominion at an equilibrium, x is solved. When Solness balances happiness and the title of master builder on the scalepans of existence, x is solved. In this way, the hero's wager answers the question: how much is the milk of human kindness worth? The answer: it is worth one crown.

VALUE AND THE COMMODITIZATION OF LIFE

By making the wager, the heroes of risk theatre reveal life's hidden value. Life, whose fundamental value was x, now assumes a known quantity, that is, the value of that against which it is staked. The value that life assumes, however, is never expressed in monetary terms. At this point, the gambling analogy falls short, and the wagers of risk theatre diverge from those of the casino. For, in the casino, gamblers make cash wagers, while in risk theatre heroes make existential wagers.

Macbeth could have staked one hundred dollars for the crown—or one million dollars, for that matter—but he does not. Instead he stakes the milk of human kindness. This is no cash wager. By betting on his humanity, he is making an existential wager. Thus, by rejecting the cash wager, tragedy rejects the commoditization of life which occurs when wage earners concede that each hour of life is worth fifteen or twenty-five dollars. Life becomes commoditized when actuaries at life insurance companies measure existence in dollars and cents. Modern life is a commoditized life where personal worth has become an exchange value. We associate ourselves with "net worth" as though money and existence were interchangeable. This is a shame.

The commoditization of life devalues and cheapens life. When one counts out life in twenty-dollar bills, life becomes a number, something abstract; it is no longer real. A life counted out in twenty-dollar bills is worth less than the paper on which it is printed. When heroes stake the all-too-human instead of cash for objects of ambition, however, they restore dignity to life by imbuing life with human value. In ages when the commoditization of life devalues life, there is a need for tragedy. Tragedy is the art that restores dignity to life; today is the right time for tragedy to rise again.

The value that the all-too-human can assume in risk theatre is limitless. This is the genius of risk theatre. Returning to Macbeth, we see that, to him, the milk of human kindness was worth a crown. But he could have just as easily exchanged it for something else. He could have, like Faustus, wagered it for world dominion. Or, he could have, like Solness, wagered it to become the master builder. Because the all-too-human is balanced against the object of ambition in the scalepans of the hero's wager, the worth of the all-too-human is limited only by the hero's imagination. As a result, and contrary to popular belief, tragedy affirms life and has the potential to imbue it with a richness only bound by the limits of daring. My friends, do you know that life, through tragedy (and only through tragedy), may take on infinite value?

There is beauty in the simplicity of a theatre where education and pleasure come together in perfect tandem. Risk theatre educates through price discovery. By setting the all-too-human and the object of desire in apposition across the balance beam of the hero's wager, risk theatre educates by revealing life's hidden value. To reveal that, however, involves risk. The hero's wager is, after all, a bet: nothing is guaranteed. Because the outcome is uncertain, there is risk. By dramatizing this risk, risk theatre entertains. When education and pleasure come together in tandem in risk theatre, human worth becomes a function of daring.

Just as audiences delight in watching "Fast Eddie" Felson or the Cincinnati Kid lay it on the line, they will delight in watching the tragic heroes of risk theatre going forth to confront the unexpected.[17] While both heroes and gamblers think

---

17   In Tevis' novel *The Hustler*, "Fast Eddie" Felson goes head to head with legendary pool hustler "Minnesota Fats" and beats him only after losing everything. The "Cincinnati Kid" is a fictional character from Jessup's eponymous novel who encounters the unexpected when he goes all-in playing stud poker against Lancey "The Man"

one outcome will happen, something else ends up happening. This "something else" is the unexpected, and it entertains by dramatizing the complete disproportion of improbable loss in the face of the probable risks that heroes and gamblers took. There is a sense of wonder in how far they go, yet how far short of the goal they fall.

STRUCTURE

By harmoniously intertwining entertainment and instruction, tragedy is able to offer the complete package as an all-in-one extravaganza. But today, tragedy is a tired art. It fails to capture the attention and publicity that it once did. This book aims to restore this revered art to its rightful throne by inviting, in nine chapters, dramatists to write risk theatre. For without the dramatist, risk theatre remains an empty stage.

Chapter 1, "Temptation, Wager, and Cast" lays out the structure of risk theatre. Since every dramatic act resembles a gambling act, I suggest that tragic drama begins with the hero's temptation, moves to the wager, and finishes with a roll of the die. The structure is tripartite.

Chapter 2, "Tempo and Tragedy," explores the tempi of risk theatre, which I categorize as *gradual, frontloaded*, and *backloaded*. In gradual tragedies, the tripartite structure progresses in clockwork. In backloaded tragedies, the temptation and wager occur near the beginning of the drama, while the wager is delayed until the end. When all of the structural

Hodges. On the verge of victory, the Kid loses all when Lancey unexpectedly "makes the wrong move at the right time."

elements occur near the beginning, the play is said to be frontloaded. In addition, I consider the effects of the *poetics of chaos*, that is, a dramaturgical technique by which the playwright primes the audience for the troika of temptation, wager, and cast to begin. I also consider the effects of time on the quality of tragedy, and classify plays accordingly as either *active* (the action takes place in the present) or *descriptive* (the action has taken place in the past and is being summarized).

Chapter 3, "Forms of Tragedy," considers the different forms that tragedy can assume, according to my classification. In *standalone tragedy*, the process of temptation, wager, and cast plays out only once. In *parallel-motion tragedy*, multiple gambling acts occur simultaneously. And in *perpetual-motion tragedy*, one cycle of the temptation, wager, and cast begets the next.

Chapter 4, "The Myth of the Price You Pay," examines the foundation myth of risk theatre, a concept that I describe as the *myth of the price you pay*. One may receive something in exchange for something and nothing in exchange for nothing, but never something for nothing. There is no free lunch.

Chapter 5, "Four Principles of Countermonetization," describes how the hero's wager, through a process that I call *countermonetization*, reveals life's value by drawing an equal sign between life and the objects of life's ambitions. I propose that my notion of countermonetization strikes back against the commoditization of life by valuing life in the human currency of blood, sweat, and tears.

Chapter 6, "The Art of the All-in Wager," contemplates how tragedy motivates heroes to take on risk. From the minor meddlers to the supernatural accoutrements of the stage, every part of the tragic machine focuses on getting heroes to go all-in. Tragedy is interested in raising the stakes because the higher the stakes, the higher life's value. And the higher life's value, the more exciting the show. Risk theatre is the art bringing together entertainment and instruction.

Chapter 7, "The Best-Laid Plans of Mice and Men," discusses the role of the unexpected, which trips up the tragic hero and upsets even the most carefully made plans.

Chapter 8, "Us and Them," contrasts tragedy with philosophy, history, and comedy. I suggest that tragedy is tragedy because it is not philosophy, history, and comedy. Inasmuch as genres—like rivalries in sports (Boston Celtics or LA Lakers), economics (capitalism or communism), and cultures (east and west)—define themselves by what they are and what they stand for, they may also define themselves by contrasting themselves with the "other" that they are not.

Chapter 9, "Why Risk Theatre Today?" explores how the instability of the meaning of the term *tragedy* throughout the ages has paved the way for my theory of risk theatre at this specific point in time.

The nine chapters may be read thematically in a tripartite structure. The first three chapters examine tragedy from a structural perspective and answer the question, "What is tragedy?" The middle section, comprising chapters 4 and 5, approaches what one might expect from reading a philosophy of tragedy, for it answers the question, "Why is tragedy what it is?" And the third section, comprising chapters 6 and 7, explores the art of writing risk theatre—otherwise known as the poetics of tragedy—and answers the question, "How is tragedy composed?" The book then concludes by affirming the uniqueness of tragedy and its role in modernity.

To labour on an original theory of tragedy instead of summarizing, commenting on, and consolidating the tradition may be a fool's errand, but for me, no pleasure or utility is greater than that of restoring the greatest show on earth to its rightful throne. Just as exuberant risk laughs out loud at the gaming tables and in the back rooms where gamblers play cards, so too theorists cannot still their beating hearts as they anticipate the ranging of powers set into action acting and reacting with the great tradition as they make wagers with their words. But should my attempt fail, a small comfort yet remains in knowing that the failure is not mine alone; others have tried to unlock tragedy's secrets and have fallen short. Welcome to risk theatre.

Edwin Wong
Victoria, August 2018

PART I
THE STRUCTURE OF TRAGEDY
HOW RISK THEATRE IS ARRANGED

1 TEMPTATION, WAGER, AND CAST

Three-part structures endure. The three-sided triangle imparts strength to bicycle frames, as well as to the girders and gussets of the Golden Gate Bridge and the Eiffel Tower. When the Romans set up forms of worship, they created the Capitoline Triad of Jupiter, Juno, and Minerva which anchored Roman religion for eight centuries. When it was superseded, it was replaced by another powerful triune: the Trinity of Father, Son, and Holy Ghost. The many variations and combinations inherent in tripartite structures form the basis of complex systems. Harmony relies on the triad of the root, the third, and the fifth. A sonata consists of three parts: development, exposition, and recapitulation. Courtship, says Ovid, is a dance in three movements: find the girl; discover whether she likes you; see if it works.[1] Three classes constitute prerevolutionary French society: the clergy, the nobility, and the Third Estate. Executive, legislative, and judicial branches underpin government. Processes, formed by a beginning, middle, and end, are also tripartite. For example, the day

---

1   Ovid, *The Art of Love*, 1.35.8.

begins with dawn, reaches its zenith at noon, and ends with night. Life represents a three-stage journey: birth, growth, and decay. In an anthropic turn, the biological metaphor of life extends to inanimate objects: corporations, empires, and dynasties are born, rise, and fall in a three-part cycle.

Risk theatre may also be viewed as a tripartite entity. Like girders and gussets, it is enduring. Like harmony, it is ever rich in its permutations and combinations. Like empire, it is a process with a beginning, middle, and end. Because tragedy is *risk* theatre, each dramatic act is a gambling act. And just as a round of betting begins with desire, moves to the wager, and ends with the die's cast, so risk theatre's dramatic sequence also follows a three-part sequence: the hero's temptation, the hero's wager, and the hero's cast.

EXAMPLES OF THE TRAGIC TROIKA

The first move in risk theatre, temptation, assumes many forms. In the case of *Macbeth*, temptation assumes the form of the witches who wait on the blasted heath. They intrigue Macbeth with prophecy:

> MACBETH. Stay, you imperfect speakers, tell
>   me more:
> By Sinel's death I know I am thane of Glamis,
> But how of Cawdor? The thane of Cawdor lives
> A prosperous gentleman; and to be king
> Stands not within the prospect of belief,
> No more than to be Cawdor. Say from whence
> You owe this strange intelligence, or why

Upon this blasted heath you stop our way
With such prophetic greeting? Speak, I charge you.[2]

After Macbeth unexpectedly becomes thane of Cawdor, the prospect of becoming king moves into the realm of belief. His ambitions are dashed, however, when Duncan names Malcolm his heir. The situation then calls for Macbeth to raise the stakes with the second part of risk theatre, the hero's wager. Lady Macbeth knows what her husband must stake:

Glamis thou art, and Cawdor, and shalt be
What thou art promis'd. Yet do I fear thy nature,
It is too full o'the'milk of human kindness
To catch the nearest way.[3]

The "milk of human kindness" for the throne: that is the hero's wager. Macbeth cannot have compassion and the throne at the same time. Finally, the die is cast as Macbeth kills Duncan. The image of casting the die captures the irreversibility of the moment: the gambling act is complete.

In Sophocles' *Oedipus rex*, a riddle tempts Oedipus. When consulted about the plague that is ravaging Thebes, Apollo's oracle dredges up the past, framing the solution in a riddle: "Relief from the plague can only come one way. / Uncover the murderers of Laius, / put them to death or drive them into exile."[4] Since Oedipus is good at solving riddles, he

---

2   Shakespeare, *Macbeth*, 1.3.70–8.
3   Ibid., 1.5.15–8.
4   Sophocles, *Oedipus the King*, in *Three Theban Plays*, trans. Robert Fagles, lines 349-51.

springs into action, but to solve the regicide is more easily said than done. The trail has gone cold. The blind prophet Tiresias obstructs the investigation, and hence Oedipus must make the hero's wager. As he rebukes Tiresias, he discloses his stake:

> Come here, you pious fraud. Tell me,
> when did you ever prove yourself a prophet?
> When the Sphinx, that chanting Fury kept her
>   deathwatch here,
> why silent then, not a word to set our people free?
> There was a riddle, not for some passer-by
>   to solve—
> it cried out for a prophet. Where were you?
> Did you rise to the crisis? Not a word,
> you and your birds, your gods—nothing.
> No, but I came by, Oedipus the ignorant,
> *I* stopped the Sphinx! With no help from the birds,
> the flight of my own intelligence hit the mark.[5]

Here is a man whose fame rests on a single exploit: outsmarting the Sphinx. Confronted with a second riddle, he resorts to intellect a second time. Though under siege by the plague and hemmed in by both the prophet (who may be a greedy charlatan) and his brother-in-law (who may have designs on the throne), he bets that his intellect can hit the mark a second time. Instead of outsmarting the Sphinx, this time he will uncover the regicide. Or so he wagers.

---

5   Ibid., lines 443-53.

The die is cast once events pass the point of no return. In a strange twist of fate, it turns out that the same shepherd who had saved Oedipus when he was a babe (he had been exposed on Mount Cithaeron) was also part of Laius' train many years later when Oedipus unwittingly killed his father. As the investigation progresses, Oedipus is brought face to face with this selfsame shepherd a third time. As the shepherd is brought in for questioning—the mysterious shepherd who had happened to be present at each existential crux, who had happened to be present when he was born, when he killed his father, and now—Jocasta realizes the point of no return fast approaches. She implores her husband to stop:

> JOCASTA. That man …
> why ask? Old shepherd, talk, empty nonsense,
> don't give it another thought, don't even think—
>
> OEDIPUS. What—give up now, with a clue like this?
> Fail to solve the mystery of my birth?
> Not for all the world!
>
> JOCASTA. Stop—in the name of god,
> if you love your own life, call off this search!
> My suffering is enough![6]

Jocasta begs him to stop because she recognizes three facts: first, that Oedipus has killed his father, married his mother, sired misbegotten children, and caused the plague;

---

6   Ibid., lines 1157-64.

second, that the shepherd knows the truth; and third, that once the shepherd speaks the truth out loud, the die will have been cast.

In Goethe's *Egmont*, Egmont, a Netherlandish aristocrat, lives under Spanish rule in the occupied Low Countries. Despite his love of freedom, he supports Margaret of Parma, the regent appointed by the occupying power, as she allows the locals sufficient freedom for commerce, agriculture, and trade to flourish. Even when his fellow citizens begin to fuss over the Spanish presence, he comes to her defence: "An honest citizen who provides for himself, honestly and industriously," says Egmont, "has as much freedom as he needs anywhere."[7] When the wave of Protestantism sweeps across the Low Countries, however, it also sweeps away economic freedom. Catholic Spain dispatches the Duke of Alba, who brings the Inquisition with him. This is too much for Egmont, who, ever the gambling man, rises to the hero's wager: "I have never disdained," he says, "even for small stakes to throw the bloody dice with my good comrades; and shall I hesitate now, when all the free worth of life is at issue?"[8] While the others flee, Egmont remains behind to uphold what few civil liberties remain. But once Alba arrives, there is no way out for Egmont: the die is cast. Not even his authority as a knight in the Order of the Golden Fleece can save him.

In Sophocles' *Antigone*, it is, paradoxically, doing the right thing that tempts or motivates both Creon and Antigone to take the hero's wager. As Thebes' ruler, Creon is obliged to

---

7   Goethe, *Egmont*, in *Plays*, trans. Anna Swanwick, p. 25.

8   Ibid., p. 31.

restore order after the civil war. Accordingly, he issues an edict forbidding the burial of traitors on pain of death. His nephew Polyneices, however, lays amongst the dead traitors. The edict places Antigone in a quandary: as Polyneices' next of kin, Antigone is obliged by the customs of Greek religion to bury her brother. A quarrel ensues. The escalating situation calls for the hero's wager. Antigone stakes her religious obligations against her civic duties:

> It wasn't Zeus, not in the least,
> who made this proclamation—not to me.
> Nor did that Justice, dwelling with the gods
> beneath the earth, ordain such laws for men.
> Nor did I think your edict had such force
> that you, a mere mortal could override the gods,
> the great unwritten unshakable traditions.[9]

Creon, on the other hand, stakes his religious scruples against his civic obligations:

> You'll never bury that body in the grave,
> not even if Zeus's eagles rip the corpse
> and wing their rotten pickings off to the throne
> of god!
> Never, not even in fear of such defilement
> will I tolerate his burial, that traitor.[10]

---

9   Sophocles, *Antigone*, in *The Three Theban Plays*, trans. Robert Fagles, lines 499-505.

10   Ibid., lines 1151-55.

By burying Polyneices, Antigone casts the die, as now she is subject to the terms of Creon's edict. Creon, in turn, casts the die by enforcing the edict: she is his niece and her condemnation sets off an irrevocable and unfortunate chain reaction within the family dynamic.

In Marlowe's *Doctor Faustus*, power tempts. Having exhausted the mortal arts and sciences, Faustus desires more:

> Philosophy is odious and obscure;
> Both law and physic are for petty wits;
> Divinity is basest of the three,
> Unpleasant, harsh, contemptible, and vile.
> 'Tis magic, magic that hath ravished me.[11]

To gain knowledge of magic, Faustus makes a pact with Mephistopheles: his soul for world dominion. He wagers that at the end of twenty-four years, he will be able to repent of his sins. The die is then cast when, after twenty-four years of vice, Faustus' heart is hardened beyond repentance, and his soul is damned for eternity.

Desire arouses temptation in O'Neill's play *Desire Under the Elms*, in which Abbie, a young wife married to an older man, becomes involved in a familial love triangle. Eben, her stepson, is young and handsome, and lives under the same roof. Eben wants Abbie—and his dad's farm as well. Abbie eventually bears Eben's child, yet her husband (i.e., Eben's father) believes the child is his. Eben, however, suspects

---

11 Marlowe, *Doctor Faustus*, 1.1.108–12. All references to *Doctor Faustus* are from the A-text of Marlowe in *Doctor Faustus: A- and B-texts (1604, 1616)*.

further deceit. He believes that she has borne a child to cuckold his father out of the farm and him out of an inheritance: the farm will bypass him and go to the new child. Abbie wagers her own motherhood to win Eben back. The baby has come between Abbie and Eben, and, in order to prove her love, she kills their child. The die is cast; nothing will ever be the same again.

Whether Greek, German, or English, from Aeschylus to O'Neill, tragedy is built from a troika of parts. Regardless of whether a play is divided into three acts (e.g., *Desire Under the Elms*), five acts (e.g., *Egmont*), or choral interludes (e.g., *Oedipus rex*), the triad remains the same, because each part corresponds to an innate feature of processes, namely, a beginning, a middle, and an end. As a dramatic process, tragedy begins with the hero's temptation, works its way to the wager, and ends with the cast.

TEMPTATION

To set the scene for the tragic hero's temptation, blanket the stage with fog. Pierce the air with alarms and gunfire. Use bloody props: freshly sawn scaffolds and effigies. Set the action against a backdrop of hellfire, and light up the darkness with the blaze of comets. Make it a time of pestilence in the hour of civil discord. Explode pattern, routine, and stability in the flash of a world gone mad, a world where the only certainty is uncertainty.

Why begin tragedy with a risk event? Tragedy begins with calamity to tempt the hero. To a hero, blood running in the streets signifies a world rife with opportunity. "Here is my chance," says the hero, "to do a hero's things." It is no accident that *Antigone* opens to the sound of the slain crying out for burial. Nor is it an accident that *Egmont* is set against the *Beeldenstorm*: rioters toppling churches and hurling statues of saints from altars. Other beginnings are equally auspicious (or at least auspicious from the viewpoint of tragedy): traitors led to scaffolds (*Macbeth*), a ghost demanding vengeance (*Hamlet*), civil war (*Seven Against Thebes*), and suppliants huddled around altars (*Oedipus rex*). Where there is calamity, there is opportunity.

Calamity throws the world into flux. As disorder rages, change accelerates. The quicker the rate of change, the higher the risk—volatility *is* risk. But for heroes, risk equals opportunity. Amid the carnage, they see uncertain outlines of the shadows cast by future possibilities. As natural-born gamblers, they are filled with desire. Put a hero in a volatile setting, and the tragedy writes itself.

If we take the hero's temptation in *Doctor Faustus*, for example, we see that the play begins by breaking pattern, routine, and stability. Faustus was hitherto engaged in the scholarly arts, perhaps preparing a lecture series on the Church Fathers or the Code of Justinian. This soon changes when Valdes and Cornelius entice him with the dark arts. Dangerous though it is, Faustus sees this temptation as an opportunity: "This night I'll conjure," he says, "though I die therefore."[12] When audiences see a magic circle, holy water, and other such props, they understand that the hero has been enticed.

---

12   Ibid., 1.1.168.

The hero's temptation becomes persuasive when structured so that spectators can see *how* and *why* the hero is tempted. Clues may be embedded in the dialogue, action, setting, or character to help spectators anticipate the outcome. Anticipated outcomes produce persuasive outcomes. *Antigone* (persuasive) and *Othello* (unpersuasive) illustrate the importance of guiding audience expectations. Sophocles uses character in *Antigone* to help spectators anticipate the development of the hero's temptation. Because action springs from character, as players reveal their personalities, they simultaneously telegraph the range of actions of which they are capable. When Creon and Antigone first make their entrance, they announce their standpoints:

CREON. Remember this:
our country is our safety.
Only while she voyages true on course
can we establish friendships, truer than blood itself.
Such are my standards. They make our city great.[13]

and:

ANTIGONE. I have longer
to please the dead than please the living here:
in the kingdom down below I'll lie forever.
Do as you like, dishonor the laws
the gods hold in honor.[14]

---

13   Sophocles, *Antigone*, in *The Three Theban Plays*, trans. Robert Fagles, lines 210-4.

14   Ibid., lines 88-92.

From his first appearance, Creon relays the impression that he is a patriot, a hard man who values country above family: to him, country is "truer than blood itself." Antigone, on the other hand, relays the impression that she is a religious zealot who values religion over life. When she buries Polyneices in the name of the gods, and when Creon condemns her in the name of the commonweal, the audience, guided by first impressions, finds the action persuasive.

In *Othello*, Iago ruins Othello, Desdemona, Emilia, Roderigo, Brabantio, Bianca, and Cassio. The contrast between the persuasiveness of the hero's temptation in *Antigone* and the unpersuasiveness of the hero's temptation in *Othello* could not be greater. Because of the inconsistencies between how Iago sees himself and how others see him, it is difficult to grasp *how* and *why* Iago acts as he does. First, Iago claims to feel slighted because Othello has passed him over for promotion. Are other officers aware of friction in the ranks? Far from it: they call him "honest Iago" and confide in him.[15] Second, Iago accuses Othello of seducing his wife. Are there hints of impropriety between Othello and Emilia? Not a trace. Third, the characters are baffled by Iago's maleficence. When they question him, he answers: "Demand me nothing; what you know, you know: / From this time forth I never will speak word."[16] If the characters themselves do not know, how could the audience know? The inconsistencies make it difficult for the audience to understand Iago's actions. Iago's temptation,

---

15   So Cassio addresses him in Shakespeare, *Othello*, 2.3.335. See also 5.2.54.

16   Ibid., 5.2.304–5.

therefore, feels unconvincing. Because it is unconvincing, *Othello* lacks the dramatic crispness of *Antigone*.

It is equally as important to win over the audience. When the audience identifies with the hero, the hero's temptation persuades. Spectators sympathize with the hero when they feel that they would have acted similarly, had they been in a similar position. Shakespeare's *Macbeth* (persuasive) and Mussato's *Ecerinis* (unpersuasive) illustrate the importance of gaining the audience's sympathy. Macbeth begins as a loyal subject, clearing the countryside of traitors. The greater ambition to be king only awakens when the witches' prophecy unexpectedly starts to fulfil itself. This extenuating circumstance mitigates his treachery. To the degree that theatregoers are susceptible to ambition, they identify with Macbeth.

Ezzelino from Mussato's *Ecerinis*, however, is no Macbeth: after learning that he is born of the devil, he takes his birthright as licence to engage in "wars, death, ruin, deceit, fraud and the perdition of the whole human race."[17] It is a bit much. Ezzelino's evil is unbounded; Macbeth's evil is bounded by qualms and uncertainties. Ezzelino craves to destroy humanity; Macbeth berates himself for turning traitor. Ezzelino is propaganda; Macbeth is a man. Theatregoers are alienated by Ezzelino's bull-in-a-china-shop antics inasmuch as they dislike propaganda.

When audiences are able to anticipate the path temptation takes (e.g., Creon and Antigone) or when their sympathies are engaged (e.g., Macbeth), the hero's temptation is

---

17 Mussato, *Ecerinis*, in *Humanist Tragedies*, trans. Gary R. Grund, lines 85-6.

persuasive. It is unpersuasive, however, when the underlying motives are unclear (e.g., Iago) or when the hero fails to win the sympathy of the audience (e.g., Ezzelino).

WAGER

The middle section of a tragic play is a preparatory act where heroes formulate the wager. For a chance to reach their desire's bourne, they lay everything on the line. They vacillate and waver before the strange opportunity, wondering whether the dice are fair. Risks are evaluated and re-evaluated. They may have false starts as the momentousness of the task becomes clear. Greed, principle, or necessity eventually overcomes doubt. Plans are laid out and strategies formulated, with contingency measures and stop switches devised to fail-safe the undertaking. The careful and crafting mind of the hero puts on a show as it prepares to take on the unknown. Each hazard must be identified; nothing can be left to chance. The middle section of the play is heavy with premonition, pregnant in expectation, and hectic in preparation.

In one notable tragedy, a woman desires to become queen. Her husband is too timid, gentle, and mindful of propriety to take the throne. To goad him along, she unsexes herself, filling her breasts with gall. To become queen, she stakes her sex: womanhood for power. This is Lady Macbeth's wager.[18] In an

---

18   From her "The raven himself is hoarse" soliloquy (Shakespeare, *Macbeth*, 1.5.38-50):

    The raven himself is hoarse

    That croaks the fatal entrance of Duncan

ancient tragedy, a young man returns home to find his father murdered and his mother the murderer. Justice demands that he avenge his father. This is Orestes' wager in Aeschylus' *Oresteia*: family for justice. In a third tragedy, one from the modern era, an oppressed woman finds love with a man who promises to run away with her to the Blessed Isles. But she is married. Her husband stands in the way, so she murders him. This is Christine's wager in O'Neill's *Mourning Becomes Electra*: matrimony for love. Thus, the hero's wager expresses tragedy's most fundamental tenet: there is no free lunch.

While the heart-wrenching sacrifice is very real, there can be no guarantees of success: this is, after all, tragedy. Through the wager, heroes determine the price they are willing to pay to achieve their desire's goal: sex for power, family for justice, and matrimony for love. Desire is up for bid, to be paid for in the currency of flesh and blood.

Vacillation usually follows the hero's wager. Macbeth, for example, has second thoughts about murdering Duncan:

> Under my battlements. Come, you spirits
> That tend on mortal thoughts, unsex me here,
> And fill me from the crown to the toe topful
> Of direst cruelty! Make thick my blood,
> Stop up th' access and passage to remorse,
> That no compunctious visitings of nature
> Shake my fell purpose, nor keep peace between
> Th' effect and [it]! Come to my woman's breasts,
> And take my milk for gall, you murth'ring ministers,
> Wherever in our sightless substances
> You wait on nature's mischief!

He's here in double trust:
First, as I am his kinsman and his subject,
Strong both against the deed; then, as his host,
Who should against his murderer shut the door,
Not bear the knife myself.[19]

Like Macbeth, Orestes also hesitates, saying, "Pylades, what shall I do? To kill a mother is terrible. Shall I show mercy?"[20] Vacillation serves two dramatic purposes. First, it wins over audiences to the side of the hero, who is often called upon to commit acts against nature. When Orestes hesitates, he acknowledges what everyone knows: to kill a mother is unthinkable. By acknowledging the consensus, he dispels the fear that he may simply be a maniac. Second, vacillation conveys the momentousness of the wager. When Macbeth protests, "I dare do all that may become a man; / Who dare [do] more is none,"[21] the stress and the strain of his undertaking are palpable: he stands on the brink of everything and nothingness. Horror at the deed collides with an overwhelming desire to have it all. The strain heralds the gravity of the impending disaster.

Vacillation eventually gives way to resolve. Sometimes it happens because fate, necessity, or external compulsion rule out other options. At other times, greed and ambition overwhelm qualms and second thoughts. Once tragic heroes have overcome their doubts, they look at the cards they have

19   Ibid., 1.7.12-6.

20   Aeschylus, *The Choephori*, in *The Oresteian Trilogy*, trans. Philip Vellacott, p. 136.

21   Shakespeare, *Macbeth*, 1.7.46-7.

been dealt. Now is the time to strategize. When heroes hold a weak hand, defensive strategies work best, and they may need some insurance. Such is the case with Orestes, who finds a surety in Apollo:

> When, later, after years of exile I came home,
> I killed my mother—I will not deny it—in
> Just retribution for my father, whom I loved.
> For this Apollo is equally answerable;
> He told me of the tortures that would sear my soul
> If I neglected vengeance on the murderers.[22]

Alternatively, risks may be hedged. In Webster's *The Duchess of Malfi*, the Duchess and Antonio, on the point of being cornered by their pursuers, decide to split ways. She elects to try her luck in Loretto while Antonio makes for Milan:

> DUCHESS. I suspect some ambush:
> Therefore by all my love I do conjure you
> To take your eldest son and fly towards Milan;
> Let us not venture all this poor remainder
> In one unlucky bottom.[23]

By thus hedging their bets, the Duchess and Antonio increase the odds that at least one of them will survive.

---

22   Aeschylus, *The Eumenides*, in *Oresteian Trilogy*, trans. Philip Vellacott, p. 163.

23   Webster, *Duchess of Malfi*, 3.5.54–8.

Alternatively, when the tragic hero holds a strong hand, offensive options open up. Prudence dictates, however, that risks be diversified, insured, or hedged all the same. It is a time for caution, as much is at stake. For example, even though the Macbeths operate from a position of power, they nevertheless frame the chamberlains for Duncan's murder and consequently murder them in turn. By murdering the suspects, they buy themselves insurance. Like the Macbeths, in O'Neill's *Mourning Becomes Electra*, Christine takes out insurance: before poisoning her older husband with a seizure-inducing drug, she tells the town gossip about his weak heart. It is their first night together after a lengthy absence; she is young and attractive. No one will be the wiser. Her strategy is ingenious: all perils have been covered.

CAST

One would think that strategy, being a well-laid plan and a goal, would increase the odds of success. But in risk theatre, strategy leads to tragedy. After the preparations have been completed, it is time for the hero's cast—so-called because the cast marks the point of no return. As Schiller recognizes, the image of the "fatal die" being thrown captures the idea of necessity, fate, "what must happen," and the inevitable stealing up on the erstwhile free agent:

> COUNTESS. But when at last the fatal die is thrown,
> The hollow mask no longer serves, they fall
> Into the mighty hands of nature, of
> The spirit that obeys none but itself,

Knows of no treaties, and will deal with them
Not on their terms, but on its own alone.[24]

So too Shakespeare turns to the image of the die in *Richard III* to signify the point of no return: "I have set my life upon a cast," says Richard, "and I will stand the hazard of the die."[25] Just like a turn down a one-way street or a word spoken in hasty anger, the cast is a visual representation of the irreversible. Just as the products of reaction when gunpowder is heated—potassium carbonate, carbon dioxide, nitrogen, and so on—can never regain their previous elemental forms after the explosion has altered their molecular arrangements, so too the cast is a spark which sets off irreparable consequences. The cast represents the moment the Rubicon is crossed: powerful forces inimical to free will are brought into motion.

In keeping with the gambling analogy, risk theatre associates the point of no return to the casting of dice, but other images are possible and equally memorable. In *Agamemnon*, Aeschylus likens the fateful moment to putting on a harness. In this play, the goddess Artemis gives Agamemnon two choices: either sacrifice his daughter and sail to Troy or disband the army in disgrace. He chooses to slaughter Iphigenia, an act which Aeschylus encapsulates into an agrarian metaphor: "Then he put on / The harness of Necessity."[26]

---

24 Schiller, *Wallenstein's Death*, in *The Robbers and Wallenstein*, trans. F. J. Lamport, p. 343.

25 Shakespeare, *Richard III*, 5.4.9-10.

26 Aeschylus, *Agamemnon*, in *The Oresteian Trilogy*, trans. Philip Vellacott, p. 49.

Like oxen before a plow, Agamemnon has yoked himself to the act's inevitable ramifications. Whether imagined as a fatal die or a harness, tragedy always approaches a critical point into which time cleaves a before and an after.

The cast takes place under a variety of circumstances. It may come as a mental breakthrough after a period of self-doubt, as in the case of Hamlet, who announces it by saying: "O, from this time forth, / My thoughts be bloody, or be nothing worth!"[27] Or it can be the product of resignation. Tired of being alive, Webster's Antonio resigns himself to withstand the hazard of the die:

> Come, I'll be out of this ague;
> For to live thus is not indeed to live:
> It is a mockery, and abuse of life.
> I will not henceforth save myself by halves,
> Lose all, or nothing.[28]

Sometimes greed prompts the cast. In Kyd's *The Spanish Tragedy*, Balthazar, after being smitten by the alluring Belimperia, announces the cast by saying: "I'll tempt the destinies, and either lose my life, or win my love."[29] Other times, the cast occurs as a function of character. "Cowards die many times before their deaths; the valiant never taste of death but once," says Caesar on the way to the forum.[30] This is Caesar being Caesar. Similarly, when the scout reports that one more

---

27 Shakespeare, *Hamlet*, 4.4.65-6.

28 Webster, *Duchess of Malfi*, 5.3.46–50.

29 Kyd, *The Spanish Tragedy*, 2.1.132–3.

30 Shakespeare, *Julius Caesar*, 2.2.32–3.

assailant waits at the seventh gate, Aeschylus' Eteocles, being full of strife and valour, relishes the chance to try the die:

> I shall stand against him myself.
> Who has a juster claim than I?
> Ruler against ruler, brother against brother,
> hater against hater, I must take my rightful place.
> Quickly, bring my armor.[31]

As Eteocles dons his armour, he puts on necessity.

AFTER THE CAST

The Unexpected

The cast serves as a transition in tragic drama between the preparations demanded by the wager and the aftermath. However, for all its pomp, the cast itself involves surprisingly little action. Think of Caesar crossing the Rubicon. Everything is changed, but nothing happens: the civil war is yet to come. As mentioned above, the tragic play culminates in the triumph of the unexpected over expectation; the aftermath of the cast then consists of unraveling all the unintended consequences. There is an adage that "the best-laid plans of mice and men often go awry." Eventually, the tragic hero comes to learn this adage well. Macbeth, for example, prepares for every contingency *except* that Birnam

---

31   Aeschylus, *Seven Against Thebes*, trans. Anthony Hecht and Helen Bacon, p. 49.

Wood should remove to Dunsinane Hill, and he was ready to fight all comers *except* one not of woman born. But that is exactly what happens. Malcolm orders the troops to cloak themselves with the wood of Birnam, and, on the ramparts, Macbeth learns that Macduff is "from his mother's womb / Untimely ripp'd."[32]

Like Macbeth, Agamemnon also falls victim to unintended circumstances. The king sacrifices his daughter, Iphigenia; the winds change; the Achaeans sail for Troy; he wages a ten-year war. He foresees the dangers of the Trojan War, but these do not kill him. The unforeseen danger is the unanticipated danger: Iphigenia's sacrifice prompts Agamemnon's wife to take a lover, and together they plot Agamemnon's murder when he least expects—a decade later on the day of his triumphant homecoming.

Similarly, in *The Hunted* (the second play in the *Mourning Becomes Electra* cycle) Christine's likely plan to swap poison in place of medicine is also unexpectedly thwarted:

> CHRISTINE. When he was dying he pointed at me
> and told her I was guilty! And afterwards she found
> the poison—
>
> BRANT. (*springing to his feet*) For God's sake, why
> didn't you—
>
> CHRISTINE. (*pitifully*) I fainted before I could hide
> it! And I had planned it all so carefully. But how

---

could I foresee that she would come in just at that
moment? And how could I know he would talk
to me the way he did? He drove me crazy! He
kept talking of death! He was torturing me! I only
wanted him to die and leave me alone!

BRANT. (*his eyes lighting up with savage satisfaction*)
He knew before he died whose son I was, you said?
By God, I'll bet that maddened him!

CHRISTINE. (*repeats pitifully*) I'd planned it so carefully—but something made things happen![33]

Something is too light a word; *everything* conspires against
her. She loses her cool, telling Mannon of the affair. Their
daughter gets out of bed and unexpectedly wanders into the
bedroom. Christine then faints, dropping the box of poison.
Her secret is out. This is tragedy's synchronicity: nature
inclines towards black swan events rather than the success
of the best-laid plans of mice and men. The peculiar thing
about risk theatre is that every time there is a storm, it is a
100-year storm.[34]

Loss and Suffering

Why is tragedy cruel and heartless, conspiring against heroes
who have every expectation of success? It conspires against
them so that others may learn its iron rule: you cannot have

---

33   O'Neill, *The Hunted*, in *Three Plays*, p. 361.

34   The concept of the unexpected in tragedy will be explored in detail
      in chapter 7.

your cake and eat it too. In addition, by stripping the hero of both the ante and the prize, what remains amounts to a naked reaction to loss, in which a pathetic awareness of what truly gives life meaning emerges. We see this awareness in the heartache that binds Brant and Christine together in a broken embrace; they rise above the angers that had moved them to murder:

> BRANT. (*dejectedly*) Aye. I suppose it's the only way out for us now. The "Atlantis" is sailing on Friday for China. I'll arrange with her skipper to give us passage—and keep his mouth shut. She sails at daybreak Friday. You'd better meet me here Thursday night. (*then with effort*) I'll write Clark and Dawson tonight they'll have to find another skipper for the "Flying Trades."

> CHRISTINE. (*noticing the hurt in his tone—miserably*) Poor Adam! I know how it hurts you to give up your ship.

> BRANT. (*rousing himself guiltily—pats her hand with gruff tenderness*) There are plenty of ships—but there is only one you, Christine!

> CHRISTINE. I feel so guilty! I've brought you nothing but misfortune!

BRANT. You've brought love—and the rest is only
the price. It's worth it a million times![35]

In this case, the characters realize that it is their love for
each other that gives life meaning. It is a valuable lesson, and
learnt at considerable expense.

Tragedy also conspires against heroes to make them suffer,
for suffering possesses a special quality that grants the sufferer authority to speak on greater themes. As a tragic play
ends, suffering reveals the nature of loss, value, and choice,
thus revealing tragedy's insight into life. Through his suffering, Eteocles, for example, gains insight into the wisdom
of despair: "If a man's lot be to suffer evil, let it be without
shame. / That is our only gain when we are dead."[36] Likewise,
as Egmont suffers, he catches a glimpse of the inscrutable
meaning of life:

The wreath has vanished! Beautiful vision, the
light of day has frightened you away! Yes, it was
they, they were united, the two sweetest joys of
my heart. Divine Freedom borrowed the form of
my beloved; the lovely girl arrayed herself in the
celestial garb of her friend. In a solemn moment
they appeared united, with aspect more earnest
than tender. With bloodstained feet the vision
approached me, the waving folds of the hem of
her robe were flecked with blood. It was my blood,

---

35   O'Neill, *The Hunted*, in *Three Plays*, p. 362.
36   Aeschylus, *Seven Against Thebes*, trans. Anthony Hecht and Helen
      Bacon, p. 50.

and the blood of many noble hearts. No! It was not
shed in vain! Forward! Brave people! The goddess
of victory leads you on! . . . And now, from this
dungeon I too shall go forth, to meet an honorable
death; I die for freedom, the freedom for which I
lived and fought, and for which, in my suffering, I
now sacrifice myself.[37]

Goethe grants the dying Egmont the realization that his
death will trigger the Dutch revolt: he dies so that others
can live free. Macbeth, too, learns as he suffers. As the end
approaches, he realizes the emptiness of the crown and lays
down the tyrant's mask:

MACBETH. Wherefore was that cry?

SEYTON. The queen, my lord, is dead.

MACBETH. She should have died hereafter;
There would have been a time for such a word.
To-morrow, and to-morrow, and to-morrow,
Creeps in this petty pace from day to day,
To the last syllable of recorded time;
And all our yesterdays have lighted fools
The way to dusty death. Out, out, brief candle!
Life's but walking shadow, a poor player,
That struts and frets his hour upon the stage,
And then is heard no more. It is a tale

---

37   Goethe, *Egmont*, trans. Anna Swanwick, pp. 78–9.

Told by an idiot, full of sound and fury,
Signifying nothing.[38]

It is not only Macbeth who walks the way to dusty death; we walk with him in solidarity. Suffering is the glue binding together players and audiences. Tragedy makes its characters suffer so that their lives may be transformed into works of art. This common sense of suffering binds together players and audiences. We suffer, says Helen in Homer's *Iliad*, "so that hereafter/ we shall be made into things of song for the men of the future."[39] Thus, the suffering tragic character becomes the hero for all tomorrow's stages.

Like the Eiffel Tower, a Haydn sonata, American government, and other complex and enduring structures and ideas, tragedy is built up from a robust troika of parts: the hero's temptation, the hero's wager, and the cast. Temptation initiates the dramatic process: an event disrupts the daily routine, thus creating opportunities. The hero's wager follows, in which, realizing the enormity of the sacrifice, the hero questions the undertaking before overcoming doubts through clever strategies. The plot culminates with the cast, or the point of no return. Unintended consequences arise, leading to a wailing and a gnashing of teeth. Suffering, however, exposes the true nature of the hero's circumstances: humanity's lot, the concerns of the gods, and the value of life. Having thus transformed the particular into the universal, the drama of

38   Shakespeare, *Macbeth*, 5.5.15-28.
39   Homer, *Iliad*, trans. Richmond Lattimore, 6.357–8.

how unintended consequences transform probable success into improbable loss comes to an end.

2 TEMPO AND TRAGEDY

As presented in the previous chapter, the tragic plot acquires its distinctive shape from its troika of parts. Temptation sets it off, it moves to the wager, and culminates in a cast. Considerable licence, however, exists in how these three parts may be arranged within a play. The tempo of risk theatre is thus dictated by how this licence is used. Depending on the arrangement of the three parts, I propose the classifications of *gradual tragedy*, *backloaded tragedy*, and *frontloaded tragedy*, each differentiated by their sense of pace. Gradual tragedies, distinguished by even intervals separating the acts of temptation, wager, and cast, move step by step. Backloaded tragedies employ a small interval between the temptation and wager, but a large interval between the wager and cast. This arrangement has the effect of pushing the cast towards the end of the play and thus placing emphasis on the ending, or the back, of the play. Conversely, in frontloaded tragedies, the troika of temptation, wager, and cast occurs in quick succession as the play opens, thus packing the action into the beginning, or the front of the play. Because three configurations of risk theatre's troika of parts are possible, tragedy plays out at one of three tempi: gradual, backloaded, or frontloaded.

THE POETICS OF CHAOS

Gradual, backloaded, and frontloaded tragedies all begin similarly, in medias res, in confusion and chaos. After the initial bout of storm and stress, however, all three tempi of tragedy aim to restore order—or at least dramatic order—as quickly as possible through the hero's temptation. As the first of the troika's elements, the temptation presages the wager and cast, and represents the first milestone on the dramatic journey. It offers a welcome respite to the theatregoers caught in the tempest of the opening moments.

The most captivating tragedies begin in a state of chaos. Chaos occupies a no-man's land between order and disorder and contains great potential—even more so than order, which grows stagnant. The dramatic potential of chaos, however, is at risk: as a liminal phenomenon caught between two states, it is inherently unstable. It will either engender order or collapse into disarray; whither and when it does is indeterminate. This uncertainty or indetermination renders chaos fascinating to an audience. When an artist uses this uncertainty to create an artistic effect, the artist engages with what I call the *poetics of chaos*, the poetics of a world teetering on a precipice.

Since the poetics of chaos relies on a sort of tension musicians call *dissonance* to create an effect, we can find examples of it by turning to the musical arts. Haydn, for example, began his oratorio *The Creation* by tone painting chaos as the inchoate sound of a symphony searching for form.[1] Cadences are unresolved. Harmonies are ambiguous. Brave and incomplete sounds caught in a maelstrom fill the auditorium. This is the poetics of chaos: music in between harmony and noise. By engaging it, *The Creation* broke every box-office record.[2] Even more arresting is Rebel's 1737 ballet *The Elements*, which opens to the sound of breathtaking dissonance: every tone of the D minor scale churning in unison. In tonality and rhythm, it possesses the requisites of harmony. The abomination of sound, however, suggests anything but. By suspending the orchestra between order and disorder, *The Elements*

---

1   In the opening movement titled "The Representation of Chaos." See the discussion in Lowe, "Creating Chaos in Haydn's *Creation*," 5:

> At this early stage of his *Creation* [i.e., bars 1-6] Haydn denies the existence of tonal organization. The music that immediately follows this chord [i.e., the unison C of bar 1] is likewise extraordinarily unusual within the stylistic conventions of the time: an unresolved dissonance and an unaccompanied melodic fragment lead only to yet another iteration of the as-yet tonally undefined A-flat major triad. Haydn's audience would have been incapable of anticipating the direction of this music, its harmonic motion lacking rational meaning. This irrationality defines Haydn's void.

2   Geiringer, *Haydn: A Creative Life in Music*, 176 quotes the correspondent of the Leipzig *Allgemeine musikalische Zeitung* reporting on the first public performance on March 19, 1799:

> On the nineteenth I heard Haydn's "Creation." Not to report to you about this good fortune (for this is what it was) would reveal either too little feeling for art or for friendship. The crowd was immense and the receipts amounted to 4088 fl. 30 kr., a sum never before collected by a Viennese theater.

harnesses the poetics of chaos to captivate the audience, who eagerly await Rebel's next move.

The poetics of chaos commands attention not only because it is subversive, but also because it represents the poetics of something about to happen. Chaos, situated on that threshold between order and disorder, is unsustainable: something must and will happen. In *The Creation*, God is about to punctuate eternity by getting down to work. In *The Elements*, the primordial substance sits on the verge of separating into the four archetypical elements of earth, water, air, and fire. Risk theatre likewise begins with the world in flux: rebellion in *Macbeth*, insurrection in *Egmont*, and plague in *Oedipus rex*. The crisis sits on a dangerous cusp: the situation is unsustainable. As risk theatre opens, out of nowhere, players burst upon the stage playing their hearts out, and a dramatic world emerges in medias res from the singularity of the mind's imagination. Like the struggle of form, thought, will, and body to free itself from the primordial bonds of formless stone in Michelangelo's series of sculptures *The Captives*, harmony, natural order, meaning, and purpose struggle to emerge from the theatrical singularity. This moment in the drama witnesses the poetics of chaos in action, a moment when terror and beauty conspire together. All is not well as risk theatre opens, for confusion, dissonance, and discord reign. The stage is a liminal world, a world on the cusp, precarious. As the audience confronts the hurly-burly, it is disoriented like a sailor in uncharted waters. The poetics of chaos commands attention by a disorientation strategy.

However, this moment of disorientation must be short lived, for the adrenalin-fueled stage of too much simultaneous activity quickly tires of itself—and tires the audience. It is too much, too soon, and too overwhelming to take in for too long. Disoriented, the audience seeks safe harbour, and art—being a hierarchy of forms and the distillation of order—happily complies. In the representation of chaos, art's artifice is turned back against itself. A D minor scale is musical, but to play all its notes in unison (as in the beginning of *The Elements*) is not. Something has to give: art called to depict chaos is art on the brink. To prevent chaos from reaching surfeit, chaos quickly yields to concord.

FROM CHAOS TO CONCORD

Returning to the examples from the musical arts, six minutes and sixteen seconds into Weil's recording of *The Creation*, we hear a tremendous C major chord ringing out as God creates light.[3] Order is restored, and the concertgoer breathes a sigh of relief. In Hogwood's rendition of *The Elements*, the seventh and last time chaos sounds out occurs five minutes and ten seconds into the recording.[4] By this time, the primal dissonance has given way to higher musical forms as earth (represented by the bass), water (flutes), air (small flutes), and fire (violins) have extricated themselves from the original morass

---

3   Haydn, *The Creation*, with Ann Monoyios (Soprano), Jörg Hering (Tenor), Harry Van der Kamp (Bass), Tölz Boys' Choir, and the Tafelmusik Baroque Orchestra, conducted by Bruno Weil, recorded Aug 31-Sep 4, 1993, Sony S2K 57965, 1994, 2 compact discs.

4   Rebel, *Les élémens*, The Academy of Ancient Music, conducted by Christopher Hogwood, recorded June 1978, L'Oiseau-Lyre 001002702, 2007, compact disc.

in D minor. Order has asserted itself. Tragedy arrives at the analogous "Let there be light" moment by laying down the hero's temptation. As the first part of the troika, the hero's temptation heralds the wager and the cast; its appearance signals that the initial dissonance is beginning to give way to the structure of the dramatic process.

To prevent chaos from reaching surfeit, the temptation is disclosed early on in all three tempi of tragedy, whether gradual, frontloaded, or backloaded. In *Doctor Faustus*, for example, Faustus meets Valdes and Cornelius at the end of act 1, scene 1. In *Hamlet*, Hamlet encounters the ghost at the end of the first act. In T. S. Eliot's *Murder in the Cathedral*, the tempters appear immediately after Becket's return to Canterbury.[5] In *The Cid*, Don Diego asks his son to duel Don Gomez—the father of his beloved—in act 1, scene 5. *Macbeth* (with a run time of approximately two and a half hours) and *Oedipus rex* (with a run time of approximately one and a half hours) are even more efficient: they get to the temptation in under ten minutes.[6]

During the opening maelstrom, the hero's temptation provides clarity for the audience. When Macbeth meets the witches, for example, the audience discerns the theme clearly as a tragedy of ambition. When Oedipus hears the riddle, the play's theme as a tragedy of knowledge is evident. When

---

5   Eliot, *Murder in the Cathedral*, p. 23.

6   In Shakespeare, *Macbeth*, directed by Rupert Goold, Macbeth encounters the witches eight minutes from the opening. Similarly, in Sophocles, *Oedipus rex*, directed by Tyrone Guthrie, Oedipus announces his intentions ("And I will start afresh, and make the dark things light") six and a half minutes in.

Hamlet encounters the ghost, it is clear to the audience that Shakespeare's drama represents a tragedy of certainty, a tragedy in which the hero will exhaust himself by trying to confirm whether the ghost is an honest ghost. When Faustus surrounds himself with his damned books, a tragedy of faith is apparent. When the tempters tempt Eliot's Becket, the audience understands the drama as a tragedy of man overcoming himself. When *The Cid*'s Don Rodrigo is summoned to duel the father of his beloved, the audience expects a tragedy of honour. In each of these cases, the temptation acts as a guide which orients the audience to the direction of the forthcoming action.

However, if the temptation is not presented within the first third of the play, the drama begins to wander. In *Death of a Salesman*, two-thirds of the play elapse before Willy is tempted to cash in on the life insurance policy:

> CHARLEY. I've got some work to do. Take care of yourself. And pay your insurance.

> WILLY. Funny, y'know? After all the highways, and the trains, and the appointments, and the years, you end up worth more dead than alive.[7]

For the first two-thirds of the play, there are no signposts. Events lack focus. Willy returns exhausted—why? He teaches his sons the art of the sale—but to what end? He sees visions of his late brother—for what purpose? When Willy

---

7   Miller, *Death of a Salesman*, p. 74.

borrows money from Charley, however, the events snap into focus as a tragedy of the American dream. Even dreams exact a price: first your dignity, then your life. Therefore, to give the play focus, the moment of temptation belongs as close to the opening as possible—but within reason. Some tragedies give away the temptation—and the rest of the plot, for that matter—in a prologue. In Euripides' *Hippolytus*, Aphrodite delivers a prologue revealing how the stepmother harbours an incestuous desire for her stepson, how the stepmother's errant desires will be revealed to the father, and how father will destroy son.[8] So too, as soon as Euripides' *Bacchae* opens, Dionysus reveals how he has driven the women mad to punish the unbelievers.[9] Spoilers sanitize the chaos of the opening sequence. The anxiety, wonder, and mystery that the initial turmoil inspires is suddenly replaced with knowledge, certainty, and ennui. The best temptations develop organically from the turbulence of the dramatic stream.

While gradual, backloaded, and frontloaded tragedies share similarities—namely, that they begin in confusion and restore order through the hero's temptation—they differ from one another in where they place the wager and the cast.

GRADUAL TRAGEDY

Gradual tragedies space out tragedy's three parts evenly. Ibsen's three-act *The Master Builder* exemplifies the gradual

---

8   Euripides, *Hippolytus*, in *Children of Heracles, Hippolytus, Andromache, Hecuba*, trans. David Kovacs, lines 1-57.

9   Euripides, *Bacchae*, in *Bacchae, Iphigenia at Aulis, Rhesus*, trans. David Kovacs, lines 1-63.

tragedy concept: temptation, wager, and cast occur with metronymic precision. Act one dramatizes master builder Solness' fear of youth:

> SOLNESS. The turn is coming. I can sense it. I feel
> it getting nearer. Somebody or other is going to
> demand: Make way for me! And then all the others
> will come storming up, threatening and shouting:
> Get out of the way! Get out of the way! Yes, just
> you watch, Doctor. One of these days, youth is
> going to come here beating on the door.[10]

Solness feels the cycle of generations passing him by. Just as he superseded Brovik, the apprentice Ragnar will consequently supersede him. But Solness senses a way to suspend this cycle: by seducing Kaja, he had been able to keep Ragnar in the fold. To seduce youth is to control youth. But, after hearing that Ragnar and Kaja plan to marry and start their own firm, Solness once again feels threatened. He therefore sees the arrival of young Hilde at the end of the first act as a new chance to remain relevant—thus the temptation.

Act 2 dramatizes the power struggle between Solness and Hilde. At what price will she be won? Hilde's ideal builder can climb as high as he builds, but Solness suffers from vertigo. Nevertheless, he is finishing a house with a tower and will prove his credentials by setting the commemorative

---

10   Ibsen, *The Master Builder*, in *Four Major Plays*, trans. James McFarlane, p. 285.

wreath atop the tower. Act 2 closes with the wager: Solness will confront his fear of heights to win Hilde.

Act 3 dramatizes the events preceding the climb up the scaffold. Hilde goads the master builder on, while Ragnar mocks him and Mrs. Solness frets. Townspeople gather round as the act ends with Solness climbing the tower: the cast. *The Master Builder* exemplifies the concept of gradual tragedy by setting the temptation, wager, and cast at even intervals. The result is that the tempo has an even flow to it.

Playwrights at leisure write gradual tragedies. Their works bear the hallmarks of ease, of having been worked over slowly and methodically. Watching one of these plays is like tramping up a manicured alpine trail: the scenery unfolds like clockwork, and sometimes the foliage obscures the view, but lookouts stationed at regular intervals reward patient hikers. Such gradual tragedies include the likes of Ibsen's *Hedda Gabler*, Goethe's *Egmont*, and Schiller's *Don Carlos*. Spontaneous, down-to-earth dialogue without excessive artifice enriches these dramas. One can imagine the private conversations in gradual tragedy as the sort overheard in a coffee shop. Because the plot develops at an unhurried and almost leisurely pace, meandering dialogue full of realism, little barbs, and playfulness shines out, as in this gem from *The Master Builder*:

HILDE. (*looks attentively at him*) You *are* ill, master builder. Very ill, I rather think.

SOLNESS. Say *mad*. For that's what you mean.

HILDE. No, I don't think there's anything much wrong with your reason.

SOLNESS. *What*, then? Out with it!

HILDE. What I'm wondering is whether you weren't born with rather a fragile conscience.

SOLNESS. Fragile conscience? What the devil's that?

HILDE. I mean your conscience is actually very fragile. Sort of delicate. Won't stand up to things. Can't bear much weight.

SOLNESS. (*growling*) H'm. What should one's conscience be like then, may I ask?[11]

Unlike backloaded and frontloaded tragedies where dialogue is used for a specific purpose—to create tension or accelerate the action—dialogue in the gradual tragedy has a more intimate quality. In contrast, certain conversations in front- and backloaded tragedies contain such excessive artifice that one cannot imagine them in real life. Dramatists write gradual tragedies when interplay between characters outshines the situations. Gradual tragedies are ones in which the journey is as important as the destination. They may be intense, to be sure, but they are less manic than frontloaded

---

11   Ibid., p. 322.

plays, such as *Macbeth*; they are also full of suspense, but less breathtaking than backloaded plays, such as *Oedipus rex*.

Gradual tragedies often borrow from historical sources (e.g., *Egmont* or *Don Carlos*) but are best suited for new and original material (e.g., *Hedda Gabler* or *The Master Builder*). When drawing on historical or mythological material which contains well-known stories and characters, a dramatist has more freedom in setting up the troika (seeing that the material is familiar to the audience). However, when creating original material, the dramatist must gradually acclimatize the audience to fresh settings, unknown characters, and novel situations. Therefore, original material perfectly suits the piecemeal unfolding of gradual tragedy.

BACKLOADED TRAGEDY

Backloaded tragedies delay the cast, as exemplified by Aeschylus's *Seven Against Thebes*. In this play, the curtain rises to a civil war between two brothers. Polyneices, backed by an army led by six champions—with himself as the seventh—has returned to reclaim Thebes, the city of seven gates. Eteocles, on the other hand, assembles seven captains to repulse them. The stakes are high, because, in addition to the customary hazards of battle, two unpredictable agents of divine justice—the Fury and the Curse—have been set into motion. Facing the triple threat of civil war, the Fury, and the Curse, Eteocles aspires to preserve Thebes and avoid the etymology underlying his name ("truly bewept" from *eteos*, "true" and *klaio*, "weep"). Thus the temptation:

ETEOKLES. If things go well for us, it's because of
    the god.
If, on the other hand,
a disaster should strike (which heaven forbid),
the moiling, the tidal groans, the sea-lamentation
would sound the name "Eteokles"
as wail and dire all through the city.
And I, Eteokles, alone the cause of weeping,
Eteokles bewept,
would be multiplied in the surge
and raving of all your voices,
and so prove fitly named
for the city of the Kadmeians.
May Zeus, Averter, forbid it.[12]

How can Eteocles keep Thebes safe? In the stylized
combat of *Seven Against Thebes*, each of the captains carries a
shield emblazoned with a heraldic, allegorical device denot-
ing the bearer's ethos, intent, and strength. Assigned by lot,
a pair of captains will fight it out at each of Thebes' seven
gates. The outcome of each of these confrontations can be
forecast—perhaps even manipulated—by skillfully interpreting the symbolic interplay between the shield devices. Thus
the wager: Eteocles bets that he can keep himself and Thebes
safe by interpreting, like a seer, the significance of the shield
devices. At the end of the opening speech, he lays down
the wager:

---

12   Aeschylus, *Seven Against Thebes*, trans. Anthony Hecht and Helen
      Bacon, lines 5-17.

> But I myself have sent out scouts, sure-footed, clear
>   of eye,
> to spy on the camp. Their reports will save me
> from all traps and deception.[13]

Through the scout (despite the plural "scouts," there is only one scout in the play), he will learn where the hostile captains have been posted and the devices they bear. With this knowledge, he can examine the matchups and determine whether the gods are on his side.

When the scout returns, the process of interpretation begins: gate by gate the scout describes the assailant: name, appearance, vaunts, and, most importantly, the shield device. Gate by gate Eteocles reaches into mythology to find an answer. If the enemy brandishes the image of Typhon and the defender has Zeus emblazoned on his shield, Eteocles concludes that heaven favours his cause: Zeus, after all, had tamed Typhon. Six times the scout reports, and six times Eteocles finds the answer. He is now at the point of maximum confidence—only the seventh gate remains. Then the dramatic marvelous happens: the scout reports that Eteocles' brother, Polyneices, is at the seventh gate. It is an unexpected turn, as Eteocles had not counted on fighting him. It is a worst-case scenario: there are rituals to purify spilt blood, but no rituals exist to purify spilt kindred blood. Since all the captains have been dispatched to the other gates, Eteocles realizes that Fate summons him to confront the Fury and the Curse. He calls for his armour, an action which leads to the point of no return: the cast.

---

13   Ibid., lines 53-5.

By the end of the opening speech (line 55), Eteocles has disclosed both the temptation and the wager. The cast, however, does not take place until line 907, when Eteocles hastens to gate seven. Thirty-eight lines separate the temptation and the wager, while eight hundred and fifty-two lines separate the wager from the cast. The lengthy span between wager and cast is what backloads the play.

Dramatists who desire audiences to sit on the edge of their seats enjoy writing backloaded tragedies, tragedies full of suspense, full of the thrill of it all. In the buildup of action and devastation, backloaded tragedies resemble southern Californian wildfires. Southern California is an area extending along the Pacific coast from the Tehachapi Mountains in the north to San Diego in the south. The region is prone to large, devastating forest fires. South of southern California is the contiguous Mexican state of Baja California. Although the vegetation and climate are similar, forest fires in Baja California are smaller and limited in scope. This is the result of different philosophies in fire suppression.[14] While Baja California has a policy of letting fires burn themselves out,

14   On the southern/Baja California fire mosaic hypothesis, see Minnich, "Fire Mosaics in Southern California and Northern Baja California," *Science* 219, issue 4590 (18 March 1983): 1287-94. Cf. Malamud, Morein, and Turcotte, "Forest Fires: An Example of Self-Organized Critical Behavior," *Science* 281, issue 5384 (18 September 1998): 1840, who find that the aggressive fire suppression policy at Yellowstone National Park prior to 1972 was a contributing factor to the 1988 Yellowstone Fires where over 800,000 acres burned. As a result, they call the accumulation of dead trees, undergrowth, and very old trees which result from aggressive fire suppression policies the "Yellowstone effect."

southern California has had a lower tolerance towards letting fires burn. But its aggressive fire suppression policy has only given the impression of safety. Each time a fire has been suppressed, dead or diseased trees, brush, and undergrowth has accumulated, increasing the odds of an unstoppable conflagration. Nature delayed strikes back with exponential force. Like fire suppression in southern California, backloaded tragedy delays nature, as it allows the pot to grow too high in the long interval between the wager and the cast. The outcome in the cases of both southern Californian wildfires and backloaded tragedies is the same: total devastation.

Backloaded tragedies include the likes of *Doctor Faustus* and *Oedipus rex*. These are the tragedies with the nail-biting, hair-raising denouements. The dramatist dams up the action in the long span between wager and cast, keeping the audience in a state of uncertainty. However, in maintaining the suspense and delaying the conclusion, realism is sacrificed. For example, *Seven Against Thebes* relies on an extended proxy battle by heraldry to delay the outcome. In *Oedipus rex*, before the recognition scene can occur, the Corinthian messenger (who knows that Oedipus has been adopted) and the shepherd (who knows the identity of Oedipus' birth parents), have to come together by a strange twist of fate. In comparison with the realism inherent in gradual tragedies, backloaded tragedies smack of artifice. In comparison with frontloaded tragedies, backloaded tragedies examine the ramifications of the gambling act in less detail (because the cast is delayed until the end of the tragedy, less time remains to explore its after-effects). Since the thrill lies more in *how* the dramatist reaches the denouement and less in *what* the denouement actually is, backloaded tragedies often take their themes from mythological and other sources where the ending is already known.

By delaying the cast as long as possible, plays such as *Seven Against Thebes* keep audiences in suspense. The art of back-loaded tragedy lies in taking an inevitable outcome (such as Eteocles and Polyneices' duel to the death) and making it seem truly random (having dispatched all the captains to the first six gates, Eteocles *has* to man the seventh gate where his brother *happens* to be). Similarly, although the outcome of *Oedipus rex* was inevitable, *how* he discovers his identity seems truly random: during the course of the regicide investigation, a messenger from Corinth arrives—seemingly out of nowhere—to report that Oedipus' parents (or who he had thought to be his parents) have died. By an uncanny coincidence, it turns out that this selfsame Corinthian messenger had handed over baby Oedipus to his adopted parents many years ago. During the course of the conversation, Oedipus learns that he had been adopted. The Corinthian messenger does not know, however, who Oedipus' birth parents are. To find out, the shepherd from whom he had received the abandoned babe would need to be summoned. This shepherd knows the identity of Oedipus' birth parents since the birth parents had charged him to abandon the baby (they did this to avoid the oracle that son would kill father). But in a second uncanny coincidence, it turns out that this selfsame shepherd is also the sole witness who can identify Laius' killer: he was part of Laius' train when Oedipus committed his ancient act of road rage. It is only at this point, after the seemingly random concatenation of unlikely encounters with characters who possess the most extraordinary knowledge, that the inevitable conclusion takes place.

Seven Against Thebes and *Oedipus rex* both develop tension through the antinomies of fate and free will; in a strange twist, fate becomes contingent on free will. By making one contingent on the other, the writer of backloaded tragedy makes the deterministic and the free more interesting because they have become counterintuitively intertwined. As such, backloaded tragedies may draw on familiar mythological or historical sources because the new thrill lies in how the dramatist intertwines fate and free will. That the ending is already known is of little consequence. Ancients did not worry about spoilers; only moderns do.

FRONTLOADED TRAGEDY

Frontloaded tragedies, such as *Macbeth*, exemplify the third and final tempo at which tragedies play out. These types of dramas situate all three parts of the troika near the beginning. In act 1, scene 3, the witches prophesy to Macbeth, tempting the hero. By act 1, scene 5, the wager is already out: the milk of human kindness for the crown. Act 1 closes with Macbeth moving offstage to murder Duncan: the cast. Although *Macbeth* contains five acts, the tripartite structure is complete by the end of the first act. The troika loads down the front of the play. Corneille's *The Cid* also exemplifies frontloading. In act 1, scene 5, Don Diego tempts his son, Don Rodrigo, by asking him to restore a father's honour. The catch is that Don Diego has been slighted by the father of

Ximena, who happens to be Don Rodrigo's beloved. In the next scene, Don Rodrigo formulates the wager:

> It is my father who's offended, and
> Ximena's father has offended him!
> What battle fierce within!
> Against my honour passion takes up arms.
> If I avenge him, then I must lose *her*.[15]

Then, in act 2, scene 2, Don Rodrigo rolls the die by challenging Ximena's father to a duel and slaying him. A whole three and a half acts continue to play out after the duel, and, for this reason, *The Cid* is an example of frontloading. Since the cast occurs early on in frontloaded plays, plenty of time remains for the denouement to unwind, a sharp contrast to tragedy in other tempi where there is less time to consider the denouement. Because the bulk of the play in frontloaded tragedy takes place after the cast, frontloaded tragedy offers an ideal vehicle for exploring a deed's after-effects—the chain of events that happen *after* the cast, that is, the repercussions. Such repercussions include the psychological or social implications of action; for example, *Macbeth* meditates on the psychology of tyranny, while *The Cid* studies the social nexus of a world run on honour.

Frontloaded tragedies begin with an explosion and end in introspection. To gauge the impact of how explosive frontloaded plays are, compare two tragedies by the same playwright: frontloaded *Macbeth* and gradual *Othello*. Because the

---

15   Corneille, *The Cid*, trans. John Cairncross, 1.6.299-303.

troika uncoils like a snake in waiting, the first act of *Macbeth* plays out a taut whirlwind of action: the rebel war, witches, the homecoming, an ambitious wife, houseguests, and then murder. In contrast, the first act of *Othello* concludes with Iago setting up Othello's temptation, thus rendering the play more methodical and less helter-skelter. Any Shakespearean tragedy begins intensely, but the intensity with which *Macbeth* opens is feverish and remarkable even by Shakespeare's standards. This effect is achieved through frontloading.

Frontloaded tragedies such as *Macbeth* and *The Cid* begin with a bang that quickly yields to a psychological or social meditation on the after-effects and repercussions of choice and decision. For this reason, playwrights concerned with what the deed does to a person or a community write in this tempo. Spoilers have little effect on frontloaded tragedy because the frontloaded tragedy specializes in examining the consequences of action. For this reason, frontloaded tragedy may also dramatize mythological and historical stories; in fact, familiar stories are helpful, as the frictional losses of expending lines that introduce characters, illustrate their connections, and set the scene may be eliminated.

TEMPO IN ACTIVE AND DESCRIPTIVE PLAYS

While considerable freedom exists in placing the temptation, wager, and cast, all three parts must be dramatized within a successful play. That is, these parts must develop and unfold within the dramatic stream of the action rather than through narration, flashback, reminiscence, or foreshadowing. They must take place in the dramatic present rather than the

play's pre- or posthistory. The cycle from temptation to cast
is the plot of the play. Because a play is an enactment of a
plot, a play must be acted out, not narrated, in order for it
to perform its function. An *active* play acts out the troika in
the dramatic present before the audience. A *descriptive* play,
however, narrates or foreshadows one or more elements of
the troika which already have taken place or are yet to come;
thus, in a descriptive play, parts of the troika occur completely extraneous to the action. Active plays are therefore
superior to descriptive plays, since the function of drama lies
in action rather than in narration. Active plays act out the
troika; descriptive plays talk about the troika.

In Aeschylus' *Persians*, for example, Xerxes is tempted
to equal his father Darius' renown in empire building.[16] He
wagers that he could do so by subjugating Greece, a victory
that can be accomplished by transporting his army across
the Hellespont into Greece. The die is cast when he yokes
together the Hellespont with an armada of ships. So far
so good. The problem is that none of the action takes part
within the play. The play is set in Susa, where Atossa and
the chorus of elders await messengers from the Greek expedition. While waiting, they summon the ghost of Darius to
interpret Atossa's troubling dreams. The audience learns of
Xerxes' temptation, wager, and cast through the dialogue
between Atossa and the ghost. The spectacle of divination
forms the play's centerpiece. Instead of dramatizing Xerxes'
desire to equal his father, the play dramatizes the spectacle

---

16   Aeschylus, *The Persians*, in *Prometheus Bound and Other Plays*, trans.
      Philip Vellacott.

of divination. Because the characters spend their time talking about, recounting, and discussing Xerxes' actions, *The Persians* is a descriptive play. Xerxes does not actually do very much: he makes a brief appearance at the end as he returns from the expedition in tatters. As such, the troika is relegated to an extracurricular position outside the stream of action. There is something of a Monday morning quarterback in descriptive plays: it is like hearing about a game rather than watching the game. Aeschylus' *Prometheus Bound* also relies on narrative rather than dramatic elements: Prometheus spends much of the play relating to his various visitors how he had dared to defy Zeus by stealing fire and teaching mortals the arts and sciences.[17]

In an active play, however, the cycle from temptation to cast occurs in the dramatic present. Macbeth, for example, does not tell the story of how the king was assassinated: he does it. Orestes in Aeschylus' *Libation Bearers* does not tell the story of how a son avenged his father: he does it. Pentheus in Euripides' *Bacchae* does not tell the story of how he challenged a god: he does it. The audience watches these crucial actions unfold. *Macbeth*, *Libation Bearers*, and *The Bacchae* prove to be more successful dramas than *The Persians* or *Prometheus Bound* because the action takes place in real time. Perhaps active plays draw in the audience more than descriptive plays for the same reason that writing experts recommend using active rather than passive verbs: they get closer to the action.

---

17   Aeschylus, *Prometheus Bound*, in *Prometheus Bound and Other Plays*, trans. Philip Vellacott.

How the troika is arranged impacts the tempo of tragedy. Frontloaded tragedies begin at a breakneck pace and end in reflection (*e.g.*, *Macbeth*). They make useful vehicles to examine the wager's often unexpected ramifications and consequences. Backloaded tragedies (e.g., *Oedipus rex*) draw out the cast until the final moments, and end in a bang. These plays find success by keeping the audience in suspense. In gradual tragedies, the troika proceeds in clockwork motion (e.g., *The Master Builder*). This configuration results in an unmatched level of realism. All three tempi may result in enduring and memorable creations if three guidelines are followed. One: present the troika through action rather than narration. Two: draw the audience in with the poetics of chaos while establishing the dramatic direction at the first available opportunity by setting down the hero's temptation. Three: match up the appropriate plot to the appropriate tempo. That is to say, if a plot focuses on the psychological deterioration of a long fall from grace, then frontload the tragedy.

3 FORMS OF TRAGEDY

The three distinct forms of tragedy that I have devised may be likened to the actions of different types of earthquakes: sometimes they shake fiercely, but briefly, and in one place. Other times, numerous quakes break out over multiple areas, rocking many places simultaneously. On yet other occasions, the incipient shock is but the first strike in a series of powerful convulsions, each of which break out like waves cresting one upon another.

Standalone tragedies, I suggest, emulate earthquakes that are one and done: they dramatize the outbreak, development, and conclusion of a single risk event, each of which consists of a temptation, wager, and cast. Standalone tragedies concentrate on an individual hero, as in the case of *Hamlet* or *Doctor Faustus*.

Tragedies that I consider to develop in *parallel-motion*, however, resemble earthquakes where the entire continental shelf crumbles into the ocean, taking with it a multitude of cities. In these plays, many risk events occur simultaneously, ensnaring a multitude of heroes in a complex web, such as in Corneille's *Cinna* or O'Neill's *Strange Interlude*.

I equate *perpetual-motion tragedies* to the faults so full of cracks that the initial convulsion fails to restore the teetering imperfect earth. To restore equilibrium, multiple aftershocks of equal or greater magnitude are required. Think of such trilogies as Aeschylus' *Oresteia* or O'Neill's *Mourning Becomes Electra*.

Like gradual, backloaded, and frontloaded tragedies, these three forms of tragedy result from different configurations of the fundamental risk theatre troika. Just as differing intervals between temptation, wager, and cast offer the possibility of those three tempi in risk theatre—gradual, backloaded, and frontloaded—so risk events can occur individually, in unison, or one after another, thus making possible my three forms of risk theatre: standalone, parallel-motion, and perpetual-motion. While the appeal of standalone tragedy lies in its dogged exploration of a single theme, parallel-motion tragedy delights by intertwining the complications of many characters. In perpetual-motion tragedy, the propagation, mutation, and transformation of a risk event through a multitude of cycles invites speculation on greater themes and offers philosophic appeal. Understanding these tempi and forms aids in grasping the very structure of risk theatre.

STANDALONE TRAGEDY

Standalone tragedy throws the spotlight on a single hero. In *Doctor Faustus*, for example, the hero Faustus stands head and shoulders above the others. Because a single hero engages in a single risk event, standalone tragedy possesses surface simplicity. Tempted to find the art that "stretcheth as far as doth the mind of man," Faustus turns to evocation and wagers his soul.[1] Standalone tragedy also pursues a single question with tenacious persistence. In *Doctor Faustus*, the question is: *how can a man fail to find divine grace when God's mercy is limitless?* By approaching this question from multiple angles, Marlowe imparts the standalone form onto *Doctor Faustus*.

Marlowe's first approach to answering the main question is that a man falls short because he is too clever. Faustus wilfully misinterprets the Bible to justify apostasy:

> FAUSTUS. When all is done, divinity is best.
> Jerome's Bible, Faustus, view it well.
> [*He reads.*] *Stipendium peccati mors est.* Ha!
> *Stipendium*, etc.
> The reward of sin is death. That's hard.[2]

Is the reward of sin death? It is if one omits—as Faustus does—the second half of the verse, which reads: "For the wages of sin *is* death; but the gift of God *is* eternal life through Jesus Christ our Lord."[3] By quoting some lines and omitting others, Faustus uses his ingenuity to twist Scripture to validate apostasy. Faustus continues by quoting 1 John 1:8: "If we say that we have no sin, / We deceive ourselves, and there's no truth in us."[4] But the intent of that passage only emerges from reading it in conjunction with the verse that follows it, one which, again, Faustus omits: "If we confess

---

1   Marlowe, *Doctor Faustus*, 1.1.63.
2   Ibid., 1.1.37–41.
3   Rom. 6:23 (King James Version).
4   Marlowe, *Doctor Faustus*, 1.1.44–5.

our sins, he is faithful and just to forgive us *our* sins, and to cleanse us from all unrighteousness."[5] The clever misreading allows him to draw the conclusion:

> Why then, belike, we must sin,
> And so consequently die.
> Ay, we must die an everlasting death.
> What doctrine call you this? *Che serà, serà*:
> What will be, shall be? Divinity, adieu![6]

If death is everlasting, is there any reason *not* to practice black magic? He has turned Scripture against itself. As such, he is too clever for his own good.

Marlowe's second approach to the question is that a man falls short because greed blinds him. As Faustus weighs the pros and cons of selling his soul, two angels vie for his loyalty:

> GOOD ANGEL. Sweet Faustus, leave that execra-
> ble art.

> FAUSTUS. Contrition, prayer, repentance—what
> of them?

> GOOD ANGEL. O, they are means to bring thee
> unto heaven.

---

5   1 John 1:8 (King James Version).

6   Marlowe, *Doctor Faustus*, 1.1.46–50.

EVIL ANGEL. Rather illusions, fruits of lunacy,
That makes men foolish that do trust them most.

GOOD ANGEL. Sweet Faustus, think of heaven and
heavenly things.

EVIL ANGEL. No, Faustus, think of honour and of
wealth. (*Exeunt.*)

FAUSTUS. Of wealth?
Why, the seigniory of Emden shall be mine.[7]

Greed blinds Faustus from God's grace.

In Marlowe's third approach, a man falls short because of
denial. Salvation is an inconvenient truth for one who traffics
with spirits. One form of denial manifests itself in disputing
hell with the devil:

FAUSTUS. Come, I think hell's a fable.

MEPHISTOPHELES. Ay, think so still, till experience
change thy mind.

FAUSTUS. Why, think'st thou then that Faustus shall
be damned?

MEPHISTOPHELES. Ay, of necessity, for here's the scroll
Wherein thou hast given thy soul to Lucifer.

---

7   Ibid., 2.1.15–23.

FAUSTUS. Ay, and body too. But what of that?
Think'st thou that Faustus is so fond
To imagine that after this life there is any pain?
Tush, these are trifles and mere old wives' tales.

MEPHISTOPHELES. But, Faustus, I am an instance to
prove the contrary,
For I am damned and now in hell.[8]

Marlowe's fourth approach: a man falls short because of shame. After Faustus avails himself of the fiend too long, he becomes jaded to the point where he claims, "My heart's so hardened I cannot repent."[9] Towards the end of the twenty-four years, his negative confession, "I do repent, and yet I do despair," similarly demonstrates how shame invalidates any genuine feeling of regret.[10] Despair, the negative form of repentance, is useless, the sickness unto death, and it forms another barrier between Faustus and divine grace.

With Marlowe's fifth approach, a man falls short because his faith is weak. At one point, Faustus turns to God: "Ah, Christ, my Saviour, / Seek to save distressèd Faustus' soul!"[11] Each time he turns to God, however, his trembling faith fails to sustain him:

MEPHISTOPHELES. Thou traitor, Faustus, I arrest
thy soul

---

8   Ibid., 2.1.130–40.
9   Ibid., 2.3.18.
10   Ibid., 5.1.63.
11   Ibid., 2.3.82–3.

For disobedience to my sovereign lord.
Revolt, or I'll in piecemeal tear thy flesh!

FAUSTUS. Sweet Mephistopheles, entreat thy lord
To pardon my unjust presumption,
And with my blood again I will confirm
My former vow I made to Lucifer.[12]

In *Doctor Faustus*, a single hero strives towards the finish line. Twenty-four years are compressed into five Jack-be-nimble acts that examine a single question. By approaching the crucial question from various perspectives, Marlowe imparts the standalone form onto *Doctor Faustus*.

Standalone tragedy is an insistent art. Driven ever forward by its own momentum, this art form is fleet, nimble, and light on its toes. It favours themes that ride right into the action: crimes of passion, the limits of ambition, and the mechanics of revenge are perennial favourites. Consequently, it risks becoming hackneyed. To maintain its dramatic fires, this form of tragedy must find ways to make trite themes novel.

This challenge confronted Shakespeare as he wrote *Hamlet*. *Hamlet* could have emerged as another run-of-the-mill tragedy starring a ghost demanding vengeance. On the surface, the story *does* appear run-of-the-mill: a ghost tempts Hamlet to avenge his father. Hamlet as avenger risks his innocence for revenge ("Taint not thy mind," warns the ghost).[13] The die is cast as he confronts Claudius. Strategy leads to

---

12   Ibid., 5.1.67–73.
13   Shakespeare, *Hamlet*, 1.5.85.

tragedy. They all die. The end. Just another average play. But we know that *Hamlet* offers more, because an *underlying* temptation plays out beneath the surface: Hamlet is infatuated with certainty. He will buy certainty at all costs. He is tempted to know whether or not the ghost is an honest ghost. He is after gnostic certainty.

> HAMLET. I'll have these players
> Play something like the murther of my father
> Before mine uncle. I'll observe his looks,
> I'll tent him to the quick. If 'a do blench,
> I know my course. The spirit that I have seen
> May be a [dev'l], and the [dev'l] hath power
> T' assume a pleasing shape, yea, and perhaps,
> Out of my weakness and my melancholy,
> As he is very potent with such spirits,
> Abuses me to damn me. I'll have grounds
> More relative than this—the play's the thing
> Wherein I'll catch the conscience of the King.[14]

He is tempted by theological certainty: if he cuts down a repentant Claudius, does Claudius' soul fly to heaven or hell? And if it flies to heaven, is what he does "hire and salary" or "revenge" proper?[15] He is tempted by fiduciary certainty: before the funeral feast grows cold, will wife be loyal to husband?[16] On the surface, Hamlet plays a revenger, but underneath it all, he is a philosopher of certainty. By layering

---

14   Ibid., 2.2.594-605.
15   Ibid., 3.3.73-9.
16   Ibid., 1.2.180-1.

an underlying temptation (for certainty) beneath the surface of what is ostensibly a revenge tragedy, Shakespeare turns good into great.

How does Shakespeare integrate the underlying temptation into the course of the play? He integrates it every step of the way. Tempted by gnostic certainty, Hamlet drops throwaway hints to test Claudius' guilt, thereby triggering Claudius' suspicion. The further Hamlet verifies the ghost's story, the more he tips his hand—even knowledge exacts an opportunity cost. When Hamlet makes a power play for absolute certainty by dramatizing the murder of his father before Claudius, he catches the king's conscience red-handed. But, by the time Hamlet feels completely sure of Claudius's guilt, Claudius is equally sure that Hamlet must be deposed.

Tempted by theological certainty, Hamlet passes up a chance at revenge. He encounters Claudius unarmed, without a guard, and with his back turned. But Claudius is praying, and Hamlet does not want to take a chance by killing Claudius repentant: his soul might fly to heaven. He forgoes the present imperfect occasion for revenge, waiting instead for a future perfect opportunity. There is a time value to action, which, once lost, is lost forever as a "could have," "should have," or "would have." There is a price to be paid for running down the clock.

Tempted by fiduciary certainty, Hamlet jeopardizes his relationships with Gertrude and Ophelia. The haste with which his mother remarried has made him wary of women. Preferring certainty in solitude to living in constant doubt, Hamlet breaks Gertrude by questioning her loyalties and directs Ophelia to a nunnery. In the heat of the moment, while questioning Gertrude, he accidentally kills Polonius. Ophelia, blindsided by the rejection, commits suicide. The cost of Hamlet's fiduciary certainty is that Laertes—Polonius' son and Ophelia's brother—now returns to avenge their deaths. Hamlet now fights on two fronts: against both Laertes and Claudius.

While ostensibly a revenge tragedy, *Hamlet* tests the hypothesis that the more certain one is, the less capable one is of action. The corollary of the thesis is that uncertainty enables action. Here, Fortinbras acts as Hamlet's foil. Having set his life on the line in a most uncertain venture for a piece of land of even more uncertain worth, Fortinbras acts with such gusto that he unexpectedly finds the Danish crown awaiting him atop the pile of bodies, one of which is Hamlet's. By testing the cost of certainty, a straightforward standalone tragedy such as *Hamlet* uncovers a hidden principle: to act is not to think; certainty kills action. Hamlet loses because he acts on certainty; Fortinbras wins because he acts on uncertainty. At Elsinore, fortune favours gamblers.

Standalone tragedy represents the most straightforward and insistent form of this art. While potentially the most dramatic of the tragic forms, standalone tragedy easily becomes trite when spectacle overcomes substance. The greater the relevance of the central question—*Hamlet*'s "What is the cost of certainty?" and *Doctor Faustus*' "How can a man fail to find divine grace when God's mercy is limitless?"—the greater the substance of standalone drama.

PARALLEL-MOTION TRAGEDY

With masterpieces such as *Doctor Faustus* and *Hamlet*, the Elizabethans perfected standalone tragedy featuring a single protagonist. If the next generation of tragedians were to make a name for themselves, they would have to come up with a form to call their own. The writers of French classical drama did exactly that by devising the type of tragedy that I call parallel motion. In parallel-motion tragedies, multiple characters experience multiple risk events. For example, Corneille's *Cinna* abounds in so many protagonists that at one moment one could say, "Emilia is the heroine," and at the next moment, "No, Cinna must be the chief protagonist." With equal justification, one could say, "This is the tragedy of Maximus" or "Augustus is the prime mover." The fluidity with which characters trade off the lead role differentiates parallel-motion from standalone tragedy, in which it would be impossible to say, "Rosencrantz is the prime mover" or "Lady Macbeth is the chief protagonist." French classical drama embraced a form of tragedy starring multiple leads, although the kernel of this parallel-motion tragedy may indeed be found in standalone tragedy (e.g., the Ophelia and Norway subplots in *Hamlet* or the Gloucester subplot of *King Lear*).

In parallel-motion tragedy, multiple risk events break out in tandem. For example, in Corneille's *Cinna*, revenge tempts Emilia, the proscript's daughter: Augustus had murdered her father. She wagers that Cinna will assassinate Augustus to win her hand. At the same time, Emilia's charm entices Cinna, who wagers his life to win her love; he thus throws the proverbial die when he convinces Augustus to hold onto empire, even while using empire as a pretext to assassinate him. Maximus, enticed by liberty, puts his money on Cinna; but he loves Emilia as well, and when he learns that Cinna is a rival, he betrays the conspiracy to get rid of Cinna. Throughout all of this action, dreams of a civilian life tempt Augustus, and he consequently wagers that he can trust his chief lieutenants, Cinna and Maximus—who happen, however, to be the chief plotters of the conspiracy. Parallel-motion tragedies make for a busy stage.

Tragedies in parallel motion often resemble jigsaw puzzles: many edges and contours must be interlocked. Augustus' pursuit of greatness must be tied to Cinna's pursuit of Emilia, Emilia's revenge, and Maximus' idealism. The pleasure of the parallel-motion tragedy lies in the skill and economy with which the dramatist interlocks divergent motives. In the case of *Cinna*, Corneille weaves his drama together by imbuing Augustus with the quality of magnanimity: despite the attempt on his life, Augustus gives Sicily to Maximus, takes in Emilia as a goddaughter, and blesses the marriage between Cinna and Emilia. By doing so, he ends Emilia's hatred, Cinna's divided loyalties, and Maximus' envy.

Characters in parallel-motion tragedy share the stage and, as a result, struggle to blossom into the full-fledged individuals of standalone tragedy. In *Cinna*, Emilia, Cinna, Augustus, and Maximus each share but a quarter of the timeshare stage. True, the protagonists of standalone tragedy also share the stage, but, on the standalone stage, the other characters only exist for their sakes. Shakespeare's Gloucester doubles King Lear, thus amplifying Lear; Lady Macbeth acts as Macbeth's evil genius. The thrill, therefore, of parallel-motion tragedy

lies in anticipating how the tessellating jigsaw pieces inter-
lock with one another, rather than in watching the rise and
fall of a solitary titan ranging the stage. It is not that parallel-
motion tragedy cannot develop characters like unto life. It
can. O'Neill's *Strange Interlude* attests to this. Surprisingly,
however, in fleshing out the characters, a play such as
O'Neill's shows why characterization forms a weak point in
parallel-motion tragedy.

For the sake of lending colour to his quartet of characters,
O'Neill stretches the dramatic form to its limits. A performance of *Strange Interlude* lasts five hours or longer.[17] The play
spans nine acts in two parts. The dramatic time frame is measured not in days, months, or even years, but by the passing
generations. In addition to standard dialogue, the characters
speak their thoughts out loud in a stream of mental footnotes
that elucidate their inner thought processes:

MADELINE. (*with the calm confidence of one who
knows*) Yes, you can bank on Gordon never losing
his nerve.

NINA. (*coldly*) I'm quite aware my son isn't a weakling—(*meaningly, with a glance at Madeline*) even
though he does do weak things sometimes.

---

17   In its 1928 Broadway premiere, *Strange Interlude* played five hours,
      not including the hour-and-twenty-minute dinner intermission.
      See Atkinson, review of *Strange Interlude*, *New York Times*, January
      31, 1928.

MADELINE. (*without lowering the glasses from her eyes—thinking good-naturedly*) Ouch! . . . that was meant for me! . . . (*then hurt*) Why does she dislike me so? . . . I've done my best, for Gordon's sake, to be nice to her . . .[18]

In the course of the play, Charlie desires Nina, Nina wants to make Sam happy, Sam wants in on the big leagues, and Darrell conducts experiments on happiness. Charlie struggles as a writer, Nina transforms from maiden to matron, Sam perseveres through failure to find the American dream, and Darrell becomes more and more entangled in his experiments on happiness (it did not help that one of his experiments consisted of making Sam a father by getting Nina with child). Each of the four leads emerges as full-fledged characters, more like Macbeth and Faustus than the cardboard cutouts in *Cinna*. But the lengths to which O'Neill has gone to achieve full characterization testify to why tragedy in parallel motion is unsuited to this end: a standard performance lacks the time necessary to develop multiple leads into full-blown personalities.[19] A tragedy in parallel motion that attempts full characterizations illustrates how art looks when it is encumbered by the limits of its own form, for the

---

18   O'Neill, *Strange Interlude*, in *Three Plays*, p. 217.

19   Atkinson, review of *Strange Interlude*, *New York Times* May 13, 1928 would even argue that five hours and nine acts is an insufficient space to develop the quartet of characters: "Although the play is in nine acts, Mr. O'Neill has no time in which to develop his characters in the round and to show us the subordinate qualities which have made them people of standing in the world."

primary delight of parallel-motion tragedy lies in seeing how the pieces of the drama connect with one another, not in the pieces themselves.

PERPETUAL-MOTION TRAGEDY

In the third form of the art, perpetual-motion tragedy, one risk event triggers the next so that "ere ever the ancient wound is healed, fresh blood is spilled."[20] Perpetual-motion tragedy comes prepackaged as a trilogy (from *tri* "three" and *logos* "story"), a set of three interconnected plays. Aeschylus' *Oresteia* trilogy, for example, comprises *Agamemnon*, *The Libation Bearers*, and *The Eumenides*.[21] Likewise, O'Neill's *Homecoming*, *The Hunted*, and *The Haunted* together form the *Mourning Becomes Electra* trilogy.[22] Each of the individual plays in the trilogy dramatizes a single risk event, and for this reason, the perpetual-motion and standalone forms are similar. How they differ is that the perpetual-motion tragedy dramatizes a succession of risk events by interconnecting three plays while standalone drama stops at a single risk event in a single play. That the risk events occur in succession and not simultaneously differentiates the perpetual-motion and parallel-motion forms.

We observe how one risk event engenders the next in *Agamemnon*: Clytemnestra avenges filicide by committing

20   Aeschylus, *Agamemnon*, in *Agamemnon, Libation-Bearers, Eumenides, Fragments*, trans. Herbert Weir Smyth, lines 1479-80.

21   The *Oresteia* originally included a fourth play, the comedic satyr-play *Proteus*, now lost.

22   O'Neill, *Mourning Becomes Electra*, in *Three Plays*.

mariticide. In the second play of the trilogy, *The Libation Bearers*, Orestes revenges his mother's mariticide by committing matricide. In the final play, *The Eumenides*, spilt maternal blood moves the Furies to pursue Orestes to Athens, which they vow to destroy unless Athena upholds their ancient prerogative to punish blood crimes.

A similar perpetual-motion process, inspired by the *Oresteia*, plays out in the *Mourning Becomes Electra* trilogy. In *Homecoming*, Christine, seeking to escape the oppression of the Mannons, takes a lover and poisons her husband. In the second play, *The Hunted*, Lavinia and Orin, their children, hunt down Christine and her lover, driving the former to suicide and murdering the latter. The third play, *The Haunted*, examines the consequences of dirty justice.

Perpetual-motion tragedies, demanding for both playwrights and audiences, are uncommon. Time-pressed audiences barely have the patience to sit through one play, let alone three. And playwrights strain to sustain a theme through a single play, let alone a trilogy. The process of creating a perpetual-motion tragedy involves more than that of a standalone tragedy, where the goal is to get in and out as quickly as possible. Perpetual-motion tragedy dramatizes a process. If standalone tragedy may be compared to a song, perpetual-motion tragedy is like a symphony.

Symphony is a process: a kernel of an idea is planted in the music and develops through tone, harmony, and rhythm. Bruckner's Ninth Symphony opens with an expansive and soaring theme. Like a Jenga tower, each time the line is repeated an element is removed until at last—unlike a Jenga tower—the long line floats impossibly on the very air. In this way, the process by which faith gathers strength finds musical expression.

Symphony is music with a message. It could be a declaration of faith. Or it could celebrate universal brotherhood, as in the case of Beethoven's Ninth. Just as symphony is the king of musical forms, perpetual-motion tragedy, speaking from a stage three plays deep, is the king of dramatic forms.

As the king of dramatic forms, perpetual-motion tragedy, like symphony, offers a larger than life message. The *Oresteia* projects a message of hope, the hope that human sensibility can triumph over the severity of Heroic Age justice. The trilogy begins with Heroic Age justice in action: because Paris had abducted Helen—his onetime host's wife—all of Troy falls. In order to punish one wanton act committed by one wanton individual, they perished by the thousands—Achaeans and barbarians alike. The fall of Troy illustrates both the effectiveness of retributive justice as a moral deterrent, as well as its staggering cost. In *Agamemnon*, the onstage presence of two peripheral characters, Cassandra—formerly a princess, now a war bride—and the grizzled Argive veteran—homesick out of his mind—testify to the cost of Heroic Age justice, which is blind to human suffering. One of the main problems with that form of justice is its appetite for retribution, which feeds on the many to satisfy the one.

Clytemnestra commits the next act of Heroic Age justice in the *Oresteia*. Her husband, Agamemnon, had sacrificed their daughter Iphigenia for a safe passage to Troy (to punish Paris). She summons the Furies (the agents of retributive justice) for help and subsequently murders Agamemnon, believing that his death balances the scales of justice.

However, because of its appetite for retribution, Heroic Age justice has the additional shortcoming of being self-perpetuating. As an example of how it perpetuates strife, after the mariticide, Agamemnon and Clytemnestra's two children, Orestes and Electra, call upon the avenging Furies for justice: "Let those who killed," prays Electra in the second play of the trilogy, "taste death for death."[23] Again, the Furies comply. After all, their task as agents of retributive justice is to preserve social order by punishing blasphemy, improprieties between guests and hosts, and blood crimes. Orestes kills his mother, reckoning that one last desperate blood crime caps the violence. But justice is insatiate, and the Furies, in turn, pursue the matricide.

From Paris and Agamemnon to Clytemnestra and Orestes, each risk event illustrates the flaw of Heroic Age justice in an increasingly interconnected world: every event touches every other event in humanity's web. Paris suffers justly, but the victims of war suffer unjustly. Agamemnon suffers justly, but his children suffer unjustly. By preserving the social order, justice destroys the social order. The crisis reaches a boiling point in the person of Orestes, who is damned if he does not avenge his father and damned if he kills his mother. Paris, Agamemnon, and Clytemnestra damned themselves, but Orestes is damned by the system.

Orestes' quandary forces the question: is there a way to give justice a more human face? The third play of the trilogy, *The Eumenides*, answers the question. After Orestes arrives in

---

23   Aeschylus, *The Choephori*, in *The Oresteian Trilogy*, trans. Philip Vellacott, p. 109.

Athens with the Furies in pursuit, Athena proposes a gentler, improved justice: a resolution of their dispute through a trial by jury. Her proposal offers a solution. Retributive justice is anger driven; trial by jury is evidence driven. Retributive justice is based on might; trial by jury is based on examination and cross-examination. Retributive justice is indiscriminate, bounded by the revenger's rage; trial by jury is discriminate: the jurors, being members of the community, have skin in the game. Retributive justice is personal; trial by jury is anonymous: the juror's ballots are unmarked. Retributive justice is the justice of the individual: the one decides the fate of the many; trial by jury reflects emerging democratic sensibilities: many members make up the jury, each negating by the mathematical rule of the law of large numbers the prejudices of the others. When the parties resolve their differences through the trial-by-jury process, the Furies are reborn as the Eumenides (the "Kindly Ones") and the process of transforming retributive to representative justice is complete, thus fulfilling the tragedy's overarching message of hope.

Characters in perpetual-motion tragedy are only dimly aware of the role they play in the overarching theme. In the *Oresteia*, for example, Orestes never witnesses the transformation of the Furies. Once acquitted, he is no longer needed. After thanking Athens and Athena, he makes an awkward exit, while the fate of Athens (which the Furies are threatening to destroy) still hangs on the line:

> ORESTES. So, Pallas, farewell;
> Farewell, citizens of Athens! May each strug-
>   gle bring
> Death to your foes, to you success and victory![24]

In this way, perpetual-motion tragedy is bigger than its characters, who are the mortal instruments of a higher process. In the *Oresteia*, while the characters pursue their vendettas, the higher process of transforming the Furies into the Eumenides takes place concurrently.

Mourning Becomes Electra plays out the *Oresteia* in reverse. The awe that Judge Mannon wields over the townsfolk and the austere portico of the Mannon household, designed in the style of a Greek temple, proclaim the distance and impartiality of justice. But the old-time vengeance lurks behind the pretence of higher justice. The name of justice may be impartial, but the angers, jealousies, and hatreds motivating it are all too partial. Each act of higher justice in *Mourning Becomes Electra* is also an act of base vengeance; thus the play sets justice on its head. In the name of justice, for example, Christine and Brant murder Mannon, who had taken Brant's share of the estate after letting his parents rot away. He deserves to die, but hatred and lust—not right, reason, and law—have moved justice. So too, Lavinia makes Christine pay for the murder of her father in the name of justice. But jealousy, not a sense of fair and reasonable conduct, moves Lavinia to seek justice. The idea of justice may be clean, but its hand is stained in blood.

---

24   Ibid., p. 173.

As the tragedy of *Mourning Becomes Electra* plays out, justice collapses back on itself. In defying her mother, Lavinia ends up becoming her mother. In rejecting his father, Orin ends up becoming his father. The play is capped off by the final implosion of justice: the shutters of the mansion—like a Greek temple in its glory—are nailed shut. Darkness entombs the house of the judge. For all of its promise, justice could not overcome the darkness of its human origins. While the *Oresteia* closes with new allegiances and new beginnings grounded on the just and the right, *Mourning Becomes Electra* closes with the Eumenides being reborn as the Furies and the Golden Age reverting back to an Iron Age. Despite their different outcomes, both plays exemplify perpetual-motion tragedy, a form of drama more about process than character.

Melpomene is tragedy's Muse, and if you will do Melpomene's work, consider applying my three forms of tragedy for the greatest effect. Playwrights with a good understanding of character—the conscious and unconscious motivations invisibly guiding action—would do well to try their hand at standalone tragedy. Those with an ear for string quartets, inventions in four parts, and counterpoint should write a multilayered parallel-motion tragedy. And finally, those who have something big to say, those to whom people, places, and things are fodder for illustrating a great idea, may consider composing a trilogy in perpetual-motion.

This concludes the structural discussion of tragedy—the question of *what* tragedy is. In order to determine *why* tragedy is what it is, we will now need to consider the philosophy of tragedy.

PART II

THE PHILOSOPHY
OF TRAGEDY
HOW RISK THEATRE WORKS

4 THE MYTH OF THE PRICE YOU PAY

Honour is bought with blood, and not
    with gold.[1]

The feeble reasoning of men's great minds
That treat the happiness of love like goods
And bid for adoration with their wealth!
It is the one thing in the bounds of earth
That cannot be exchanged for anything
But its own self. Love is the price of love.
It is the only diamond I possess
That I must either give away or hide;
Much like the merchant, who, to spite a king,
And since the whole of Venice could not pay,
Returned his pearl to the enriching sea
Rather than fix a price beneath its worth.[2]

Here is the foundation myth of tragedy, the *myth of the price you pay*. Like other myths, it imparts human

---

1   Marlowe, *The Jew of Malta*, in *The Complete Plays*, 2.2.56.

2   Schiller, *Don Carlos*, in *Don Carlos and Mary Stuart*, trans. Hilary Collier Sy-Quia and Peter Oswald, 2.8.712-23.

significance and meaning onto nature—by itself so distant, foreign, and elusive—by translating, arranging, selecting, idealizing, and highlighting the seemingly random phenomena of the perceptible world into a tale. Like other myths, it finds patterns in the jumble of the natural world. Like other myths, it is not so much a true or a false story, but a story deserving to be told, and told more for the sake of the telling than for the facts. The myth of the price you pay is a modern myth, one you will not find elsewhere because it is of my own devising, devised to translate the philosophy of tragedy into a memorable narrative.

Three related stories make up the myth of the price you pay. The first story starts with hunter societies and ends with the emergence of the first international markets in the early Bronze Age. It describes how things came to be valued in terms of opportunity cost—to have one thing is to give up another—and how, in the long course of time, a price came to be set upon human life. The myth of the price you pay begins when the idea of opportunity cost—normally applied to physical goods in the material world—is applied to the all-too-human.

The second story takes place in Bronze Age Greece and tells the tale of Sarpedon, Glaucus, and Achilles. It recounts how—in the prototragedy of the *Iliad*—Sarpedon and Glaucus monetize life and Achilles stands up to reject that monetization of life.[3] But for Achilles to do so, he had to pay the price all the same. His rejection forms the basic premise of tragedy: while human values cannot be bought with gold,

---

3   On the *Iliad* as the original tragedy, see Plato, *Republic* 598d.

they can indeed be bought with blood. The *Iliad*, I will argue, showcases the myth of the price you pay in action.

The third story maps the second story onto history. It tells the tale of how Croesus' invention of coinage in the sixth century BC increased material wealth but degraded the spirit: increases in material wealth all came at the expense of the spirit. A century after the invention of coinage, Sarpedon and Glaucus' view had prevailed: life had become fully monetized. At that point, the degraded masses clamoured out for redemption. Art, as the arbiter of human values, answered the call and gave the world tragedy. By using Achilles' rejection of life's monetization as a template, tragedy rose up to champion life by dramatizing the purchase of human values with blood, not gold.

THE FIRST STORY: HUNTER SOCIETIES TO INTERNATIONAL MARKETS

The myth of the price you pay begins with hunter societies. In hunter societies, like is worth like: the value of a beaver is worth a beaver, and a deer a deer, for example. A beaver could trade for a beaver or a deer for a deer. More often, however, one thing is traded for another: a beaver for a deer, for instance. The question then arises of how to establish their values relative to one another. The answer lies not far from the manner in which schoolchildren are taught how to combine fractions that contain unlike quantities: find a common denominator. The common denominator in the production of beaver and deer is labour: both beaver and deer take time to prepare. If it takes twice the time to prepare a beaver as it does to prepare a deer, one beaver naturally exchanges for, or is worth, two deer.[4] Because time is limited, when the hunter chooses to prepare a beaver, the option to prepare two deer is foregone; the unexercised option for two deer is the opportunity cost of one beaver.

Built into the myth of the price you pay is the idea that cost represents the negative part of choice, and that the cost must be paid as part of the process of choosing. It is a *quid pro quo*: there is no free lunch. Choice is decision, and decision, derived from the Latin verb *caedere* "cutting away from," implies that what is cut away is lost. The hunter brings home *either* one beaver *or* two deer, but not one beaver *and* two deer. Because opportunity cost is involved in choosing one beaver *or* two deer, a price can be set on beaver and deer.

In the hunter society, the objective opportunity cost of labour made it possible to value materials according to the cost of production, but at that stage assigning value to human life was not yet possible. As mentioned above, one beaver is

---

4   Following Smith, *The Wealth of Nations*, 1.6:

> In that early and rude state of society which precedes both the accumulation of stock and the appropriation of land, the proportion between the quantities of labour necessary for acquiring different objects seems to be the only circumstance which can afford any rule for exchanging them for one another. If among a nation of hunters, for example, it usually costs twice the labour to kill a beaver which it does to kill a deer, one beaver should naturally exchange for or be worth two deer. It is natural that what is usually the produce of two days' or two hours' labour, should be worth double of what is usually the produce of one day's or one hour's labour.

worth two deer because the option of two deer is foregone when one beaver is chosen. But what is foregone when one chooses life? Because the question is senseless, human life could not be expressed as a quantity of beaver, deer, or anything else. Over time, however, more sophisticated valuing mechanisms emerged that would enable markets to set a price on life.

Once trade expanded beyond the confines of sequestered hunter societies and an international marketplace emerged, the rising complexity of transactions overwhelmed the capacity to express worth by means of labour time. Sometimes one trading partner would increase productivity by, say, using a fan system instead of sun-drying pelts. At other times, beaver and deer were traded for species whose dwindling stocks commanded an endangered premium. Or it could be that one nation experienced a recessionary glut of labour, while its booming neighbour faced a labour shortage: the time value of labour could be mismatched. Or perhaps merchants formed guilds, imposing tariffs on imports and distorting the objective value of labour. The more trade expanded, the more the idea of valuing goods by labour time became obsolete.

As the international marketplace emerged, a supranational standard to which the worth of goods are pegged arose, thus antiquating the process of assigning value to goods by tabulating man-hours. In mercantile societies, the supranational standard may be a gold standard; in statist societies, it may be a fiat currency; in agrarian societies, it could be an oxen standard. Subjectivity and objectivity distinguished the old from the new systems. Valuing by labour time is an objective system: if it takes three days, three days will always equal three days. However, valuing by a gold standard, fiat currencies, or oxen is a subjective system: gold, paper, and oxen have no intrinsic worth. Their value is based on perception; depending on the evaluator, the item could be worth everything or nothing. The move from absolute value (objective man-hours) to perceived value (subjective currencies) resulted in an important consequence: placing a value on human life was now possible.

THE SECOND STORY: THE *ILIAD*

The *Iliad* captures the moment when sequestered hunter societies gave way to an emerging agrarian world order. Cyclopean walls and proud settlements atop rocky crags were displacing the nomadic road warrior life. Tribal hierarchy and isolation were giving way to cross-border shopping and international treaties. Yet, amid change, the old ways persisted in the numerous traditional vestiges, such as Ajax' seven-layered cowhide shield and Nestor, the wise old advisor from bygone days. In this way, the *Iliad* captures a critical junction between legend and history, between the Mycenaean world of the past and the Archaic period that was yet to come. The *Iliad*'s account of the meeting between Argive Diomedes and Lycian Glaucus shows how, as the world grew, it became possible to put a price on human life by using an oxen standard.

Like traders arriving at the market to exchange beaver for deer, Diomedes and Glaucus have arrived at Troy. But they have come to Scamander's banks not to transact beaver for deer, but to exchange—as heroes do—life for life. When they meet on the battlefield, the audience expects Diomedes, a king fighting for the Achaeans, to kill Glaucus, a squire fighting for the Trojans. In the hierarchical structure of the *Iliad*, a soldier falls to a squire, a squire falls to a king, and a king falls to a god. But something strange happens when they meet.

In the preamble to the one-on-one duel, Homeric combatants relate their lineage. That they take the care to recount their family histories when death hovers near is one of the endearing traits of the epic. After Glaucus recites his genealogy, Diomedes realizes that their grandfathers had been guest-friends: a two-handled gold cup sits in his house, a gift from Glaucus' grandfather to his grandfather, who gave in return a bright scarlet belt. In a surprise turn, Diomedes proposes, in lieu of taking Glaucus' life, a gift exchange to renew the ancestral friendship:

"Let us avoid each other's spears, even in the
    close fighting.
There are plenty of Trojans and famed companions
    in battle for me
to kill, whom the god sends me, or those I run
    down with my swift feet,
many Achaians for you to slaughter, if you can do it.
But let us exchange our armour, so that these others
    may know
how we claim to be guests and friends from the
    days of our fathers."
So they spoke, and both springing down from
    behind their horses
gripped each other's hands and exchanged the
    promise of friendship;

> but Zeus the son of Kronos stole away the wits
>   of Glaukos
> who exchanged with Diomedes the son of
>   Tydeus armour
> of gold for bronze, for nine oxen's worth the worth
>   of a hundred.[5]

As a surrogate to combat, the gift exchange reflects the balance of power between Diomedes and Glaucus that otherwise would have been revealed in the duel—with one notable exception: the duel reveals the *absolute* superiority of one over the other, for one dies while the other lives. The gift exchange, however, reveals the *quantitative* disparity of their worth down to the accuracy of the unit of measurement used. Since an oxen standard is used, the quantitative disparity between their worth can be measured down to the accuracy of one oxen. Whether one warrior's value equals three times or ten times that of his opponent in combat, in killing or being killed only the *absolute* superiority of one over the other is known. The gift exchange, however, reveals the disparity in their worth *by degree*. Diomedes gives Glaucus brass arms worth nine oxen and receives in exchange gold armour worth one hundred oxen. Subtracting nine from one hundred oxen leaves a difference of ninety-one oxen. Since Glaucus escapes the encounter with his life, the difference of ninety-one oxen *is* the inferred value of Glaucus' life.[6]

---

5   Homer, *Iliad*, trans. Richmond Lattimore, 6.226–36.

6   Though the idea that Glaucus negotiates for his life through the gift-exchange mechanism is unattested in the *Iliad*, such an

What had prevented the hunter society from pricing out existence was its use of labour time to calculate worth. Since labour time and life were equivalent, to measure one against the other would have been as helpful as showing the sun with a lamp, a mountain by a stone, or the ocean by a drop of water: something cannot be defined against itself. What had changed in the world of the *Iliad* was its adoption of an international oxen standard. Since the purchasing power of oxen, paper money, gold, and other symbols of notional value is based not on an objective anthropomorphic constant (i.e., labour time) but rather on a subjective idea of notional value, anything imaginable could be valued—including human life.

Oxen, dollars, and gold—as symbols of notional value—could proxy whatever the imagination desired, whether it be thirty shekels for a slave, a king's ransom, or *wergild*, the compensation paid by the killer to the victim's family. By a strange twist, the piece of paper or lump of metal that lacked intrinsic value was not worth nothing but rather, could be

---

interpretation is at least as old as Horace, *Satires*, in *The Complete Works of Horace*, trans. Charles E. Passage 1.7.12-18, who writes:

> Rage was so fierce between mighty Achilles and lofty-souled Hector,
> Scion of Priam, that only the death of the one or the other
> Could have concluded it, simply because, on the score of their prowess,
> Each was ranked foremost. If two who are cowards get into a jangle,
> Or if a poorly matched pair get involved—Diomédes when faced with
> Glaucus the Lycian, for instance,—the weaker backs down and may even
> Placate the other with gifts.

worth anything. Life had now become monetized, had become something tradable, like pork bellies on the Chicago Mercantile Exchange. It had become a commodity.

The Shadow Market and the Invention of Tragedy

The *Iliad* demonstrates through Diomedes and Glaucus' gift exchange how life could be monetized. Something, however, in the human spirit rejects the monetization of life and finds it most distasteful. So, in addition to demonstrating how life could be monetized, Homer also gave expression to the countermonetary spirit, and he does so in the story of how Achilles is wooed back into battle. Not for all the wealth of the world would Achilles return to the field. But when he does come back, he comes back for the sake of friendship, and, in doing so, he shows that, besides the conventional market exchange, there is an alternate exchange, one which sets value without tabulating labour hours or counting out greenback dollars. This alternate exchange I call the *shadow market*, and it is there that Achilles goes to set friendship's value. Achilles' story is important because it exemplifies the countermonetary foundation of tragedy: human things are bought with blood, not gold.

The *Iliad* begins as Achilles debates whether to return home. He has withdrawn from the Trojan War, a consequence of having been insulted by Agamemnon, his commander-in-chief. Capitalizing on Achilles' absence, the Trojans score stunning victories and push the Achaeans back to their ships. On the verge of defeat, Agamemnon bribes Achilles to return, offering a base bid with two escalating clauses. It begins with:

Seven unfired tripods; ten talents' weight of
    gold; twenty
shining cauldrons; and twelve horses,
    strong, race-competitors
who have won prizes in the speed of their feet.
    That man would not be
poor in possessions, to whom were given all these
    have won me,
nor be unpossessed of dearly honoured gold; were
    he given
all the prizes these single-foot horses have won
    for me.
I will give him seven women of Lesbos, the work of
    whose hands is
blameless, whom when he himself captured strong-
    founded Lesbos
I chose, and who in their beauty surpassed the races
    of women.
I will give him these, and with them shall go the
    one I took from him,
the daughter of Briseus. And to all this I will swear
    a great oath
that I never entered into her bed and never lay
    with her
as is natural for human people, between men
    and women.

The first escalator follows:

All these gifts shall be his at once; but again,
    if hereafter
the gods grant that we storm and sack the great city
    of Priam,
let him go to his ship and load it deep as he pleases
with gold and bronze, when we Achaians divide the
    war spoils,
and let him choose for himself twenty of the
    Trojan women
who are the loveliest of all after Helen of Argos.

which in turn is followed by the second:

And if we come back to Achaian Argos, pride of the
    tilled land,
he may be my son-in-law; I will honour him
    with Orestes
my growing son, who is brought up there in abun-
    dant luxury.
Since, as I have three daughters there in my strong-
    built castle,
Chrysothemis and Laodike and Iphianassa,
let him lead away the one of these that he likes,
    with no bride-price,
to the house of Peleus, and with the girl I will grant
    him as dowry
many gifts, such as no man ever gave with
    his daughter.
I will grant to him seven citadels, strongly settled:
Kardamyle, and Enope, and Hire of the grasses,

Pherai the sacrosanct, and Antheia deep in
    the meadows,
with Aipeia the lovely and Pedasos of the vineyards.
All these lie near the sea, at the bottom of
    sandy Pylos,
and men live among them rich in cattle and rich
    in sheepflocks,
who will honour him as if he were a god with
    gifts given
and fulfil his prospering decrees underneath
    his sceptre.[7]

Of all the heroes, Achilles is in the unique position of
having alternate fates. If he fights the Trojans, he will win
fame but die young. If, however, he returns home, he will live
to a ripe old age in obscurity.[8] The implication of his alternate fates is that if he accepts Agamemnon's offer, he would,
in effect, be exchanging his life for seven tripods, ten talents
of gold, seven cauldrons, twelve horses, and so on. Though
worth more than Glaucus' ninety-one oxen, his life would
have become monetized nonetheless. But Achilles rejects his
offer, and, what is more, makes it clear in his rebuttal that he
sets life's value above material consideration:

I hate his gifts. I hold him light as the strip of
    a splinter.

---

7   Homer, *Iliad*, trans. Richmond Lattimore, 9.122-56.
8   Ibid., 1.505, 9.410-6.

Not if he gave me ten times as much, and twenty
     times over

as he possesses now, not if more should come to
     him from elsewhere,

or gave all that is brought in to Orchomenos, all
     that is brought in

to Thebes of Egypt, where the greatest possessions
     lie up in the houses,

Thebes of the hundred gates, where through each
     of the gates two hundred

fighting men come forth to war with horses
     and chariots;

not if he gave me gifts as many as the sand or the
     dust is,

not even so would Agamemnon have his way with
     my spirit

until he had made good to me all this heartrend-
     ing insolence.[9]

By demanding that Agamemnon pay him back for "heart-rending insolence," Achilles rejects the monetization of life.[10] Now, you will remember that, on the basis of labour time, the exchange of deer and beaver can be set to a two-to-one

---

9   Ibid., 9.378-87.

10   On Achilles' rejection of the offer, see Schein, *The Mortal Hero*, 109-10:

> Achilles presents radically the problem of how to measure worth: Agamemnon cannot buy off someone who is totally alienated, cannot offer him sufficient "honour" for his life. [...] He forces to the surface the real moral question of the poem: what, in a heroic world, is the true measure of value?

ratio because it takes twice the time to prepare a beaver. And, on the basis of labour time, if the preparation of a set of brass arms takes the same time as it takes to prepare nine oxen, the set of brass arms can be valued at nine oxen. But how is heartrending insolence to be valued? The catch is that it cannot be valued in terms of labour time, for it resides in a separate and higher category of things. By asking to be compensated for heartrending insolence, Achilles asserts that even if Agamemnon were to include all the wealth of Ormus and Ind, his payment would still be insufficient:

> For not
> worth the value of my life are all the possessions
>   they fable
> were won for Ilion, that strong-founded citadel, in
>   the old days
> when there was peace, before the coming of the
>   sons of the Achaians;
> not all that the stone doorsill of the Archer holds
>   fast within it,
> of Phoibos Apollo in Pytho of the rocks.
>   Of possessions
> cattle and fat sheep are things to be had for
>   the lifting,
> and tripods can be won, and the tawny high heads
>   of horses,
> but a man's life cannot come back again, it cannot
>   be lifted

nor captured again by force, once it has crossed the
teeth's barrier.[11]

With these words, Achilles affirms the supreme dignity of
life against Glaucus' penny-pound existence. Glaucus and
Diomedes had sold out life; Achilles reaffirms its sanctity.

If life should not be valued in gold, how can it be valued?
The answer lies in Achilles' return to the field. Though
money could not move him, Achilles nevertheless returns,
and of his own accord. The story is well known: the dete-
riorating Achaean position puts the fleet at risk; Patroclus
begs Achilles to arm; Achilles desists but relents; he lends
Patroclus his immortal arms with a warning not to confront
Hector; Patroclus drives the Trojans back; he approaches
Hector; he dies. When Achilles hears the news, he takes to
the field. All that glitters could not move him, but in the end
friendship did. As Patroclus' friend, Achilles hated Hector for
taking his life, felt shame that he was not there to ward off
the death crush, and felt a duty to avenge him. His return
makes a bold, countermonetary statement: friendship is a
human value weightier than gold, more valuable than oxen,
and greater than the wealth of the world. Friendship is equal
in worth to Achilles' life, the life that he forsakes when he
takes to the field.

The stories of Diomedes, Glaucus, Agamemnon, and
Achilles illustrates that two sorts of marketplaces exist.
There is a conventional marketplace where life can be
exchanged for heads of oxen and gold bars can make good

11   Homer, *Iliad*, trans. Richmond Lattimore, 9.400-9.

an insult. This is the marketplace of Agamemnon, Diomedes, and Glaucus. In this marketplace, life is another commodity. Then there is an alternate exchange, a shadow market, where the all-too-human changes hands. In the shadow market, traders exchange human concerns such as fame, friendship, anger, ambition, duty, honour, loyalty, and heartache. Instead of oxen, gold, or dollars, in the shadow market, they trade kinship for power, buy truth at the cost of grief, and forfeit love to sate ambition. The invention of tragedy occurs when Achilles turns to the shadow market to satisfy friendship at the cost of his own life.

The inability to express the value of existence in terms of gold or heads of oxen forms the *sine qua non* of tragedy; tragedy acts as an exchange of the last resort when all of the other marketplaces fall short. Tragedy reveals the value of the psychic constituents of life—joy, camaraderie, desire, ambition, dignity, and so on—not in monetary terms but in the terms of the opportunity cost of losing the next best thing. Achilles, for example, could not honour Patroclus and also hold onto his own life. Because he gives up his life to honour Patroclus, the transaction reveals that Achilles values friendship as much as he values life. Transactions in the shadow market are therefore tragic because they involve existential costs. In tragedy, no one has cake and eats it too.

THE THIRD STORY: CROESUS

The *Iliad* contains two competing worldviews: Agamemnon, Diomedes, and Glaucus' worldview, where existence can be monetized and Achilles' worldview, which sets life above monetary consideration. The third story in the myth of the price you pay tells of how the idea that silver and gold could be used to purchase life and the all-too-human came to prevail. The development and spread of coinage in the centuries following the Trojan War gives this view an economic foundation. But not all was well, and an urgent need arose for a champion to rise up to assert the dignity of human values in the face of the monetization of all values. The third story tells of how this champion emerged in the art form of tragedy, and it begins in the sixth century BC with Solon and Croesus, whose meeting is well known; the depiction, however, of Croesus' invention of coinage leading to the rise of tragedy results from my own devising.

In the *Histories*, Herodotus recounts the meeting between Solon, one of the Seven Sages of Greece, and Croesus, the ruler of Lydia.[12] He recounts how Croesus' worldly success had transformed Sardis from a backwoods county into an international hub and how illustrious visitors paid Croesus tribute at the Lydian court. One such dignitary was the Athenian lawmaker Solon. When Croesus, the wealthy king of Lydia, asked his wise visitor Solon, "Who is the happiest man?", Croesus had expected Solon to name him happiest, for he possessed the greatest wealth. Upon being told by Solon that fickle fortune precludes a man from being called happy until his final day, his estimation of the wise lawmaker diminished. Many years later, however, Croesus came to appreciate Solon's wisdom as he stood bound to his funeral pyre, an empty emperor of an empty empire, defeated by

---

12   Herodotus, *The Histories*, trans. Aubrey de Sélincourt, 1.29-33.

Cyrus the Great.[13] All this Herodotus relates. But before his encounter with Solon, after annexing the Phrygians, Mysians, Mariandynians, Chalybians, Paphlagonians, Thracians, Carians, Ionians, Dorians, Aeolians, and Pamphylians, Croesus faced a happier problem: how to keep so many ethnicities content within his empire.[14]

And now for my part of the story, more a myth than a story, as it is not attested in Herodotus or anywhere else. One viable solution was for Croesus to foster trade. Prosperous states are stable states. But trade hitherto was burdensome. It was time consuming for traders to match up the cost of production in their labour time to the labour time of others' products. There were other complications besides. One beaver for two deer is simple enough. If the beaver hunter requires ten deer, he can bring five beavers. But what if the beaver hunter only requires one deer? Or what if the deer hunter needs beavers in January, and the beaver hunter needs deer in June? Croesus realized that, in order to overcome these Neolithic constraints holding back trade, he had to find a way to break apart *the object of trade* from *the store of value*.

Previously, the object of trade (e.g., the beaver pelt) and the store of value (e.g., labour time) were equivalent. In a swords-to-ploughshares moment, Croesus decided to make use of all of the surplus brass weapons and gold arms. After the wars of conquest, the empire felt secure. On the west, the Minoan thalassocracy had long been declining: the Mediterranean lay soft and still. On the east, the River Halys

13   Ibid., 1.86.
14   Ibid., 1.28 for all the peoples Croesus subdued and added to Lydian empire.

formed a natural boundary between Lydia and Persia; only a fool would muddy her waters with soldier's boots and horses' hooves. Croesus therefore decided that metal would be the new store of value, and thus the idea of coinage was born.

In addition to the abundance of metal, there were other advantages to making metal into a store of value. Malleable and durable enough for everyday use, metal could act as an independent store of value and therefore act as a catalyst in economic transactions, thus facilitating trade. Coinage could consequently increase trade in several ways. First, it could make trade more convenient: instead of carrying around beaver, the buyer could simply carry a coin purse. Second, it could speed up the transaction: coins act in essence as an IOU that could be used at any time with any market participant. For example, the problem of the deer hunter who needs beavers in January and the beaver hunter who needs deer in June may be eliminated since the coins could stand in proxy for the deer until the beaver hunter receives the physical delivery in June. The problem of fractional deer and other ratio mismatches, as outlined above, is also avoided: an appropriate coin of the perfect size and denomination could be created to facilitate any trade. For all of these reasons, the idea of coinage seemed good to Croesus.

Having struck prototypes of the first coins, Croesus showed them to Solon, who happened to be on his famous tour, and naturally wanted the sage's opinion. After admiring the allure of the first brass and gold tokens, Solon asked, "What will these coins be worth, which of themselves serve no utility?" After a moment of consideration, Croesus replied, "Because they will be distributed far and wide, the value of the coins will float, their value set by the collective sum of all the market participants." Pleased at the clever stroke, he continued, "Yes, the marketplace will regulate their value through commerce, and they will be worth *desire* itself." To which Solon replied, "Desire? Thou fool! Did you consider the heart of man? Appetite will devour the spirit, as some buy up souls with indulgences while others measure achievement by net worth, blinded by desire, like new Midases." Croesus had no reply but instead thought to ask Solon whether he was the happiest man alive. From there it was all downhill. In the coming years, Croesus' prediction that coinage would boost trade proved correct. Solon, however, was also correct: the increase in trade corresponded directly to the debasement of the spirit.

Both Solon and Croesus' predictions would come to fruition in the ancient city of Athens. In the fifth century BC, Athens was a portrait of commerce. Container vessels droned in Piraeus harbour around the clock. The Acropolis was paved in gold, and the treasuries overflowed. Though a mere city-state, Athens bruised the Persian invaders to such an extent that one observing the wreckage after the Battle of Salamis or the bloodied steppes of Plataea or Marathon would have thought Athens to have been ten times her actual size and Persia one-tenth. How did Athens become mistress of the Mediterranean? In short, the silver mines of Laurium.[15] The only city-state with an unlimited supply of

---

15   The contribution of Laurium to the rise of the Athens as a world power was well known enough for Aeschylus to name it in *The Persians*, in *Prometheus Bound and Other Plays*, trans. Philip Vellacott, p. 129 as one of the reasons Athens prevailed over Persia:

mineral wealth, Athens controlled desire. In stamping coins, she stamped desire: of all the ancient city-states, she alone could make desire manifest. Athens was the unexpected beneficiary of Croesus' idea to use metal as a store of value. But not all was golden.

As Athens industrialized, deforestation accelerated the erosion of the black pasture and ploughland forevermore into the Saronic Gulf with the result that the Attic peninsula became a barren crag.[16] As industry and commerce advanced, fishermen and farmers gave up the safety of the land and the coast, sailing further and further into the unpredictable sea, goaded onward by greed. In tapping the riches at the Laurium mine, men, women, and children were transformed into slaves numbering the tens of thousands who clawed the earth in the name of desire.[17] The dark side of trade was tyranny, mercantilism, slavery, and the growing number of

> ATOSSA: Besides their men, have they good store of wealth at home?
> CHORUS: They have a spring of silver treasured in their soil.

16   See Plato, *Critias* 111a-d where Critias laments the effects of soil erosion in Athens, due in part to flooding and accelerated by deforestation.

17   Thucydides, *History of the Peloponnesian War* 7.27 estimates that, in 413 BC, 20,000 slaves worked the Laurium mine. On the working conditions in the mines, see Murray, "Life and Society in Classical Greece," in *The Oxford History of Greece and the Hellenistic World*, 265:

> The skeletons and evidence of living 300 feet underground in tunnels fed with air through downdrafts created by fires halfway up the shafts, the niche for the guard at the mine entrance, and the fact that the tunnels were so small that the face workers must have crawled and knelt at their work

widows and orphans from the merchants who had sailed too far and too late. Such was the price of desire. But the price was too high as possessions grew to master the possessor. When merchants sailed during the winter, risking their lives in the name of profit, possessions have possessed the possessor. Other contradictions arose. When Athens enchained the captives of war—all the sad Andromaches and Hecubas—at the Laurium mine to fund the fight for freedom, a contradiction arose. When Athens demanded tribute from her neighbours to maintain her own freedom, a contradiction arose. Amid the monetization of fifth century Athens, a spirit of dissent arose.

The Debt to Nature

As the spirit of dissent grew, it sought a voice. It remembered Achilles' scorn of lucre and how he had turned to the alternate exchange of the shadow market to find the true meaning of value. Looking further, it came to the realization that the shadow market extended beyond just Achilles. Everywhere, a debt to nature existed according to which the all-too-human was paid for in the currency of blood, sweat, and tears, not by senseless metal tokens. The spirit of dissent now remembered Hector and how he had paid the price for his *aristeia*, his "finest moment," by running into Achilles at the Scaean gate at the worst possible moment, exhausted, without spear, and without squire. It was as though Hector owed a debt to nature for his earlier heroics, a debt that he discharges by his blood. The spirit of dissent remembered how Helen paid for

---

while all porterage was carried out by pre-adolescent children, reveal the truth.

her bewitching beauty by being everywhere hated.[18] She paid the price in tears. It remembered Sarpedon and how he paid the price for sitting at the first place at the feast by fighting in the first ranks of battle.[19] He paid the price in blood and sweat. It remembered many things in addition, remembered how, for the glory of leading the allied forces, Agamemnon was called to sacrifice his firstborn. It remembered how the Achaeans paid for the sack of Troy by being shipwrecked on the homeward voyage. Even many years later, they would continue to pay when New Troy, rising as Rome, conquered Greece. And finally, it remembered how even the singer of tales had a price to pay: Homer, in order to hear the hexameter song, gave up his sight.[20] Blindness was Melpomene's price for a song. Whether Homer's story is true or apocryphal is of little consequence; that it was remembered thus testifies to the pervasiveness of the myth of the price you pay. For all of nature's gifts, she exacts a price in return. All of these

18   Homer, *Iliad*, trans. Richmond Lattimore 3.154-80.

19   Ibid., 12.309-21.

20   The tradition, drawing cues from the anonymous *Homeric Hymn to Delian Apollo* (a work attributed to Homer) and the *Odyssey*, asserts that Homer was blind. In the *Homeric Hymn to Delian Apollo*, in *The Homeric Hymns*, trans. Sargent, p. 19, the singer claims to be "a blind man who lives on the rugged island of Chios." In Homer, *Odyssey*, trans. Richmond Lattimore, 8.62-5, the singer Demodocus—who some see as being autobiographical—is described as being blind:

> The herald came near, bringing with him the excel-
> lent singer
> whom the Muse had loved greatly, and gave him both
> good and evil.
> She reft him of his eyes, but she gave him the sweet
> singing art.

remembrances exemplify the myth of the price you pay, and the spirit of fifth century Athenian dissent elevated these remembrances into the art form of Greek tragedy to restore a human price to human values.

Thomson, in a rare extended discussion of the relationship between money and tragedy, reaches a similar conclusion. To him, tragedy also strikes back against the monetization of human values:

> When money was first introduced, it was recognised as a new power destined to increase in an unprecedented degree man's control over Nature. "Man is money": such was the saying of a citizen of one of the first Greek states to strike a coinage. There is nothing money cannot buy; there is nothing the man with money cannot become. But this new power was soon seen to be ambivalent. As Sophokles wrote:
>
> > Money wins friendship, honour, place
> >   and power,
> > And sets man next to the proud
> >   tyrant's throne.
> > All trodden paths and paths untrod before
> > Are scaled by nimble riches, where the poor
> > Can never hope to win the heart's desire.
> > A man ill-formed by nature and ill-spoken
> > Money shall make him fair to eye and ear.
> > Money earns man his health and happiness,
> > And only money cloaks iniquity.

And so we find the same poet denouncing money
as the root of all evil:

> Of all the foul growths current in the world
> The worst is money. Money drives men
>   from home,
> Plunders great cities, perverts the
>   honest mind
> To shameful practice, godlessness and crime.[21]

THE MYTH OF THE PRICE
YOU PAY AND TRAGEDY

Cost understood objectively—the number of oxen it takes to buy a suit of armour, how many deer exchange for a beaver, and so on—is economics. It is a science. Economics seeks to find a monetary value for everything it runs across. Glaucus' life is worth ninety-one oxen. A certain amount of cash makes good slander. And so on. Cost understood subjectively—the sacrifices one makes to be immortalized in song, the opportunity cost of helping a friend, and so on—is tragedy. It is an art. Tragedy rejects the monetization of human concerns and sets the concerns of the spirit above material wealth. Because tragedy posits that human values are to be understood in human terms, it must turn to a different market, the shadow market, to set a value on the all-too-human. In the shadow market, concerns such as honour, desire, ambition, loyalty, heartache, grief, and joy change hands. When they change

---

21   Thomson, *Aeschylus and Athens*, 352.

hands, their relative value is revealed. Tragedy, I therefore propose, is an economics of the final resort that examines the opportunity cost involved in being alive.

In the same way as the epic hero Hector pays nature back for his *aristeia* with his late and unexpected meeting with Achilles, the tragic hero likewise comes into being to settle an account and return the debt to nature. Nature has blessed Sophocles' Oedipus, for example, with monster-taming and oracle-defying intelligence. But there is a cost, and only when he tears out his eyes and his wife suicides does he balance the existential ledger. Like Achilles establishing the value of friendship by giving up his own life, Oedipus prices out intelligence by making a transaction known as the hero's wager on the shadow market.

Every action can be expressed in terms of a human cost and a monetary cost. Tragedy examines the human cost. It leaves the monetary cost to the economists. Take Xerxes' actions in Aeschylus' *Persians*, for example: Xerxes had dared to yoke together the Hellespont, thereby joining Asia and Europe by a bridge of floating ships and uniting two continents that nature meant to keep apart. The monetary cost of his pride may be measured in the cost of the engineering, the armada, the tackle, and the manpower. It is certainly a substantial number, but that is not what Aeschylus dramatizes. Instead, he dramatizes the human cost: the lamentations over the dead and Xerxes' loss of dignity as he returns to the gilded court in tatters.

Tragedy presents a roll call of those who have paid the price. Some pay the price for love. Others do so for an ideal. Some come to the theatre for the power and the glory.

Others come to find vengeance. Love, idealism, power and glory, and vengeance: these are some of the more common human concerns traded on the shadow exchange. To attain them, heroes ante what they hold most dear in the hero's wager. The more they value the objects of their ambition, the more they sacrifice: that is how tragedy determines worth.

So, how much does love cost? In O'Neill's *Desire Under the Elms*, Abbie loves Eben, but he is not convinced of her love. He thinks that she feigns desire to steal the farm. To prove her love, Abbie has to turn to the shadow market: in tragedy, money and the conventional market are of little use. Eben and Abbie have a child whose birth initiates a power play over the ownership of the farm and serves as a source of friction. To prove her love and allegiance to Eben, Abbie smothers their babe. In the conventional market, labour cost determines worth, but in the shadow market, worth is determined by sacrifice. Because Abbie sacrifices a mother's love for Eben's love, the value of Eben's love equals their child in the same way as one beaver, for example, equals two deer. In tragedy, one cannot have love and what is given up in order to attain this love: these are the economics of tragedy.

For love to be deemed true love, an opportunity cost must be identified—the loss of the foregone alternative that could have been chosen instead of love. Tragedy can conceive of neither free lunch nor free love. Because true love entails an opportunity cost, a play such as Euripides' *Alcestis* becomes possible. To save her husband's life, Alcestis offers to die in his place. In this exchange, we learn that her husband's life is worth what she exchanges in its place: her youth and happiness.

How much does it cost to be an idealist? In O'Neill's *Long Day's Journey into Night*, Edmund, to deny God, gives up hope and thus sacrifices his peace of mind on atheism's altar. In Albert Camus' *The Just Assassins*, Dora, to liberate Russia, renounces the carefree dreams of a young girl. In Camus' *Caligula*, the emperor, to find true freedom, renounces family, rejects friendship, and casts himself outside of society. In *Prometheus Bound*, Prometheus, to lay down the new world order, leaves behind his band of brethren, one buried alive and the other crushed under the pillars of heaven and earth. In Sophocles' *Antigone*, two idealists vie with one another. Creon, to become patriot, sacrifices family and religion. Antigone, on the other hand, to honour family and the nether gods, renounces her civic obligations. Though some may find it grim, tragedy takes back existence by demonstrating that what is worth possessing cannot be monetized. If Shakespeare's Brutus (in *Julius Caesar*) pays five dollars to become a master Stoic, it is unclear how much Stoicism is worth in human terms. But if Brutus watches Portia swallow burning coals in order to perfect Stoicism, then it becomes absolutely clear how much Stoicism is worth. Tragedy makes its characters pay not out of cruelty, but to assign a value to humanity's dreams and aspirations.

How much does the power and the glory cost? To control men's destinies, Ibsen's Hedda Gabler relinquishes her autonomy to Brack, who has other designs on her. In Sophocles' *Philoctetes*, young Neoptolemus, to be hailed as a hero, sacrifices his honour, conning the crippled Philoctetes out of his conquering bow like a used-car salesman. To rise to the heights of statecraft, Racine's Titus bids farewell to romance and Berenice. For a Scottish crown, Macbeth exchanges the milk of human kindness. To become the god of war, Marlowe's Tamburlaine sets his gentle heart upon war's altar. To achieve power incarnate, Faustus hardens his heart. To buy influence at the royal court, Racine's Mattan sells out his faith, exchanging the true God for a false idol and an idolatress' ear.

How much does vengeance cost? According to the rule of risk theatre, something for something and nothing for nothing. Nothing ventured and nothing revenged, but for a price tragedy sells revengers satisfaction. When Euripides' Jason wrongs Medea, Medea lays her motherhood on the line. To kill their children is hurtful, but as long as it hurts Jason more, she attains satisfaction. In Middleton's *The Revenger's Tragedy*, Vindice, to become a better revenger, lays his filial and fraternal bonds to pawn, bribing his own mother to pander his sister. Webster's Bosola, to redress wrongs done to the Duchess of Malfi, sacrifices his good nature and personal security. In the spirit of "nothing ventured, nothing gained," Seneca's Atreus in *Thyestes* takes no chances and throws in the kitchen sink, venturing honour, shame, right, good, loyalty, and righteousness to revenge the wrongs done him by his brother, who had seduced away his wife and kingdom.

While tragedy most often sets a price on the human assets and desires such as love, idealism, power and glory, and vengeance, its scope extends to cover *any* human concern, such as trust. Goethe's Egmont, for example, wagers that his knighthood in the Order of the Golden Fleece can save his life, but, as it turns out, he pays for his trust with his life. Or take happiness. Nina in O'Neill's *Strange Interlude* buys happiness by neglecting to inform her husband that his best friend fathered their child: happiness comes at the price of honesty. Or consider a principle as abstract as moral certainty. Hamlet, for example, sacrifices his capacity for action in exchange for proof of Claudius' guilt. Due to the breadth of human concerns, the size of the shadow market is at least as large as, if not larger than, that of the conventional market.

Though some tragic transactions can take place in both the conventional and the shadow markets, the shadow market *exalts* life. Sex can be bought on the conventional market, but to buy true love one turns to the shadow market. A vote can be bought on the conventional market, but to buy conviction one turns to the shadow market. Investiture and paying one's dues are similar, but investiture trades on the conventional market, while dues trade on the shadow market. Although blood money and revenge appear similar, blood money belongs to the conventional market, while revenge trades on the shadow market. The conventional market debases life, while the shadow market exalts it.

Some characters pay the price out of passion; others do it for the power and the glory. Some are revengers and tyrants, while others have mild and timid natures. But for whatever reason they pay the price, they pay because opportunity cost is inherent in choice. *Either* the delights of motherhood *or* sweet revenge. *Either* the stroke of swift revenge *or* moral certainty. *Either* the Scottish crown *or* the milk of human kindness. When opportunity cost is inscribed onto life, tragedy begins. For power, heroes pay in the broken bonds of kinship; for truth, they pay with grief; for one love, they lose another love; and for one dream, they lose another dream, so that all hopes and ambitions lie broken, sundered, and in tatters. This is the fundamental state of the tragic world. The myth of the price you pay may consist of a mere story, but it holds true insofar as opportunity cost and choice do exist. Lear gets many things wrong, to be sure. But he hits on the awesome truth when he says: "Nothing will come of nothing."[22] *Everything* costs something.

In dramatizing the myth of the price you pay, tragedians cast their creations into the shadow market so that they may trade the essence of mortality. In the process, tragic heroes lose what is dear to them so that we, the audience, may be reminded that human concerns bear human costs.

22   Shakespeare, *King Lear*, 1.1.90.

5 FOUR PRINCIPLES OF COUNTERMONETIZATION

A round the time monetary exchange grew sophisticated enough to transact human existence (e.g., the payment of blood money) or the affairs of the heart (e.g., Agamemnon bribing Achilles), I suggest that a spirit of *countermonetization* arose in dissent. Just as simony degrades ecclesiastical office and indulgences cheapen salvation, monetization dirties life by reducing it into a financial object, whether a gold coin, oxen, or stock certificates. Countermonetization is my term for the movement which sought to restore the sanctity of life by forbidding the use of money in existential transactions. To achieve its objectives, it needed to find a vehicle through which it could voice its critique. That vehicle was the tragic theatre.

As discussed in the previous chapter, when theatre troupes in the fifth century BC began dramatizing shadow market exchanges to separate the aesthetic and economic realms, tragic theatre arose as an alternate exchange to weigh the value of the all-too-human. Tragedy routed its trades through the shadow market because money in the shadow market is a counterfeit currency: blood, sweat, and tears comprise the true legal tender. If, for example, Jason exchanges life and limb to obtain the Golden Fleece, he is operating in the shadow market. There is a tale to be told. But it makes for a poor tale were he to have purchased the fleece from Hudson's Bay for $14.99—this sort of exchange takes place on the conventional money market. Drama proved an ideal countermonetary vehicle because shadow market transactions, being full of pathos, engage audiences: heroes enter the shadow exchange, wager dear things, and confront the unexpected. There is plenty of opportunity for lights, camera, and action.

Those who do Melpomene's work are entrusted with the important task of reckoning life's value in terms of the opportunity cost lost in the pursuit of objects of ambition. When risk theatre adheres to my four principles of countermonetization, it fulfils its mandate to affirm life's sanctity. First, the use of money is to be rejected. Second, payment by blood, sweat, and tears must be paid in full. Third, the price cannot be paid on a whim, but must be paid after great deliberation, and, even then, with reluctance. Fourth, payment must be made by the protagonist. This chapter explores how tragedy engages these four principles.

THE FIRST PRINCIPLE: REJECTION OF MONEY

Since tragedy acts as a valuing mechanism for concepts beyond the monetary pale, the best tragedies reject the authority of money outright. Such is the case in *The Master Builder*:

HILDE. What is so terrible?

SOLNESS. All this I somehow have to make up for. Pay for. Not in money. But in human happiness. And not with my own happiness alone. But also with others'. Don't you see that, Hilde? That's the price my status as an artist has cost me—and others. And every single day I have to stand by and watch this price being paid for me anew. Over and over again—endlessly![1]

and in *The Changeling*:

BEATRICE. I pray, bury the finger, but the stone
You may make use of shortly; the true value,
Take't of my truth, is near three hundred ducats.

DE FLORES. 'Twill hardly buy a capcase for one's
    conscience, though,
To keep it from the worm, as fine as 'tis.[2]

and in *Medea*:

JASON. I shall not argue any more of this case with you. But if you wish to get some of my money to help the children and yourself in exile, say the word, for I am ready to give with unstinting hand, and also to send tokens to my friends, who will treat you well. You would be a fool not to accept

---

1   Ibsen, *The Master Builder*, in *Four Major Plays*, trans. James McFarlane, p. 316.

2   Middleton and Rowley, *The Changeling*, 3.4.41–5.

this offer, woman. Forget your anger and it will be
the better for you.

MEDEA. I will accept no help from your friends nor
will I take anything from you, so do not offer it. The
gifts of a base man bring no benefit.[3]

In the *Iliad*, Achilles rejects Agamemnon's compensation package because he deems that human considerations
such as heartache and self-esteem are inappropriate objects
for financial exchange. After all, how can money stand in as
a substitute for peace of mind or life?[4] Solness, De Flores,
and Medea follow Achilles' lead in rejecting the authority
of money in human transactions: Solness pays for his art
with happiness, De Flores places conscience above monetary
considerations, and Medea would rather preserve her dignity
than exchange it for hush money. Their stances fall in accord
with the first principle.

Despite tragedy's countermonetary bias, money does play
a role, albeit infrequently. It changes hands, for example, in
Ford's *'Tis Pity She's a Whore*:

SORANZO (*gives money*).
Here's gold, here's more; want nothing. What
    you do
Is noble, and an act of brave revenge.
I'll make ye rich, banditti, and all free.

3   Euripides, *Medea*, in *Cyclops, Alcestis, Medea*, trans. David Kovacs,
     lines 609-18.
4   Discussed in chapter 4.

BANDITTI. Liberty, liberty![5]

and in Kyd's *The Spanish Tragedy*:

PEDRINGANO. I swear to both by him that made
us all.

LORENZO. In hope thine oath is true, here's thy
reward, (*gives him money*)
But if I prove thee perjured and unjust,
This very sword whereon thou took'st thine oath
Shall be the worker of thy tragedy.[6]

At first appearances, it would seem that *'Tis Pity She's a Whore* and *The Spanish Tragedy* break the first principle of countermonetization, for money changes hands. The banditti equate money with freedom, and Pedringano's loyalty goes to the highest bidder. In the final examination, however, the banditti and Pedringano illustrate the failure of money to articulate human worth: the banditti and Pedringano have it all wrong. Far from being role models, they represent the scum and offal, the worst the human race has to offer. That they are the ones who can be bought testifies to money's shortcomings in counting out the human ledger.

A different example of money being used to illustrate money's inadequacy occurs in O'Neill's *Long Day's Journey into Night*. In a heart-to-heart conversation with his son,

5   Ford, *Tis Pity She's a Whore*, in *Six Renaissance Tragedies*, 5.4.8–11.
6   Kyd, *The Spanish Tragedy*, in *Six Renaissance Tragedies*, 2.1.89–93.

Tyrone divulges his greatest regret, one he had kept silent until now:

> TYRONE. That God-damned play I bought for a song
> and made such a great success in—a great money
> success—it ruined me with its promise of an easy
> fortune. I didn't want to do anything else, and by
> the time I woke up to the fact I'd become a slave to
> the damned thing and did try other plays, it was too
> late. They had identified me with that one part, and
> didn't want me in anything else. They were right,
> too. I'd lost the great talent I once had through
> years of easy repetition, never learning a new part,
> never really working hard. Thirty-five to forty thou-
> sand dollars net profit a season like snapping your
> fingers! It was too great a temptation. Yet before
> I bought the damned thing I was considered one
> of the three or four young actors with the greatest
> artistic promise in America.[7]

By performing the same role year in and year out, Tyrone has monetized his artistic potential. For a stipend of $35-40,000 per year (the sum of which in the 1880s would be the equivalent to a high six-figure income in 2016), he has given up the artist that he could have been.[8] His exchange

---

7   O'Neill, *Long Day's Journey Into Night*, pp. 152–3.
8   The character of James Tyrone is based on O'Neill's actual father, the actor James O'Neill, who had made a fortune playing Dantès in a stage adaptation of Dumas' *The Count of Monte Cristo*. After the over-whelming reception to his performance, he signed a contract in 1883

takes place in the conventional market. It is not tragedy. But the subsequent realization that the transaction does not go the other way, that the hundreds of thousands cannot buy back human potential defines tragedy. His realization parallels and recalls the story of the biblical Judas, whose tragedy Rembrandt realizes in his painting *Judas Returning the Thirty Silver Pieces*.

Judas' story exemplifies the shortcomings of money. Like Tyrone, Judas, in betraying Christ, converts the sacred into the profane and monetizes what should not be monetized:

> Then went one of the twelve, called Judas Iscariot,
> went unto the chief priests, and said unto them,
> What will ye give me, and I will deliver him
> unto you?[9]

In his negotiations with the chief priests, Judas has set a value on Christianity. For thirty shekels, he relinquishes his place in Christendom.

---

promising one thousand a week as well as a box office percentage. He would go on to perform the role over six thousand times over three decades. See O'Neill, *James O'Neill*, 96. Based on the inflation conversation factor of 0.042 by Robert Sahr at Oregon State University, $35,000 in 1883 would be the equivalent to $830,000 in 2016. See Sahr, "Inflation Conversion Factors for Years 1774 to Estimated 2027," accessed July 12, 2017, http://liberalarts.oregonstate.edu/spp/polisci/faculty-staff/robert-sahr/inflation-conversion-factors-years-1774-estimated-2024-dollars-recent-years/individual-year-conversion-factor-table-0.

9   Matt. 26:14-5 (King James Version).

Judas' exchange of his faith for thirty shekels is an economic rather than a tragic transaction. But his subsequent realization that money is a false measure of what has been sold makes for first-class tragedy:

> Then Judas, which had betrayed him, when he
> saw that he was condemned, repented himself, and
> brought again the thirty pieces of silver to the chief
> priests and elders, saying I have sinned in that I have
> betrayed the innocent blood. And they said, What
> is that to us? See thou to that. And he cast down
> the pieces of silver in the temple, and departed, and
> went and hanged himself.[10]

Like Tyrone, Judas comes to understand the limitations of money, but understands too late. In both cases, their remorse makes it clear that money is a poor measure of human value.

In his painting *Judas Returning the Thirty Silver Pieces*, Rembrandt reveals the extent of tragedy possible in Judas' late realization.[11] The artist captures the brief moments in the biblical narrative between "he cast down the pieces of silver" and "he went and hanged himself." The coins lie scattered haphazard on the lower floorboards as a testimony to their worthlessness. Judas also occupies the lower plane

---

10   Matt. 27:3-5 (King James Version).

11   Rembrandt, *Judas Returning the Thirty Silver Pieces*, 1629, oil on oak panel, 79 x 102.3 cm, Mulgrave Castle, Lythe, North Yorkshire, England, accessed July 12, 2017, https://commons.wikimedia.org/wiki/File:Judas_Returning_the_Thirty_Silver_Pieces_-_Rembrandt.jpg.

of the painting. Wild and tattered, he appears more animal than man. A portrait of penitence, hands cupped in suppliant prayer, he attempts to buy back his humanity. But the high priest turns away in a violent, contrapposto stance, disdain evident in how he rejects the suppliant with the palm of his outstretched hand. Despite the economic exchange, Rembrandt's depiction makes it clear that, in some cases, money can be used to show money's shortcomings.

In both Tyrone and Judas' cases, the inability of money to buy back what has been lost underscores the need of an alternate marketplace to value human considerations. The true cost of Tyrone's lost artistic promise is his daily regret, and the true cost of Judas' Christianity is his soul.

Because tragedy is a vehicle of countermonetization, it rejects cash in accordance with my first principle. It can reject cash outright, as Solness does in *The Master Builder*. If a cash transaction does take place, however, two possibilities remain: either the characters who accept cash are scoundrels (e.g., Ford's banditti), or, if they are not scoundrels, they subsequently realize the inanity of ascribing monetary value to the all-too-human (e.g., O'Neill's Tyrone).

THE SECOND PRINCIPLE: PAYMENT IN FULL

My second principle of countermonetization requires that the payment of blood, sweat, and tears be paid in full. In other words, what the hero wagers must be irrevocably lost. When Macbeth, for example, wagers the milk of human kindness for the throne, he gets the throne but the milk is spilt: the murder of Duncan fundamentally corrupts him in an irreversible manner:

> MACBETH. Will all great Neptune's ocean wash
>   this blood
> Clean from my hand? No; this my hand will rather
> The multitudinous seas incarnadine,
> Making the green one red.[12]

Loss must be irrevocable because such a loss proves that there is no free lunch: *either* the crown *or* the milk of human kindness, but not both.

Bolt's *A Man for All Seasons*, Aeschylus' *Prometheus Bound*, and Sophocles' *Antigone* also illustrate the second principle in action. In *A Man for All Seasons*, More, by refusing to endorse Henry VIII's divorce, places his life at risk to uphold his Catholic faith. He dies a martyr, and in dying demonstrates that tragedy knows no middle ground: *either* his faith *or* his life, but not both.

Prometheus Bound likewise demonstrates the second principle. To lay down the new world order, Prometheus leaves his brethren behind—Typhon buried alive under Etna and Atlas crushed under the pillars of heaven and earth. Their burdens leave an eternal blot on Prometheus' conscience. That the new world order is bought at such a cost testifies that the price of choice is real: *either* the new order *or* the bands of brotherhood, but not both.

---

12   Shakespeare, *Macbeth*, 2.2.57–60.

Antigone also illustrates how choice results in irrevocable loss. When Antigone advocates family, she cuts her ties with the city. And when Creon advocates public duty, he cuts his ties with family. *Either* family *or* duty, but not both.

Why is it important for the price to be paid in full? The tragedian's task is to establish the value of the all-too-human through the art form of tragedy. When tragedians make their protagonists pay in full, they communicate the seriousness of their undertaking. By doing so, they give credibility to tragedy's function as a dead serious valuing mechanism. To understand the full implications, take a look at the shortcomings of *defective tragedy*, my term for tragedies where the price is paid, but only in part.

Deus ex machina: Defective Tragedy

Set against the Macbeths and the Mores are the characters in deus ex machina tragedies who pay the price in part. These tragedies are defective because they violate the second principle: at the play's conclusion, a god descends from the machine to return the price that has been paid. When the price is paid in part, tragedy's credibility as a valuing mechanism falters, as the unfortunate impression is given that the price is not right—the books are cooked.

Euripides' *Alcestis* and Sophocles' *Philoctetes* illustrate the effects of price distortion in deus ex machina tragedies. In *Alcestis*, the heroine Alcestis voluntarily dies so that her husband, Admetus, may live. So far so good. But the demigod Heracles eventually wrests her forfeit life back from Death. Alcestis and Admetus are happily reunited, but the all-important myth of the price you pay has been violated:

Alcestis has demonstrated her devotion without paying the full price, and thus her sacrifice seems a mere mirage. The spirit of tragedy has left the building.

Price distortion likewise takes place in *Philoctetes*. Young Neoptolemus desires to bask in the kudos of military glory. He is, after all, Achilles' son, and, as Achilles' son, has large shoes to fill. He decides to embark on a covert mission to acquire Philoctetes' bow, the ancient equivalent of the atom bomb, for it is prophesied that this bow, and only this bow, will end the Trojan War. Neoptolemus succeeds in swindling the bow from Philoctetes, and, in the process, sacrifices his integrity in order to gain military acclaim. In the end, however, Neoptolemus relents and returns the bow to Philoctetes. In doing so, he pays the price, relinquishing military glory to gain back his integrity. He tries to persuade Philoctetes to bring the bow to Troy of his own free will but is unsuccessful. But then the god descends from the machine: as the play ends, Heracles comes down from heaven and persuades Philoctetes himself to bring the bow to Troy. The covert operation proves an even bigger success than the previously planned theft, as it results in the return of the master archer *and* the bow. This results, however, in a violation of the myth of the price you pay: Neoptolemus maintains his integrity *and* enjoys military kudos. How can tragedy be tragic when you can have it all?

I suggest that *Alcestis* and *Philoctetes* are examples of defective tragedy, as price distortion takes place when the hero has his cake and eats it too. The myth of the price you pay forbids free lunches. Go back, for a moment, to the two traders transacting beaver and deer. In a typical transaction, they exchange one beaver for two deer. The beaver hunter, having given up a beaver, leaves with two deer, and the deer hunter, having given up two deer, leaves with a beaver. All is well. But now imagine the incongruity of the scene if the beaver hunter somehow leaves with two deer *and* a beaver while the deer hunter also leaves with two deer *and* a beaver. Well, a similar incongruity takes place in *Alcestis* and *Philoctetes*. If desire comes without sacrifice—if the gods fulfil every wish—what is the cost of desire? Probably not much. In contrast with sugarcoated deus ex machina tragedies are the tragedies where the hero pays in full. In these plays, because the wager is irrevocably lost, we learn, without a shadow of a doubt, the true cost of being. Macbeth cannot be king and drink the milk of human kindness: that is the *price* of the crown. More cannot be friends with the king *and* satisfy his Catholic conscience at the same time: that is the *cost* of conscience.

That deus ex machina tragedies are defective does not imply all "happy ending" tragedies are so. Although deus ex machina tragedies have happy endings, not all happy ending tragedies are defective. Consider Corneille's *Cinna*. Although it ends with a happy group hug and a sigh of relief, it resembles *Macbeth* more than *Alcestis* because the price has been paid in full: in this case, there is a cost to the happy ending. At first glance, *Cinna* appears to violate the second principle which states that the price of blood, sweat, and tears must be paid in full: Augustus has his cake in being sovereign and eats it too by being friend to all; Cinna maintains his honour while also holding onto life; Emilia finds a husband in Cinna and a new father in Augustus, and so on.

However, *Cinna*'s happy ending contrasts with the degraded happy endings of defective tragedy where the god returns the price that has been paid. In *Cinna*, Augustus pays for the happy ending by overcoming his nature and all of the natural inclinations that allowed him to school Brutus, sink Pompey, vanquish Lepidus, unman Antony, and launch wave upon wave of bloody and deadly proscriptions. In a last-ditch show of clemency, Augustus binds the conspirators to him: this is how he pays the price. By lavishing the conspirators with gifts, he relinquishes his pride to those who serve him. The happy ending comes at the cost of Augustus' authority, the authority of the crown. So while deus ex machina tragedies are indeed ineffective, some tragedies that end well fulfil tragedy's countermonetary mandate.

THE THIRD PRINCIPLE: PRICE NOT PAID ON A WHIM

The third principle of countermonetization prescribes that the price cannot be paid on a whim, but must be paid after serious deliberation, and, even then, with great reluctance. Like the first two principles, this third principle exists to maximize our sense of life's worth: tragedy, despite the loss of life, fights everywhere to exalt life. Rodin's sculpture *The Burghers of Calais*, which depicts a tragic moment in Calais' history, shows how the gesture of reluctance can increase the perception of life's value.[13] In 1347, Calais had fallen after

---

13   Rodin, *The Burghers of Calais*, 1895, bronze, 201.6 x 205.4 x 195.9 cm, Town Hall, Calais, France in Rodin, *Rodin on Art and Artists: Conversations with Paul Gsell*, 27.

a difficult, year-long siege by the English. The conqueror, Edward III, made an overture: if six of the city's leaders voluntarily gave up their lives, the citizens would be spared. The sculpture captures the moment when the six volunteers walk out to the gallows pole.

In Rodin's depiction, the first three burghers hasten out with headstrong and deliberate steps. The latter three, in contrast, wander out with slow and stuttering steps. The contrasting gaits provides a valuable clue in how the burghers value their lives. One interpretation—and one which Rodin rejects—is that the first three are greater heroes and that the latter three are lesser heroes because they display a lack of nerve. Rodin's own interpretation is that the reluctant burghers are held back not so much by a failure of nerve (they have, after all, volunteered), but rather by a higher estimation of all that they leave behind.[14] The more one values life, the more hesitantly one approaches the hazards inimical to life. In this way, the gesture of reluctance communicates how precious life is, and this is what we are after in risk theatre.

Bull-in-a-china-shop Tragedies

In tragedy, when the hero pays the price with a devil-may-care heedlessness by rushing into the hour of doom, such an attitude gives the unfortunate impression that human worth amounts to little. These plays I call *bull-in-a-china-shop*

---

14   Rodin, *Rodin on Art and Artists: Conversation with Paul Gsell*, 36:
      While these three men of Calais may be less brave than
      the three first, they do not deserve less admiration. For
      their devotion is even more meritorious, because it costs
      them more.

tragedies and their failure is that they undervalue the all-too-human. For example, when the Duchess propositions her stepson Spurio in Middleton's *The Revenger's Tragedy*, the speed at which they consummate their affair leaves the impression that matrimony and modesty are hardly worth anything.[15] However, if we compare a similar situation in Euripides' *Hippolytus*, we notice that Phaedra's reluctance to confess her stray love for Hippolytus signals how highly she values her good name and the ties of marriage. That she would rather die than dirty her reputation testifies to the high value she confers on her human assets.[16] From the perspective of those who love life, *Hippolytus* is superior to *The Revenger's Tragedy* because it exalts the value of all-too-human pride and self-worth.

Senecan protagonists are often found in bull-in-a-china-shop tragedies since they are especially reckless of their fortunes. The fervour with which Atreus in the tragedy *Thyestes* parts with reputation, honour, shame, law, goodness, loyalty, and righteousness in order to revenge himself on his brother makes it reasonable to infer that he values those qualities at the price of mud.[17] However, if we compare Atreus with Macbeth or More, for example, we see that Macbeth gets

15 Middleton, *The Revenger's Tragedy*, 1.2.192. The play's authorship is debated and variously ascribed to Thomas Middleton or Cyril Tourneur, with the possibility that it is neither.

16 Euripides, *Hippolytus*, in *Children of Heracles, Hippolytus, Andromache, Hecuba*, trans. David Kovacs, lines 373-430.

17 For the long list of human qualities Atreus wagers to revenge himself on his brother Thyestes, see Seneca, *Thyestes*, in *Oedipus, Agamemnon, Thyestes, Hercules on Oeta, Octavia*, trans. John G. Fitch, lines 176-335.

across the idea that the milk of human kindness is a most valuable possession as he vacillates, debating again and again whether he ought to sacrifice compassion for the crown.[18] So too More conveys the worthiness of what he stands to lose as he perfects the most circumspect defences against those who would harm him.[19]

Great sacrifices proceed andante because much consideration must be given to precious things. Rodin's three reluctant burghers walk to the scaffold andante; Macbeth's thoughts and second thoughts emerge andante. Small sacrifices, however, proceed presto because little consideration is afforded to foibles. The three headstrong burghers walk to the scaffold presto; Seneca's protagonists rush into doom presto. It would seem that those who go quickly have little to leave behind.

THE FOURTH PRINCIPLE: PROTAGONIST PAYS THE PRICE

The question of *who* should pay the price remains. Because tragic action revolves around payment, it makes sense for the lead character to foot the bill, or, at the very least, the greater

---

18   On Macbeth's vacillation, see Shakespeare, *Macbeth*, 1.7.1-82 (where Macbeth backs down but is goaded on by Lady Macbeth) and 2.1.33-64 (the "Is this a dagger which I see before me" soliloquy where he gives voice to indecision one final time).

19   In Bolt's play, More seeks to avoid condemnation by keeping his political opinions to himself. This way, when tried in a court of law, his guilt, if any, could only be inferred, but never proven. Since More is a political figure, the dramatic tension rises as friends, enemies, family, and court busybodies attempt to tease out his political views.

portion of the bill. That way the protagonist and the action come together to answer tragedy's central question: what are human assets worth?

In Racine's *Athaliah*, Mattan, a former prophet of Jehovah, pays the price. The cult of Baal flourishes in the royal court, and for the sake of the court, Mattan has turned apostate, exchanging God for an idol. But his secret heart knows that Baal is a fraud, and the knowledge wracks him with guilt. Mattan exchanges the true faith for worldly power on the shadow market. This transaction shows the valuing mechanism of risk theatre at work. The problem, however, lies not with the transaction but with the transactor: Mattan is a secondary character. His sacrifice detracts from the play's two principal characters, Athaliah and Jehoida.

Athaliah and Jehoida vie for control of Joash, the infant pretender to the throne of Judah. They pay, however, less of a price than does Mattan. Jehoida, in fact, hardly pays *any* price. He restores Joash to the throne and cuts down the Baal cult with barely a scratch. As for Athaliah, her sacrifice is interesting but insufficient. She exchanges ruthlessness and authority for mercy and sympathy, and regains her humanity at the cost of becoming soft. She shows weakness and falls prey to Jehoida; thus, the queen of spades dies the queen of hearts. By dying, however, she regains her humanity. Though she pays the price, her price is less than what Mattan pays: for him there is no redemption. Because the leading characters (Athaliah and Jehoida) pay less than the secondary character (Mattan), the tragedy unhappily diverts the audience's attention away from the central action of the play—Athaliah and Jehoida's fight over the infant pretender.

When the haves leave the tab for the have-nots, it detracts from the delight of dining; in the same way, when lead characters pay less than their share, it diminishes the pleasure of risk theatre. Since tragedy as risk theatre concerns itself with paying the price, audiences anticipate that the leading characters will pay. If those characters who have less bear the burden, the action wanders; but when the leading characters shoulder the cost, the action proceeds in a straight line towards the goal. In many successful dramas, however, multiple characters pay the price, a device that does not necessarily detract from the dramatic thrust of the play. The trick is to ensure that the lead pays a higher share.

Egmont and *A Man for All Seasons* both pull off this trick successfully. In *Egmont*, both Egmont and Ferdinand pay the price; but Ferdinand acts as an adjunct, while Egmont pays the greater price as the protagonist. To make it clear that Egmont pays the greater price, multiple scenes throughout the play showcase the richness of all Egmont stands to lose: motley tradesmen gather around to recount Egmont's tales of glory, Egmont's beloved dotes on him day and night, and Egmont's peers talk of him with respect and admiration. Even Ferdinand, the son of his nemesis, befriends and embraces him. Egmont's depiction emphasizes all that he has to lose: the camaraderie of the citizens of Brussels, the love of Clara, and the fellowship of his peers.

Young Ferdinand, who experiences his own demitragedy, stands in contrast to Egmont. Ferdinand wants to become a great figure of state like his father, the peerless Duke of Alba. His first assignment requires him to lead Egmont into his father's trap. However, the catch is that Ferdinand must befriend and then betray Egmont. After Ferdinand succeeds in befriending Egmont, he learns that betrayal is easier said than done. To come of age, Ferdinand forfeits the innocence of youth, but Egmont loses his life; thus, the cost that Egmont bears is higher than that of Ferdinand. The result is that the spotlight stays focused on where the play shines the brightest: on the main character Egmont, the resolute hero.

Tragedy also plays alongside demitragedy in *A Man for All Seasons*. To uphold his principles, More experiences the major tragedy by losing his life, which, by all accounts, was the best of lives: he enjoyed his wife's love, his daughter's devotion, Norfolk's friendship, and the respect of both friends and enemies. Multiple scenes dramatize the richness of all his intangible assets. In contrast to More, Rich, obsequious and ambitious, perjures himself to bring down More during the culminating trial:

> RICH. I said, "Ah, but I will put you a middle case. Parliament has made our King Head of the Church. Why will you not accept him?"

> NORFOLK. (*strung up*) Well?

> RICH. Then he said Parliament had no power to do it.

> NORFOLK. Repeat the prisoner's words!

> RICH. He said, "Parliament has not the competence." Or words to that effect.

CROMWELL. He denied the title.

RICH. He did. (*All look to* More, *but he looks to* Rich.)

MORE. In good faith, Rich, I am sorrier for your perjury than my peril.

NORFOLK. Do you deny this?

MORE. Yes! My Lords, if I were a man who heeded not the taking of an oath, you know well I need not to be here. Now I will take an oath! If what Master Rich has said is true, then I pray I may never see God in the face! Which I would not say were it otherwise for anything on earth.[20]

Rich's perjury unravels More's twofold strategy of keeping his head by silence (when possible) and by equivocation (when necessary). With dexterity More had skated around his adversaries' dangerous questions, finding shelter in the letter of the law. But the law fails him when Rich willfully gives false testimony while under oath. More is undone by Rich's perjury. But in a final moment of clarity, he sees into Rich's minor tragedy and calls him on it:

MORE. I *have* one question to ask the witness. (Rich *stops.*) That's a chain of office you are wearing.

---

20   Bolt, *A Man for All Seasons,* pp. 155–6.

(*Reluctantly* Rich *faces him.*) May I see it? (Norfolk *motions him to approach.* More *examines the medallion.*) The red dragon. (*To* Cromwell) What's this?

CROMWELL. Sir Richard is appointed Attorney-General for Wales.

MORE. (*Looking into* Rich's *face, with pain and amusement.*) For Wales? Why, Richard, it profits a man nothing to give his soul for the whole world... But for Wales—![21]

For the sake of a position in the court, Rich has given up his soul, an obsequious and arrogant soul worth a thin dime. Because he is a worm, his loss pales in comparison with More, who leaves behind a treasure trove of riches: a chancellorship made greater by integrity, a devoted wife, a loving daughter, and faithful friends. Because More's tragedy costs him more than what Rich pays in his minor tragedy, the action and the protagonist converge together in a show of dramatic unity.

Those with the Most Pay the Price

For a long time, it has been felt that tragedy tells the story of kings and queens. Even back in the early Middle Ages, Isidore of Seville, in his encyclopedia *Etymologies*, wrote that trage-dians were the ones who sang about the sorrowful deeds of kings.[22] I believe that this longstanding tradition is due in part

---

21   Ibid., p. 158.
22   Isidore of Seville, *The Etymologies of Isidore of Seville*, trans. Stephen A. Barney, W. J. Lewis, J. A. Beach, and Oliver Berghof, 18.45.

to an intuitive understanding of the myth of the price you pay. Tragedy relates the deeds of kings because kings were perceived as being able to pay the price.

From serf to peasant and from peasant to merchant and craftsman, from farmer and fisherman to knight, lord, lady, bishop, and baron, up each rung on the ladder to the crown, the capacity to pay the price increases from rung to rung. The proportionate loss experienced when a poor man loses his shirt equals the loss of a kingdom for a ruler, but a king's absolute loss is greater, as he pays out not only his own blood, sweat, and tears, but also the blood, sweat, and tears of all those tributary to him. By standing on the shoulders of all those supporting them, kings bear the greatest outlays. The beggar's loss is a thrift shop tragedy, while the king's loss makes for the greatest show on earth. When beggars die, there are no comets seen, but the heavens themselves blaze forth the death of princes.

As the wheel of history charges forwards, much has changed and will continue to change. Modern royalty now consists of the members of the Forbes 400, politicians, Wall Street tycoons, industrialists, magnates, and artists—the Rothschilds, Kennedys, Madoffs, Jobses, Onassises, and Goulds. Although they are not kings, they constitute the new royalty because they can pay the price. The new royalty makes fitting subjects for those who do Melpomene's work. Though kings have lost their lustre, the rules for the new royalty remain the same. First, blood, sweat, and tears are legal tender in the shadow market; money is a counterfeit currency. Second, payment in full please; your layaway plans are not welcome. Third, make the price worth something by deliberating over it long and hard. And fourth, the protagonist—to take centre stage—must bear the burden of paying the price. By engaging these principles, tragedy's counter-monetization imbues life with meaning.

PART III

A POETICS OF TRAGEDY

HOW TO WRITE RISK THEATRE

6 THE ART OF THE ALL-IN WAGER

Here are the seven telltale signs of tragedy. First, heroes tend to be either proud and cocksure egocentrics or hopeless idealists. Second, nurses, aides, attendants, advisors, pedagogues, and confidants dispense unbecoming, if not downright malign advice. Third, starring roles are filled by kings, queens, and other one-percenters. Fourth, supernatural appurtenances, such as ghosts and oracles, litter the stage. Fifth, passions run white hot. Sixth, heroes claim to suffer woes "greater than mortal man has ever borne."[1] Seventh, the

---

1   The phrase is from the Middle Comic poet Timocles fragment 6, which is quoted in Athenaeus, *The Deipnosophists*, vol. 3, trans. C. B. Gulick 6.223b-d:

> The comic poet Timocles, speaking of the many ways in which tragedy is useful in the conduct of life, says, in *Women at the Dionysia*: "Good sir, harken, if haply I shall tell you the truth. Man is a creature born to labour, and many are the distresses his life carries with it. Therefore he has contrived these respites from his cares; for his mind, taking on forgetfulness of its own burdens, and absorbed in another's woe, departs in joy, instructed withal. Look first at the tragedians, if it please you, and see what a benefit they are to

curtain rises to scenes of adultery, murder, destruction, war, famine, and plague. Damnation is in the air. I call these signs collectively the *commonplaces of tragedy*.

I will argue that the commonplaces of tragedy, which I consider part of the deep structure of risk theatre, motivate heroes to go all-in. When heroes go all-in, they load up the hero's wager with dizzying levels of risk. Since risk and uncertainty are intertwined, high risk makes for high drama: the greater the risk, the more uncertain the outcome. In addition, by taking on inordinate levels of risk, heroes can fulfil tragedy's mandate as a valuing mechanism because it is only when risk runs riot that they get the price right when they lay down their wagers in tragedy's high-risk, high-stakes show.

The Price is Right

This brings us to a most interesting question: when is the price right? To get the price right means going all-in, but not willy-nilly. When one wagers things of great consequence for things of little consequence, the price is not right. For example, when Eilert in Ibsen's *Hedda Gabler* sacrifices a lifetime of work for the pleasure of a night out on the town

---

everybody. The poor man, for instance, learns that Telephus was more beggarly than himself, and from that time on he bears his poverty more easily. The sick man sees Alcmeon raving in madness. One has a disease of the eyes—blind are the sons of Phineus. One has lost his son in death—Niobe is a comfort. One is lame—he sees Philoctetes. One meets misfortune in old age—he learns the story of Oeneus. For he is reminded that all his calamities, which are "greater than mortal man has ever borne," have happened to others, and so he bears his own trials more easily."

or when Xerxes in Aeschylus' *Persians* puts the best of the Persian youth at risk to conquer a barren crag called Hellas, the price is not right. Eilert undervalues his manuscript, and Xerxes undervalues the best of the Persians. They have left too much money on the table. The reward is incommensurate with what they have put at stake.

Also, when one wagers things of little consequence for things of equally trite consequence, the price is not right. For example, when the new god Dionysus in Euripides' *Bacchae* squabbles with mortals, he gives the unfortunate impression that he has too much time on his hands. In wagering his dignity to prove his godhead, he leaves himself open to rebuke from the very mortals he chastises:

> CADMUS. Dionysus, we entreat your mercy: we have
> wronged you!

> DIONYSUS. Late is your knowledge of me: you did
> not have it when you needed it.

> CADMUS. We recognize this. But you chastize us
> too harshly.

> DIONYSUS. Well, I was treated with contempt
> though a god.

> CADMUS. Gods ought not to be like mortals in
> their tempers.[2]

---

2   Euripides, *Bacchae*, in *Bacchae, Iphigenia at Aulis, Rhesus*, trans. David Kovacs, lines 1344-8.

The only response Dionysus can muster is that it was done by the will of Zeus. In this exchange, he had too much to lose and too little to gain.

When one wagers things of little consequence for things of the highest consequence, the price is still not right. For example, when Helen in Euripides' *Helen* hoodwinks an unwanted suitor for a coveted passage home or when Ruffus in Verardi's *Ferdinand Preserved* sacrifices a pittance to usurp the crown, they wager too little. There is great pleasure in watching heroes gamble at the no-limit tables, but there is little pleasure in watching heroes win a little here and lose a little there at the nickel-and-dime tables. Tragedy, because it is entertainment, asks heroes to go big or go home.

Only when heroes risk things of great consequence for equally consequent items do they get the price right. Heroes, like Faust, who put up souls to gain the world, fulfil the all-in wager by daring to make life great. By counterbalancing the soul against all the world has to offer, they fill the human vessel with value: in Faust's reckoning, one soul is worth the whole cosmos. The price is right when life is valued high and set in glory—that is tragedy's mandate and purpose as art.

Intangible concepts, such as the soul; qualities, such as mercy or dignity; and feelings, such as friendship or sympathy, all belong to humanity and are difficult to value. But when the hero dares to go all-in, he or she signals a belief in life, in its goodness, and that the all-too-human has as great a value as that which it is set against on the other side of the wager. What other art, besides tragedy, "the gravest, moralest, and most profitable" of poems, can equate the worth of one soul to the whole cosmos?

The hero of the all-in wager is the one whose life is ambition's peer. Like Corneille's Don Rodrigo, these heroes entertain by their brashness: "I rashly challenge a victorious arm," says the young Don Rodrigo to the grizzled veteran, "But, since my heart is high, I've strength to spare."[3] Like Goethe's Faust, such heroes are fearless, natural-born gamblers:

> My spirits rise, my powers are stronger, clearer,
> As from the glow of a refreshing wine.
> I gather heart to risk the world's encounter,
> To bear my human fate as fate's surmounter,
> To front the storm, in joy or grief not palter,
> Even in the gnash of shipwreck never falter.[4]

Though mortal, they know no limits: "My name is Faust," says the magician point-blank to the eternal earth spirit, "in everything your equal."[5] Here is tragedy, the way it is meant to be played.

Heroes who find risk attractive—whom I call *risk-on* characters—entertain, but have one shortcoming: because they are far removed from day-to-day life, they are unconvincing. Audiences demand plausible characters, characters verisimilar to life, characters who react in the same way that audiences themselves would react, were they to find themselves in a similar situation. Plausible characters, however, are unsuited for the stage of tragedy because they opt for a middling life

---

3   Corneille, *The Cid*, in *The Cid, Cinna, The Theatrical Illusion*, trans. John Cairncross, 2.2.415-6.

4   Goethe, *Faust: Part One*, trans. Philip Wayne, p. 46.

5   Ibid., p. 48.

and a salaried position, carefully balancing risk with reward, hedging bets, insuring against loss, and diversifying ambitions into many baskets. They do not go all-in and are indifferent to "gathering heart to risk the world's encounter," preferring a white-picket fence to Melpomene's delirious wagers. They are more likely to be reading the fine print on Allstate insurance policies than shaking their fist at the gods or scaling the golden walls of heaven. This leads to the playwright's catch-22. While tragedy demands characters full of fire, realistic characters—like Miss Julie—carry insurance against it:

> JEAN. Don't you know it's dangerous to play
> with fire?

> MISS JULIE. Not for me; I'm insured.[6]

The commonplaces of tragedy arose as a solution to this conflict facing the tragic playwright. By encouraging heroes to bet big, they allow the implausible hero plausibility. With the help of the commonplaces, the hero can take on risks greater than those ten ordinary mortals could bear, yet remain like to life. The commonplaces achieve their effect through a combination of the three c's: *confidence*, *capacity*, and *compulsion*. Confidence is the faith that moves mountains. Capacity is measured by the hero's abilities and resources, or—continuing with the analogy of moving mountains—by the mountain-moving excavators and explosives at the ready.

---

6   Strindberg, *Miss Julie*, in *Miss Julie and Other Plays*, trans. Michael Robinson, p. 81.

Compulsion is that which is felt when desperate times call for desperate measures: when buried under an avalanche, the mountain must be moved. Normally, risk is a four-letter word with a negative connotation. The three c's, however, transform risk into opportunity. When risk becomes opportunity, the circumstances are right for the protagonist to risk everything. The three c's furnish the preconditions for risk to run riot.

THE FIRST COMMONPLACE

The Proud Hero

The proud and cocksure hero, the expert in love with function, exemplifies my first commonplace of tragedy. Like Formula One drivers, they put their lives on the line because they have expertise and daring: as experts they are expected to drive at dizzying speeds. Sophocles draws on the first commonplace when motivating Oedipus to lay it on the line. In *Oedipus rex*, Oedipus takes on extraordinary risks to lift the plague. To lift the plague, he must expel the secret and insidious regicide walking among the Thebans. He successively interviews priest, prophet, brother-in-law, wife, messenger, and slave to get at the truth. As each interview draws the truth closer, Oedipus risks damning himself, alienating his wife and children, plunging Thebes into civil war, and jeopardizing the Corinthian line of succession because he does not understand that he himself is the regicide. As knowing voices implore him to stop, the dangerous risks he takes on become clear:

TIRESIAS. Just send me home. You bear your burdens,
I'll bear mine. It's better that way,
please believe me.

and,

JOCASTE. Stop—in the name of god,
if you love your own life, call off this search!
My suffering is enough.

or,

SHEPHERD. No—
god's sake, master, no more questions![7]

How can Oedipus press on in the face of such danger? That is Sophocles' catch-22. The tragedian solves it by turning to the first commonplace of tragedy: employ a cocksure hero whose expertise fits the crisis. Oedipus fits the bill. After all, he had relayed right from his opening lines a presumptuous confidence:

Here I am myself—
you all know me, the world knows my fame:
I am Oedipus.[8]

---

7   Sophocles, *Oedipus the King*, in *The Three Theban Plays*, trans. Robert Fagles, lines 364-6, 1162-4, and 1279-80.

8   Ibid., lines 7-9.

Theatre knows no bolder entrance than Oedipus' "I am Oedipus." *How* he acquired world fame emerges in the exchange with Tiresias:

TIRESIAS. This day will bring your birth and
 your destruction.

OEDIPUS. Riddles—all you can say are riddles, murk
 and darkness.

TIRESIAS. Ah, but aren't you the best man alive at
 solving riddles?

OEDIPUS. Mock me for that, go on, and you'll reveal
 my greatness.[9]

Oedipus' fame arose from unriddling the Sphinx. His skills in inquiring, deducing, inferring, and problem solving are second to none. His evident satisfaction at having dispatched the Sphinx ("You all know me, the world knows my fame") further points to his delight in fulfilling his function as a solver of riddles.

Since Oedipus' entire being basks in the glories of inquiry, deduction, inference, and solution, the audience expects him to step up to the plate when confronted with a riddle—risk be damned. So, to motivate Oedipus to lay it on the line, Sophocles presents the crisis as a riddle. From Apollo's cryptic command to reopen the investigation into Laius'

---

9   Ibid., lines 499-502.

death to the lack of an investigation in the first place, the plague appears as a riddle which must be solved. Then, little by little, from the unexpected resistance Oedipus encounters during the investigation to the old oracle that he would sleep with his mother and kill his father, the riddle of the plague gives way to the riddle of Oedipus' existence. But, since Oedipus is the expert riddler, when the crisis presents itself to him as the enigma of his own existence, he cannot stop, nor is he expected to stop, since, by solving the riddle, he is fulfilling his natural-born function.

The first commonplace also allows an all-in hero such as Shakespeare's Caesar to rise to the occasion. Although grave danger awaits Caesar in the Capitol, he has more than sufficient warning to avoid the impending catastrophe. First, the soothsayer tells him to "beware the ides of March."[10] Then there are the multiple signs encouraging him to avoid the Capitol. The heart is missing from the sacrificial animal. His wife has nightmares of his statue running blood. Spirits walk the streets. Birds shriek out of season. A lioness whelps in the streets. Graves yield up their dead. Tempests rain blood. A lesser hero would do the plausible thing: stay home. But Shakespeare does not need a lesser hero. He needs an all-in hero, a defiant nature to fuel the tragic machine, a hero who can be counted on to escalate rather than resolve the crisis. To create a lifelike character with a knack for overcoming common sense, prudence, caution, logic, trepidation, and good advice, Shakespeare turns to the first commonplace

---

10   Shakespeare, *Julius Caesar*, 1.2.23.

and imbues Caesar with a proud and egocentric nature that delights in dominion:

> CAESAR. I rather tell thee what is to be fear'd
> Than what I fear; for always I am Caesar.

and,

> CAESAR. Caesar shall forth; the things that
>   threaten'd me
> Ne'er look'd but on my back; when they shall see
> The face of Caesar, they are vanished.

and,

> CAESAR. Cowards die many times before
>   their deaths;
> The valiant never taste of death but once.

or,

> CAESAR. I could be well mov'd, if I were as you;
> If I could pray to move, prayers would move me;
> But I am constant as the northern star,
> Of whose true-fix'd and resting quality
> There is no fellow in the firmament.[11]

---

11   Ibid., 1.2.211-2, 2.2.10–2, 2.2.32-3, and 3.1.58–62.

Since Caesar is portrayed as a brave, forceful, lionhearted, and steadfast individual who is capable of overcoming any contingency, he is expected—like the Formula One driver—to stake whatever it takes. Like Oedipus, a certain egocentric perspective allows Caesar to brush aside common sense, prudence, caution, trepidation, good advice, and other untragic attributes. The first commonplace is a valuable tool in the tragedian's toolbox because, through confidence—one of the three c's—it allows heroes to take on inordinate risk, yet remain like to life.

Many years ago—and perhaps still today—schools taught that a character's pride is the tragic flaw. Pride equals hubris, and hubris is wrong. Having done wrong, the hero suffers. Oedipus took pride in being clever and paid the price. Caesar took pride in being Caesar and died. These types of moralizing interpretations result from *ex-post* interpretations, that is, an after-the-fact understanding possible only after the events have already played out. Ex-post twenty-twenty hindsight is unavailable at decision time. Heroes must operate based on past experiences and forecasts: they operate *ex-ante*, or before the fact.

To blame Oedipus and Caesar for relying on what had worked in the past is a blame-mongering, ex-post interpretation. It is an "I hate to say it, but I told you so" interpretation filled with the same hubris that it rejects. Its hubris is that it asks heroes who act before the fact to understand the situation from an after-the-fact perspective. My theory of risk theatre rejects the blame-mongers' interpretation. As a series of gambling acts, tragedy prefers egocentrics because they make bigger bets. Playwrights do not create proud heroes so that critics can blame them for their pride; rather, heroes must be proud because proud natures delight in going all-in.

The Idealist

Idealists who are beholden to liberty, law, God, or such notions as tradition, democracy, communism, capitalism, and the various other -*isms* are drawn by their nature towards the all-in. Because idealists jump at opportunities to walk the talk, they gravitate towards risk. Celebrated examples of idealists include Antigone and Creon in Sophocles' *Antigone*. The conflict between Antigone and Creon arises in the aftermath of the Theban civil war. One of Oedipus' sons, Eteocles, died while defending Thebes; the other, Polyneices, died attacking Thebes to reclaim his birthright. Creon, the regent, issues a proclamation: Eteocles is to be buried with full pomp, and Polyneices is to be left for beasts to devour. Antigone, however, wants to ensure that *both* of her brothers are buried.

Grievous risks stand in Antigone's way. Her sister tries to talk her out of it:

> ISMENE. Now look at the two of us, left so alone . . .
> think what death we'll die, the worst of all
> if we violate the laws and override
> the fixed decree of the throne, its power—
> we must be sensible. Remember we are women,
> we're not born to contend with men. Then too,

we're underlings, ruled by much stronger hands,
so we must submit in this, and things still worse.[12]

The chorus likewise rebukes Antigone for her daring: "You went too far, the last limits of daring— / smashing against the high throne of Justice!"[13] Since the playwright's task is to draw the heroine to the top of risk's rickety ladder, Sophocles employs the first commonplace by drawing attention to Antigone's idealistic streak:

> ANTIGONE. I will bury him myself.
> And even if I die in the act, that death will be
>   a glory.
> I will lie with the one I love and loved by him—
> an outrage sacred to the gods! I have longer
> to please the dead than please the living here:
> in the kingdom down below I'll lie forever.[14]

When someone says that they have longer to please the dead than the living, they have licence to go all-in.

Like Antigone, Creon is also an idealist. He champions order, law, and the ship of state above all else:

> CREON. Remember this:
> our country *is* our safety.
> Only while she voyages true on course

12 Sophocles, *Antigone*, in *The Three Theban Plays*, trans. Robert Fagles, lines 70-7.
13 Ibid., lines 934-5.
14 Ibid., lines 85-90.

can we establish friendships, truer than blood itself.
Such are my standards. They make our city great.[15]

His idealism gives him licence to lay it all on the line, and
he does so as he rebukes the town prophet:

CREON. You'll never bury that body in the grave,
not even if Zeus's eagles rip the corpse
and wing their rotten pickings off to the throne
of god![16]

Because Creon acts as the great patriot, he easily champions
civil law over religious law, no matter the hazard involved.

THE SECOND COMMONPLACE:
MINOR MEDDLERS & (UN)HELPFUL ADVISORS

What if the story requires a moderate hero, one who is not
overly cocksure or ideology bound? What if the hero needs
to be more prudent and less reckless, more sensible and less
senseless? The solution lies in the second commonplace
of tragedy: the trusted sidekick, embodied by all the aides,
attendants, and advisors who goad heroes into going all-in
with unbecoming advice. As Goethe's Iphigenia understands,
friendship inspires confidence and confidence incites sallow
hearts to act:

---

15   Ibid., lines 210-4.
16   Ibid., lines 1151-3.

IPHIGENIA. How precious is the presence of a friend,
His words of certainty, whose heavenly power
The lonely person lacks and, lacking, sinks back
Listless. Locked in the heart, thoughts and decisions
Ripen slowly; having someone near,
Who cares, will bring them swiftly to fruition.[17]

In Seneca's *Thyestes*, Thyestes receives an invitation from his brother Atreus welcoming him home and offering him a share of the throne. Thyestes, knowing his brother, suspects a trap. Besides, years of exile have taught him the pleasures of simple living. To him, the throne means little and, if anything, is a liability. To goad Thyestes on, Seneca places next to him a trusted advisor-type figure (who happens to be Thyestes' son, Tantalus):

TANTALUS. What is it? Father walks listlessly, in a daze; he keeps looking round and hesitating.

THYESTES. Why the impasse, my spirit? Why wrestle so long with such an easy decision? Can you trust the most unreliable of things, a brother and a throne? Are you afraid of evils you have already conquered and tamed? Running from hardships you have turned to advantage? By now it is pleasant to be "wretched"! Turn back while you may, and rescue yourself.

---

17   Goethe, *Iphigenia in Tauris*, in *Plays*, trans. Frank Ryder, p. 127.

TANTALUS. What is forcing you, father, to walk away from sight of your fatherland? Why fold your arms against such blessings? Your brother returns to you with his anger cast aside, gives you back a share in the throne, joins together the limbs of this dismembered family, and restores you to yourself.[18]

Through the second commonplace of the unhelpful advisor, Thyestes is persuaded to trade secure poverty for uncertain power.

In *Hippolytus*, Euripides makes use of the second commonplace to motivate Phaedra. Phaedra, through the machinations of Aphrodite, has fallen in love with her stepson. Her low tolerance for risk, however, prevents her from acting on her feelings, and she resolves, instead, to die a quiet death as she pines away. To goad her on, Euripides places next to her a trusty sidekick in the person of the nurse. The nurse coaxes out Phaedra's secret and tells Hippolytus. He is horrified. Now, to preserve her honour, Phaedra must act. She goes all-in and frames Hippolytus for rape. Without the nurse's advice, Phaedra would have gone risk-off, preferring death to action; with the nurse's advice (and the subsequent disclosure of her illicit feelings), Phaedra's appetite for risk surges. By offering trustworthy if misleading advice, the second commonplace succeeds in promoting risk.

---

18   Seneca, *Thyestes*, in *Oedipus, Agamemnon, Thyestes, Hercules on Oeta, Octavia*, trans. John Fitch, lines 421-33.

THE THIRD COMMONPLACE: KINGS AND QUEENS

"God's sharp lightnings fly to stagger mountains," writes Aeschylus.[19] "When beggars die, there are no comets seen; / The heavens themselves blaze forth the death of princes," says Shakespeare.[20] These lines exemplify what I deem the third commonplace of tragedy, that is, the curious overrepresentation of kings, queens, and other wealthy and powerful characters in tragedy: Hamlet, *Prince* of Denmark; Oedipus, *King* of Thebes; the *Duchess* of Malfi; Don Carlos, *Prince* of Spain; Thomas Becket, *Archbishop* of Canterbury; and so on. The pool of tragic heroes draws from the elite because they are the ones with the greatest capacity to take on risk. It is hard to be the hero of the all-in wager on an empty stomach. To go big, one must have capital, whether one has invested in oneself, has aristocratic capital, capital in wealth, or human capital.

Case in point is Fergus in Norton and Sackville's *Gorboduc*. Gorboduc, King of Britain, has abdicated, his sons are slain, civil unrest rises, and the throne lies vacant. Fergus, Duke of Albany, covets the crown. To seize the crown, however, involves risks greater than those ordinary mortals are accustomed to bear. Fergus, however, uses his capital to underwrite the risk:

> FERGUS. And Britain land, now desert left alone
> Amid these broils uncertain where to rest,

---

19   Aeschylus, *Agamemnon*, in *The Oresteian Trilogy*, trans. Philip Vellacott, p. 59.

20   Shakespeare, *Julius Caesar*, 2.2.30-1.

Offers herself unto that noble heart
That will or dare pursue to bear her crown.
Shall I, that am the Duke of Albany,
Descended from that line of noble blood,
Which have so long flourish'd in worthy fame
Of valiant hearts, such as in noble breasts
Of right should rest above the baser sort,
Refuse to venture life to win a crown?
Whom shall I find enemies that will withstand
My fact herein, if I attempt by arms
To seek the same now in these times of broil?
These dukes' power can hardly well appease
The people that already are in arms.
But if, perhaps, my force be once in field,
Is not my strength in power above the best
Of all these lords now left in Britain land?
And though they should match me with power
        of men,
Yet doubtful is the chance of battles joined,
If victors of the field we may depart,
Ours is the sceptre then of Great Britain;
If slain amid the plain this body lie,
Mine enemies yet shall not deny me this,
But that I died giving the noble charge
To hazard life for conquest of a crown.
Forthwith, therefore, will I in post depart
To Albany, and raise in armour there
All power I can: and here my secret friends,
By secret practice shall solicit still,

To seek to win to me the people's hearts.[21]

Fergus goes all-in, staking his capital as a surety. Hailing from a line of valiant hearts, he owns ancestral capital. As Duke of Albany, he has military capital: the conscripts await their summons. As an able orator, he claims human capital: secret friends stand ready. Capital burns a hole in his pocket, calling him to arms.

THE FOURTH COMMONPLACE: SUPERNATURAL ELEMENTS

When the hazard proves too great for mortals to bear, the invisible world acts as a backstop of the last resort. My fourth commonplace consists of the supernatural appurtenances of the stage such as witches, ghosts, and oracles. These appurtenances can be quite useful in unleashing risk events. When Orestes, for example, shirks from killing his mother to avenge his father, all Pylades has to do to restore Orestes' nerve is to remind him of the oracle:

> CLYTEMNESTRA. Down with your sword, my son!
> My own child, see this breast:
> Here often your head lay, in sleep, while your
> soft mouth
> Sucked from me the good milk that gave you life
> and strength.

ORESTES. Pylades, what shall I do? To kill a mother
   is terrible.
Shall I show mercy?

PYLADES. Where then are Apollo's words,
His Pythian oracles? What becomes of men's
   sworn oaths?
Make all men living your enemies, but not the gods.

ORESTES. I uphold your judgement; your advice
   is good.[22]

Supernatural appurtenances make the meek bold. Set the supernatural in the path of one who exercises caution in every undertaking, and even he becomes brazen, as we see in Macbeth's encounter with the witches:

MACBETH: Speak, if you can:—what are you?

1 WITCH. All hail, Macbeth! hail to thee, Thane
   of Glamis!
2 WITCH. All hail, Macbeth! hail to thee, Thane
   of Cawdor!
3 WITCH. All hail, Macbeth! that shall be
   King hereafter.[23]

---

22   Aeschylus, *The Choephori*, in *The Oresteian Trilogy*, trans. Philip Vellacott, p. 136.
23   Shakespeare, *Macbeth*, 1.2.47-50.

Macbeth begins the play fighting traitors in the king's name. When a credible source tempts him with the crown, however, Macbeth will risk turning traitor to wear the crown.

Supernatural appurtenances increase the appetite for risk by increasing confidence. Witches and oracles can access the world core, have occult knowledge, can see into the future, and recall the forgotten past. They have insider information. Their tips remove uncertainty, baiting heroes to take on more than they can handle:

> 2 APPARITION. Be bloody, bold, and resolute: laugh
>   to scorn
> The pow'r of man; for none of woman born
> Shall harm Macbeth. *Descends.*
>
> MACBETH. Then live, Macduff; what need I fear
>   of thee?
> But yet I'll make assurance double sure,
> And take a bond of fate: thou shalt not live,
> That I may tell pale-hearted fear it lies,
> And sleep in spite of thunder.
> Thunder. third apparition, *a Child crowned, with a*
>   *tree in his hand.*
> What is this,
> That rises like the issue of a king,
> And wears upon his baby brow the round
> And top of sovereignty?
>
> ALL. Listen, but speak not to't.

3 APPARITION. Be lion-mettled, proud, and take
  no care
Who chafes, who frets, or where conspirers are:
Macbeth shall never vanquish'd be, until
Great Birnam wood to high Dunsinane hill Shall
  come against him. *Descend.*

MACBETH. That will never be:
Who can impress the forest, bid the tree
Unfix his earth-bound root? Sweet bode-
  ments! good![24]

Superior intelligence transforms risk into opportunity. Recognizing this principle, heroes go all-in when the spirits speak.

THE FIFTH COMMONPLACE: PASSIONS RUNNING WHITE HOT

Certain emotions heighten our tolerance for risk. Because risk runs riot once care and prudence have been soused in wine, my fifth commonplace involves the fiery heroes who are drunk on passion, such as Balthazar, a character from Kyd's *Spanish Tragedy.* As Kyd readies Balthazar to roll the die, he ravishes him with Bel-imperia's beauty. Once Balthazar feels the rush of blood, he is ready for the hero's enterprise: "I'll tempt the destinies," he says, "and either lose my life, or

---

24   Ibid., 4.1.79-96.

win my love."[25] In Shakespeare's *Othello*, the title character's "constant, loving, noble nature" makes him ill-suited to carry out crimes of passion.[26] No problem: Shakespeare turns to the fifth commonplace and puts him "into a jealousy so strong / That judgement cannot cure."[27]

Anger works just as well as romantic passion to spur on the hero. Webster, in *The Duchess of Malfi*, uses anger to unleash the mild-mannered Antonio. When Antonio's land is appropriated and wife murdered, he is ready to risk everything to play at the high-limit table:

> ANTONIO. This night I mean to venture all
>   my fortune
> Which is no more than a poor lingering life
> To the Cardinal's worst of malice.

He is fired up to the extent that, two scenes later, he can still be found reaffirming his appetite for risk:

> Come, I'll out of this ague;
> For to live thus is not indeed to live:
> It is a mockery and abuse of life.
> I will not henceforth save myself by halves,
> Lose all, or nothing.[28]

---

25   Kyd, *The Spanish Tragedy*, 2.1.132-3.

26   Shakespeare, *Othello*, 2.1.289.

27   Ibid., 2.1.301-2.

28   Webster, *The Duchess of Malfi*, 5.1.62-4 and 5.3.46-50.

Shame is another emotion which motivates the tragic hero. In Corneille's *The Cid*, Don Rodrigo feels the pang of shame when he finds out that the Count has, with impunity, slapped his aged father. For Don Rodrigo to confront the Count, however, is an undertaking fraught with danger: not only is the Count a superior swordsman, but he is also the father of his beloved. But, because Don Rodrigo is fired up over the slight, he leaves it all on the table and duels the Count. Euripides' Medea is also goaded on by the sting of shame. When her husband gallivants away with a young princess, she puts her children at risk to make him pay. The emotions—whether passion, jealousy, anger, or shame—fire up meek and reserved natures into committing acts of reckless abandon.

THE SIXTH COMMONPLACE: CONSOLATIONS GONE WRONG

Consolers say, "Not to you alone" while sufferers claim to have suffered woes "greater than mortal man has ever borne."[29] I suggest that this banter forms the sixth commonplace of tragedy. In Euripides' *Hippolytus*, for example, after

---

29 On woes "greater than mortal man has ever borne," see note 1. The saying *non tibi hoc soli*, "not to you alone" was, and perhaps still is today, a popular consolation, see Cicero, *Cicero on the Emotions: Tusculan Disputations 3 and 4*, trans. Margaret Graver, 3.79:

> Nor is it a very dependable method of consolation—although it is certainly used a great deal and is often beneficial—to say, "You are not the only one to have this happen." This medicine is indeed beneficial, as I said, but not always or for everyone: some spit it out.

Phaedra dies, the chorus of Trozen women comforts Theseus with tragedy's stock consolation: "My lord, it is not upon you alone that these ills have come: you have lost a trusty wife, but so have many others."[30] Instead of feeling comforted, however, Theseus reacts by pouring out his grief:

> Ah me, how wretched am I at your death, luckless
> man that I am, what a grief to my house I have
> seen, grief that cannot be endured or uttered![31]

So too, in Sophocles' *Electra*, when the chorus consoles Electra on the death of her father:

> CHORUS. You are not alone, dear child, in the sorrow
> Which moves you more than the others who share
>   your home;
> Your nearest kin, your sister Chrysothemis,
> And Iphianassa, they are not tired of life.

she replies:

The sufferer in tragedy falls into the category of those who spit it out.

30 Euripides, *Hippolytus*, in *Children of Heracles, Hippolytus, Andromache, Hecuba*, trans. David Kovacs, lines 834-5. In his commentary on these lines, Barrett calls it "a commonplace of consolation," pointing out that Euripides uses similar consolations in *Alcestis* and *Medea*, see Barrett, *Euripides, Hippolytos*, ad loc.

31 Euripides, *Hippolytus*, in *Children of Heracles, Hippolytus, Andromache, Hecuba*, trans. David Kovacs, lines 844-6.

ELECTRA. What use is there
In comfortable words?
Leave me alone,
Kind sisters, there is no escape
From this. My sum of woe
Outruns all reckoning.[32]

Or, in Shakespeare's *Hamlet*, when Claudius consoles Hamlet on the death of his father,

CLAUDIUS. 'Tis sweet and commendable in your
    nature, Hamlet,
To give these mourning duties to your father,
But you must know your father lost a father,
That father lost, lost his . . .

he replies:

HAMLET. O that this too too sallied flesh
    would melt,
Thaw, and resolve itself into a dew!
Or that the Everlasting had not fix'd
His canon 'gainst [self-]slaughter! O God, God,
How [weary], stale, flat, and unprofitable
Seem to me all the uses of this world![33]

---

32   Sophocles, *Electra*, in *Electra and Other Plays*, trans. E. F. Watling, pp. 73 and 75.

33   Shakespeare, *Hamlet*, 1.2.87-90 and 1.2.129-34.

This consolation, "not to you alone," functions by asking the sufferer to sympathize with other sufferers. For example, if the sufferer happens to be a wife who has lost a husband, tragedy's stock consolation would ask her to be mindful of all the other widows who have suffered. By asking for sympathy amongst sufferers, the consolation binds the sufferer to the universe of suffering.[34] Having bound the sufferer to others, it dilutes grief, taking away the sufferer's prerogative. As drops are to the sea, so are the sufferer's tears in relation to the boundless ocean of human suffering.

But there is a paradox in suffering that gets in the way of the good intentions of those who deliver tragedy's stock consolation. The paradox is that the sufferer wants more suffering, not less. Each sufferer wants, with his suffering, to be the most exalted sufferer, and competes with other sufferers to be the king of pain, such as, for example, Io and Prometheus in *Prometheus Bound*:

Io. Why should I go on living? Why not hurl myself
At once down from this rocky cliff, be dashed
    in pieces,
And find relief from all my pain? Better to die
Once, than to suffer torment all my living days.

---

34   Cf. Keller, *Peace at Eventide*, 1:

We bereaved are not alone. We belong to the largest company in all the world—the company of those who have known suffering. When it seems that our sorrow is too great to be borne, let us think of the great family of the heavy-hearted into which our grief has given us entrance, and, inevitably, we shall feel about us their arms, their sympathy, their understanding.

PROMETHEUS. Then you would find it hard to bear
    my agonies,
Since I am fated not to die. Death would
    have brought
Release. But now no end of suffering is in sight.[35]

Prometheus looks askance at Io's pain because her toils detract from his own. To wear the crown, the sufferer must concentrate suffering by undergoing woes "greater than mortal man has ever borne." Great woe empowers sufferers and gives them licence to indulge in their secret desire, which is to rebuke all of existence:

PROMETHEUS. O Earth, my holy mother,
O sky, where sun and moon
Give light to all in turn,
You see how I am wronged![36]

Great woe gives sufferers a proof against caution and emboldens them to enact, like the suffering Lear, the terrors of the earth:

LEAR. You see me here, you gods, a poor old man,
As full of grief as age, wretched in both.
If it be you that stirs these daughters' hearts
Against their father, fool me not so much
To bear it tamely; touch me with noble anger,

---

35   Aeschylus, *Prometheus Bound*, in *Prometheus Bound and Other Plays*, trans. Philip Vellacott, p. 42.

36   Ibid., p. 52.

> And let not women's weapons, water-drops,
> Stain my man's cheeks! No, you unnatural hags,
> I will have such revenges on you both
> That all the world shall—I will do such things—
> What they are yet I know not, but they shall be
> The terrors of the earth![37]

To do the terrors of the earth is to go risk-on.

When tragedy mixes together consolers and sufferers, like a chemist combining potassium and water, the reaction explodes. Sufferers do not want to be consoled, because, in a paradoxical way, suffering is their most precious possession. Consolers, however, want to rehabilitate sufferers by taking away the sufferer's prerogative, but in the process of doing so, they take, as it were, the bone from the dog:

> JOCASTA. And as for this marriage with
>   your mother—
> have no fear. Many a man before you,
> in his dreams, has shared his mother's bed.
> Take such things for shadows, nothing at all—
> Live, Oedipus,
> as if there's no tomorrow![38]

In this scene from *Oedipus rex*, Jocasta tries to console Oedipus with the stock "not to you alone" consolation ("Many a man before you ... has shared his mother's bed").

---

37   Shakespeare, *King Lear*, 2.3.272-82.

38   Sophocles, *Oedipus the King*, in *The Three Theban Plays*, trans. Robert Fagles, lines 1073-8.

But Oedipus, far from being soothed, becomes—like a dog without a bone—more livid. Because she has tried to remove his most precious anxieties, he feels a greater urgency to go all-in: "Listen to you? No more," he replies, "I must know it all, must see the truth at last."[39] With these words he seals his doom, pushing the investigation past the point of no return. The tragic consolation acts as a brilliant decoy. Far from having a calming effect, it leverages heroes' anguish into action. By doing so, the sixth commonplace drives heroes to bet the farm.

THE SEVENTH COMMONPLACE: DANGEROUS AND UNCERTAIN TIMES

No tragedies depict domestic bliss, but many portray families rent apart. No tragedies depict orderly succession, but many portray incapable heirs and collapsing dynasties. No tragedies depict happy shepherds, but many portray famine and plague ravaging the countryside. My seventh and final commonplace comprises the uncertain, dangerous, and turbulent situations prevalent in tragedy. I propose that risk theatre prefers dangerous and uncertain settings not because, as some suppose, tragedy is an unhappy art, but because tragedy is a risk art. Because desperate times call for desperate measures, volatile settings increase the appetite for risk-taking, thereby transforming run-of-the-mill heroes into heroes of the all-in wager.

Risk comes at a price: the potential for loss. During good times, the upside of risk is as small as the downside is large.

---

39   Ibid., lines 1168-9.

During times of political, social, and economic stability, the prudent tactic is to minimize risk by diversifying, insuring, or hedging against it. "My ventures are not in one bottom trusted," says the prudent merchant: he diversifies away the risk of loss by shipping his merchandise in multiple ships.[40] Chances are that a storm will not sink every vessel. When risks cannot be diversified away, they may be insured against. Homeowners who do not have the luxury of owning multiple properties in multiple locations may insure against fire by purchasing property insurance. Finally, when risks cannot be insured, they may be hedged. Farmers, for example, hedge against falling wheat prices by using forward contracts to lock in the price of future sales. Diversification, insurance, and hedging strategies, however, are predicated on the orderliness of a stable, steady-state world. They protect up to the limits of *anticipated* disasters. When *unanticipated* helter-skelter breaks out, however, they fail. When the hundred-year storm strikes, every bottom is shipwrecked. Diversification fails. During the Great Fire of London, the insurance house itself goes up in flames. Insurance fails. When the levee breaks, destroying the harvest, the farmer hangs himself—the forward contract obligates him to sell the crops which have been washed away. Hedging has failed.

Extraordinary situations are commonplace in the tragic theatre because, in extraordinary situations, risk skews to the upside: not taking risks incurs *greater* risk than sitting still or maintaining conventional strategies. Take the game of baseball. Fools go for a home run when they can get by with a

---

40   Shakespeare, *The Merchant of Venice*, 1.1.42.

hit. But at the bottom of the ninth down three with two outs and bases loaded, the prudent hitter goes for the grand slam because all the other choices result in certain loss. So too, in the game of football, the "Hail Mary" pass (where the quarterback throws a long desperation pass into the end zone) is a hazardous low-probability and interception-prone affair. But when a team is down a touchdown and far from the end zone, the further the clock ticks down, the more attractive the "Hail Mary" option becomes. Extraordinary situations encourage risk by compulsion, the last of the three c's: as the seconds tick down, not to throw the "Hail Mary" pass incurs the greater risk of certain loss.

In tragedy, when a storm rolls in, it is the hundred-year storm. When a flood occurs, it is a biblical flood. When sickness strikes, it is the Black Death. Outlier events—witch trials in Salem (Miller's *Crucible*), Britain rent in three (Shakespeare's *King Lear*), plague in Cadiz (Camus' *State of Siege*), or civil war in Thebes (Aeschylus' *Seven Against Thebes*)—are the norm in tragedy because the greater the disequilibrium, the more attractively priced risk becomes. When the world is ablaze, risk's enticements more than compensate for its blandishments.

Consider how the setting of *The Crucible* encourages risk. The year is 1692, on the eve of the greatest witch-hunt in American history. The town is Salem, a frontier settlement in colonial Massachusetts established some forty years prior. During this time, feuds have arisen and skeletons have gathered in the closets. Bad blood flows between the Putnam and the Nurse clans.[41] The town reverend, Parris, a vengeful and unlikeable character also caught between the factions, hangs onto his position by the skin of his teeth.[42] Parris also worries about his niece Abigail, who, after being discharged by the Proctor household, cannot find employment. Despite being ignorant of the brief affair between his niece and Proctor, Parris has heard the rumours.[43] Now, despite the centrifugal forces tearing the community apart, counterbalancing centripetal forces were binding the community together. Salemites shared a common set of puritan beliefs. Also, as an outlying town, to survive meant pooling together resources and wits. Most of the time, the centripetal forces cancelled out the centrifugal forces, preserving the status quo. The witch-hunt changed all that.

Most of the time, despite the family feud, the Putnams would not have dared to charge Rebecca Nurse with the deaths of their children, nor would they have accused her of sending her spirit out to harm others.[44] Most of the time, despite his desire to assert authority, Parris would not have dared to assist magistrates set on hanging his parishioners.[45] Most of the time, despite his honest nature, Proctor would not have dared to publicize his lechery.[46] Most of the time, despite her desire to become Proctor's wife, Abigail would not have dared to plant evidence of witchcraft against

41   Miller, *The Crucible*, pp. 23-4.
42   Ibid., pp. 1-2, 9, 12-3, 27-8.
43   Ibid., pp. 9-10.
44   Ibid., pp. 24-5 and 69.
45   Ibid., pp. 81-115.
46   Ibid., pp. 105-6.

Proctor's wife.[47] But everything changes when the witch-hunt gets underway.

The rules of the witch-hunt are simple. Those suspected of witchcraft who refuse to confess are hanged. Like all invisible crimes, the balance of power favours the plaintiff. Those who confess are spared. There is a catch: the act of confession includes perpetuating the cycle of accusations. It stands that, if one has associated with witches, one can bring them to light. During the witch-hunt, an accuser could, with impunity and threadbare evidence, send the accused to the gallows, particularly if the accused has high moral standards and refuses to confess to bogus charges. This is the first way in which the setting of *The Crucible* encourages risk. We can see this process in action when the Putnams accuse Rebecca Nurse of using supernatural force to murder their babies.[48] Under normal circumstances, they would not have dared to question Rebecca's moral integrity: her acts of charity were famed throughout Salem and the neighbouring towns.[49] But in these outlier circumstances, they accuse her. She hangs.

The situation also prompts an aggressive response from Reverend Parris. The epicentre of the crisis puts Parris in an awkward spot. Betty, his daughter, was one of the girls caught conducting the heathen ritual. Abigail, his niece, was the girls' ringleader. Tituba, his slave, had a reputation for being able to conjure the dead, and she had been caught leading the ceremony.[50] Both Parris' credibility and his job were at

---

47   Ibid., pp. 59-60 and 70-5.
48   Ibid., pp. 69, cf. 24.
49   Ibid., pp. 34.
50   Ibid., pp. 13 and 17.

stake. When he discovers how effective the witch trials are at augmenting his flagging authority, he suppresses—even if it means that his parishioners should hang—the attempts to expose the witch-hunt as a sham.[51]

Unlike the busybody Parris, John Proctor is a no-nonsense individual who lives on the town's outskirts to avoid Salem's partisan politics. But the dramatic setting likewise induces him to abandon conventional strategies. Proctor had a brief affair with Abigail some seven months before the events of the play, an affair he would prefer to keep quiet. When Abigail charges his wife with witchcraft, his only recourse is to demonstrate to the court that Abigail had trumped up the charges in order to supplant his wife. But, to save his wife, Proctor has to expose Abigail's true motives, and this involves revealing that he is a lecher. The attempt to save his wife is bought at the cost of his good name.[52]

Then there is Abigail, who makes a bold gambit of her own. Rumours of impropriety prevent her from finding employment after being discharged from the Proctor household. Not only that, as the play begins, she has been caught conducting heathen rituals in the woods with her friends, two of whom have fallen into a strange catatonic stupor. The town suspects witchcraft, a hanging crime. She wagers that she can avoid hanging by charging other townsfolk with witchcraft. She also wagers that she can find legitimacy by becoming John Proctor's wife.[53] Although Proctor is married, to get rid of his wife during the witch trial is a small matter: all she has to do

51   Ibid., pp. 81-115.
52   Ibid., pp. 105-6.
53   Ibid., pp. 58-9 and 105-6.

is accuse her. To those in dire straits, there is little to lose and everything to gain by attempting the "Hail Mary" play.

By setting *The Crucible* on the eve of the greatest witch-hunt in American history, Miller incentivizes his characters to dare greater things, whether for good or bad. In the play's overture, Miller describes how the setting of the play contributes to the risk-on environment:

> The witch-hunt was not, however, a mere repression. It was also, and as importantly, a long overdue opportunity for everyone so inclined to express publicly his guilt and sins, under the cover of accusations against the victims. It suddenly became possible—and patriotic and holy—for a man to say that Martha Corey had come into his bedroom at night, and that, while his wife was sleeping at his side, Martha laid herself down on his chest and "nearly suffocated him." Of course it was her spirit only, but his satisfaction of confessing was no lighter than if it had been Martha herself. One could not ordinarily speak such things in public.
> Long-held hatred of neighbors could now be expressed, and vengeance taken, despite the Bible's charitable injunctions. Land-lust which had been expressed before in constant bickering over boundaries and deeds, could now be elevated into the arena of morality; one could cry witch against one's neighbor and feel perfectly justified in the bargain. Old scores could be settled on a plane of heavenly combat between Lucifer and the Lord; suspicions

and the envy of the miserable towards the happy could and did burst out in the general revenge.[54]

CONFIDENCE, CAPACITY, AND COMPULSION

A good working model of tragedy gives an account of *what* the commonplaces of tragedy are and *why* they are necessary. Though each tragedy is unique, I suggest that seven motifs contribute to the success of tragedy. Heroes are of above average intelligence, confident, frequently ambitious, and prone to wrath. They suffer woes "greater than mortal man has ever borne." They hail from royal stock or are independently wealthy. They have trusty sidekicks who dispense reassuring advice. They operate in volatile settings. Supernatural appurtenances divulge classified information.

Through confidence, capacity, or compulsion, these seven commonplaces encourage heroes to assume risk in a realist theatre. Make heroes confident enough to roll the die or give them something to believe in. If they waver, have the trustworthy aide speak out words of encouragement. Goad them on with witches and oracular utterances. Should that not suffice, souse them in the wine of passion or strike them down with unbearable calamities. Give them access to the wealth of nations, armies, and all that glitters. Should further prodding be required, destroy everything they hold dear. Spurred on by one or by a combination of the seven commonplaces, heroes will ultimately go all-in. That is the art of the all-in wager.

---

54   Ibid., pp. 5-6.

7 "THE BEST-LAID PLANS OF MICE AND MEN"

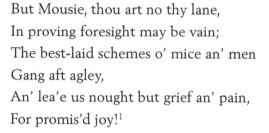

But Mousie, thou art no thy lane,
In proving foresight may be vain;
The best-laid schemes o' mice an' men
Gang aft agley,
An' lea'e us nought but grief an' pain,
For promis'd joy![1]

Tragic heroes are brighter, better informed, better accoutred, and better looking than the competition. They outwit, outmuscle, and outmanoeuvre adversaries. They have friends in high places, mobilize on a dime, fight with air superiority, and attack with the strength of ten men. They play to win because they take well-calculated risks. But when heroes wager their souls, they lose their souls. When they gamble their lives, they lose their lives. When the hero stakes the milk of human kindness on becoming a king, he falls short: becoming a tyrant is the best he can do. Despite every advantage, heroes' best-laid plans go awry. There is a

---

1   Burns, "To a Mouse, On Turning Her Up In Her Nest with The Plough," in *The Complete Illustrated Poems, Songs & Ballads*, lines 37-42.

complete disproportion of *improbable* loss in the face of the *probable* risks that heroes took. A paradox of expectation results: heroes count on winning, and should win, but instead of winning, lose everything.

How do tragic heroes lose? They lose because they expect one thing, but out of left field, something else happens. They are caught flat-footed. The thing that they expect will happen is, in their eyes, a high-probability event; it is likely. But what actually happens is a low-probability event, something that is, as Darrell says in O'Neill's *Strange Interlude*, "a thousand to one against it."[2] What actually happens is unexpected, and, as a result, all is lost.

Risk theatre is the dramatization of how more things can happen than what the hero anticipates will happen. Beneath tragedy's surface simplicity—the rueful choruses, ghosts clamouring for revenge, and choleric tyrants—lies its deep structure, which, although hidden from plain sight, nevertheless leaves telltale signs. Just as lifeguards can infer the presence of an undertow by watching swimmers being swept out to sea, theatregoers who watch heroes being swept out into the void—heroes who enjoyed every advantage—can infer that, beneath tragedy's surface simplicity lies a great dark power inimical to heroes' best-laid plans which contrives that, every time, the least expected outcome happens, whether it be a thousand to one or a million to one against.

In day-to-day life, the unexpected happens all the time. A knock on the door at a late hour. Black Monday. Or a strange lump in the back of the throat. It could be 9/11. Or

---

2   O'Neill, *Strange Interlude*, in *Three Plays*, p. 229.

it could be the day JFK died. Littlewood's Law states that, in day-to-day life, we should expect, on average, an event with odds a million to one against it about once a month.[3] Not so in theatre. Unlike the open-ended reality of everyday life, theatrical reality is a constrained reality—more like the Gardens of Versailles than the open country. From the lighting to the furnishings to a dropped handkerchief, everything within theatre's constrained reality is set there on purpose by the dramatist demiurge. Though the handkerchief seems to fall randomly, there is nothing random or accidental about its fall, which is a deliberate accident planted on the stage by the playwright to create a "lights, camera, and action" effect. Thus, to coerce the truly unexpected from theatre's

---

3   Littlewood's Law emerges from his discussion of coincidences and improbabilities in Littlewood, *Littlewood's Miscellany*, 103-5. There he defines remarkable coincidences as events with a probability of one in a million, and gives examples of how common they are. One of his examples is a story of how the astrophysicist Eddington received misprinted coordinates of a new comet. To Eddington's surprise afterwards, when he looked at the place indicated in the misprint, he saw a new comet. Freeman Dyson, one of Littlewood's students at Cambridge, explains how the law works in *The Scientist as Rebel*, 273:

> The proof of the law is simple. During the time that we are awake and actively engaged in living our lives, roughly for eight hours each day, we see and hear things happening at a rate of about one per second. So the total number of events that happen to us is about thirty thousand per day, or a about a million per month. With few exceptions, these events are not miracles because they are insignificant. The chance of a miracle is about one per million events. Therefore we should expect about one miracle to happen, on the average, each month.

constrained reality is a challenge. Strindberg succeeded in *The Father*, where, in the final scene, the captain suddenly and inexplicably drops dead. Here, Strindberg had the benefit of writing under the banner of a naturalist theatre committed to unflinching realism.[4] Not all theatre, however, can handle such a vulgar display of unexpectation. Within theatre's constrained reality, unmotivated or insufficiently motivated events tend to jar the audience. Theatre functions as a game where dramatists tee up expectations and audiences anticipate outcomes. The rules dictate that dramatists have an obligation to telegraph outcomes. The truly unexpected breaks the compact between dramatist and audience. Instead of the truly unexpected, I suggest that what theatre needs is the *foreseen surprise*. Like the captain in *The Father*, Evans in *Strange Interlude* suddenly drops dead. Heart attack. Interspersed comments on Evans' weight and blood pressure, however, have prepared the audience for that eventuality. He drops dead suddenly, but not inexplicably. Instead of being truly unexpected, his death is a foreseen surprise. In risk theatre, it is the foreseen surprise which trips up the protagonist's best-laid plans. This chapter explores the strategies risk theatre uses to integrate foreseen surprises seamlessly into the action. The terms *foreseen surprise* and *unexpected* will be used interchangeably to denote events such as Evans' heart attack which, while generally anticipated by audiences, catch characters off guard.

---

4   Strindberg, *The Father*, in *Miss Julie and Other Plays*, trans. Michael Robinson, 3.7.

The first strategy of tripping heroes' intentions involves the brute-force attack of divine intervention: heroes will one thing; fate and the gods will another. The second strategy involves gnostic limits or errors. The hero can run aground on the limits of knowledge because not everything can be known: "There are more things in heaven and earth," says Hamlet, "than are dreamt of in your philosophy."[5] Furthermore, even when events may be foreseen, errors of induction—basing future expectations on past results—or heuristic errors—using mental shortcuts in complex situations—may produce surprising outcomes. The third and final broad class of strategy involves waylaying heroes' expectations with the unintended consequences of their actions. Unintended consequences can arise from tight coupling, feedback, and the Maginot Line mentality. A tight coupled plan is one in which every part of the plan is interconnected to the degree that a failure in any one part cascades down the chain, ruining everything. Feedback involves the nonlinear and acausal modification of a system or process by its own results and effects: in other words, feedback occurs when a process is altered by the endogenous effects of its internal dynamics. In drama, feedback arises when characters interact with one another. Feedback amplifies the misunderstandings between characters, and their misunderstandings, in turn, lead to surprise endings. Feedback is most effective in the parallel-motion form of tragedy where there are multiple protagonists who can misinterpret one another. The Maginot Line mentality also produces unintended consequences and

---

5   Shakespeare, *Hamlet*, 1.5.166-7.

occurs when two options are open to the enemy, but the enemy chooses option three. The Maginot Line mentality derives its name from the French war minister between the World Wars who second-guessed his German counterpart. Maginot knew that Germany was chaffing under the punishing conditions of the Treaty of Versailles: it was a question of *when*, not *if*, Germany would retaliate. If, thought Maginot, he were the German war minister, he would try to cripple France's industrial heartland by invading through the southeastern border. To protect Alsace-Lorraine and neutralize the threat, Maginot therefore lay down impenetrable fortifications known as the Maginot Line. With the southeastern border secure, the only other option would be to attack France through the neutral Benelux countries, an act that would mobilize the Allies. Maginot believed that the Germans had two options: go through the Maginot Line or the Low Countries. The Germans, however, chose option three: they went through the impassable Ardennes Forest, which, because it was impassable, had been left open. By choosing the unforeseen option, the Germans outflanked the Maginot Line and turned the best of fortifications into the worst of liabilities. Paris, contrary to expectation, fell within a month.

Divine interference, the limits of knowledge, errors of induction, heuristic errors, tight coupling, feedback, and the Maginot Line mentality: these are the strategies tragedians use to upset heroes' best-laid plans.

DIVINE INTERFERENCE

Old-time Attic tragedy brings about the unexpected, otherwise known as the foreseen surprise, by exploiting the power differential between mortals and immortals. In Euripides' *Bacchae*, a ninety-eight-pound weakling arrives at Thebes spreading a seditious cult. Pentheus, the warrior-king, has every expectation of trouncing the newcomer: at the prime of manhood, he fights before the home crowd and has at his beck and call slaves, guards, archers, and soldiers. But when the effeminate stranger turns out to be the god Dionysus, Pentheus' expectations are dashed. Contrary to expectation, he is torn apart limb by limb.

In another of Euripides' tragedies, *Hippolytus*, the cross purposes between mortals and immortals turn every expectation upside down. Phaedra marries Theseus; Aphrodite makes her long for Theseus' son. Hippolytus devotes himself to the chaste hunt; Aphrodite ensnares him in the affairs of the lusty court. The nurse prays to Aphrodite; Aphrodite hexes her. Phaedra makes a last-ditch attempt to preserve her honour; Artemis lays her lie bare. Theseus believes Hippolytus has betrayed him and curses his son; Artemis demonstrates Hippolytus' innocence. In their cold war, Artemis and Aphrodite trip up their human counterparts' best-laid plans.

Besides the brute-force attack, dramatists have more subtle means of employing the divine to thwart heroes. In *Seven Against Thebes*, Aeschylus weaves the underlying design of randomness into what is fated to bring about the unexpected, yet foreseen outcome (foreseen to the audience, not to the characters). To combine randomness and fate, Aeschylus draws on the ancient Greeks' belief that chance was not truly random, but part of fate's design and a reflection of the gods' will. In the game of knucklebones, for example, the belief was widespread that the "Aphrodite" or "Venus" throw (1, 3, 4, and 6 on four dice) lands at the goddess' prompting.[6] In another example, when Hector challenges the Achaeans to a duel, they select a champion by casting lots. They did so because they believed that the lot, imbued with numinous significance, would reveal the grand design as it leapt out of the helmet.[7] They were not let down: Ajax trounces Hector. So too, on the eve of apportioning the world, Zeus, Poseidon, and Hades drew lots to determine who should have dominion over the sky, the sea, and the underworld.[8] The three

---

6   Cicero, in refuting the popular belief, testifies to its prevalence. See Cicero, *On Divination*, in *On Old Age, On Friendship, On Divination*, trans. W. A. Falconer, 2.121:

> Nothing is so uncertain as a cast of dice and yet there is no one who plays often who does not sometimes make a Venus-throw and occasionally twice or thrice in succession. Then are we, like fools, to prefer to say that it happened by the direction of Venus rather than by chance?

7   Homer, *Iliad*, trans. Richmond Lattimore, 7.171-89.

8   Ibid., 15.184-92:

> Then deeply vexed the famed shaker of the earth spoke to her:
> "No, no. Great though he is, this that he has said is too much,
> if he will force me against my will, me, who am his equal
> in rank. Since we are three brothers born by Rheia to Kronos,
> Zeus, and I, and the third is Hades, lord of the dead men.
> All was divided among us three ways, each given his domain.

brothers drew lots neither because they were equals nor from some pretense of democracy, but because—like the Achaeans in the previous example—they believed that the great design would reveal itself through randomness. Their belief would be proved correct, as their assignations by lot resulted in a lasting and stable cosmic order, the first since the cosmos had come into existence.[9] This same belief—that randomness is only apparently random—pervades *Seven Against Thebes*.

The play begins as seven champions, led by Polyneices, prepare to lay siege to Thebes, the city of seven gates. Polyneices has returned to reclaim the city from his brother, Eteocles. Inside the city, Eteocles readies the defences. The scout, whom he has sent to spy on his brother Polyneices' camp, reports that the invaders are in the process of assigning gates to each of the seven champions:

SCOUT. As I was leaving
they were casting lots, each to divine by fortune

I when the lots were shaken drew the grey sea to live in
forever; Hades drew the lot of the mists and the darkness,
and Zeus was allotted the wide sky, in the cloud and the
    bright air."
See also, Apollodorus, *The Library of Greek Mythology*, trans. Robin Hard, 1.2.1.

9   In Hesiod's *Theogony*, the first cosmic order (established by Gaia and Uranus) and the second cosmic order (established by Cronos and Rhea) were both overthrown. Cronos brings the first order to an end by castrating Uranus. The Olympians, led by Zeus, bring the second order to an end by imprisoning Cronos and the other Titans in Tartarus. See Hesiod, *Theogony*, in *Theogony, Works and Days, Shield*, trans. Apostolos N. Athanassakis, lines 133-82 and 453-725.

against which of our gates he would lead
his battalions.[10]

The gates are assigned by lot, which is to say that the assignations are anything *but* random; the will of the gods and nature's underlying order, as we recall, reveals itself through the lot. To repulse the invaders, Eteocles assembles seven defenders, one for each of the gates. Judging from the images of lottery and chance that dominate the play, the process of assigning defenders to their gates is also random. For example, Eteocles, as he comments on the matchup between Hippomedon and Hyperbius, claims that it is the god of luck and chance who has brought them to the fourth gate: "Hermes," he says, "by divine reason, has matched this pair."[11] Similarly, Eteocles, in his comments on the matchup between Tydeus and Melanippus at the first gate, says that "the chances of battle are as dice in the hands of Ares."[12] A gambling reference also occur as Eteocles declares that he will assemble "six men, myself the seventh" to defend the gates: to roll a seven with two dice as 6 + 1 was considered an ominous throw.[13] Whether the random process of selecting defenders to their gates is done by lot, divination, or some

---

10   Aeschylus, *Seven Against Thebes*, trans. Anthony Hecht and Helen Bacon, lines 77-9. See also lines 458, 522, 566, and 706.

11   Ibid., line 625. On Hermes' capacities, see the notes accompanying Hecht and Bacon's translation, ad loc.: "Hermes is, among other things, a god of luck or fortunate coincidence."

12   Ibid., line 511.

13   See Roisman, "The Messenger and Eteocles in the *Seven Against Thebes*," *L'antiquité classique* 59 (1990) 22: "6 + 1 was considered an unlucky throw in the six sided dice."

other method is unclear, but it is clear that we are to understand a lottery process at work.[14]

The worst-case scenario—and one that the audience
would be familiar with since it formed part of the myth—
only occurs if brother confronts brother at the seventh
and final gate: the earth would drink consanguine blood,
the resulting pollution would drive the Furies into action,
Oedipus' curse would be fulfilled, and Laius' ancestral guilt
would be freed to hunt down its next victim, the hapless
Antigone. Why the seventh gate?—because, if the brothers
should find themselves stationed against one another at gates
one through six, they could avoid the worst-case scenario by
substituting another captain. But at the seventh gate, since
the captains have all been assigned, it would be too late for
substitutions. If they find themselves stationed against one
another at the final gate, the die is cast.

The odds of rolling two sixes on two six-sided dice are
1:36, a figure arrived at by multiplying the probabilities of

---

14   Hermann, "Eteocles' Decision in Aeschylus' *Seven against Thebes*,"
      in *Tragedy and Archaic Greek Thought*, 58ff. convincingly argues that
      Eteocles decides by lot during the shield scene itself, e.g., as the
      Scout announces each of the attacking captains, Eteocles draws a
      lot to determine the defender and then interprets the tale of the
      tape. Hermann's conjecture solves an interesting problem that has
      bedeviled the play, which is: why does the shield scene seem so
      undramatic and static? He solves the problem by suggesting that the
      shield scene is far from undramatic, as Eteocles is busy casting lots.
      Since the stage directions have not survived, Hermann's conjecture
      must remain a conjecture, but a very plausible and appealing one
      that heightens the dramatic tension to the nth degree by making
      risk palpable.

rolling a six on a single die together: the outcome of two independent rolls is the product of their individual probabilities. Based on this analogy, if the odds of each of the brothers being posted to the final gate are 1:7, the odds of them both being posted to the final gate are 1:49, the product of each of their individual probabilities of being posted to the final gate. That they should meet at the highest gate, therefore, is a low-probability event, something that happens one out of forty-nine times, or just over two-percent of the time. In a simulation with seven attackers, seven defenders, and seven gates, the odds that the brothers *do not meet* at the final gate would occur, on average, forty-eight out of forty-nine times, or just under ninety-eight percent of the time: this would be the expected outcome. That they *do not meet*, therefore, is, to a gambler, like money in the bank. Should they meet, it would be unexpected, similar to drawing the dead man's hand in a poker game: possible, but unlikely. Aeschylus could not, of course, have calculated these odds, for probability theory lay another two millennia away. But the ancients, as Aristotle attests, could grasp that some odds were better than others.[15] Aeschylus did exactly that: in perceiving that the chances of Eteocles and Polyneices meeting at the seventh gate is very small, Aeschylus brings about a rather dramatic foreseen surprise when he brings the encounter to pass.

The great central episode (the "shield scene") contains the key of how Aeschylus makes the known outcome surprising.

15　Aristotle, *On the Heavens* 292a29: "To succeed in many things, or many times, is difficult; for instance, to repeat the same throw ten thousand times with dice would be impossible, whereas to make it once or twice is comparatively easy."

The episode takes place between Eteocles and the scout.[16] The scout describes the attackers one by one: station, appearance, mannerisms, boasts, and, most importantly, the shield device. After learning the attacker's identity, Eteocles draws a lot, announces the defender and, like a seer, interprets the occult details of the matchup to determine who the gods favour. He wagers that, like his father Oedipus, he can solve the riddle of each of the matchups and guide Thebes to safety. In the stylized combat of *Seven Against Thebes*, if one combatant carries the device of Typhon and the other the device of Zeus, it is a sign that heaven favours the latter: just as Zeus had tamed Typhon, whoever bears the Zeus device can be expected to prevail. To Eteocles' great satisfaction, that exact scenario just happens to play out at the fourth gate.[17] As Eteocles interprets the matchups gate by gate, he grows ever more confident, finding that, if the attacker is impious, someone who "abuses and berates Apollo's priest," the defender happens, by a sort of synchronicity, to be "a noble man who honours the throne of Reverence."[18] Or, if the attacker resembles the race of giants in appearance, the randomly posted defender bears the "goodwill of Artemis" and the other Olympian gods.[19] To Eteocles, their duel will repeat the Gigantomachy, the battle in which the gods slew the giants. Eteocles is heartened as the matchups unfold, because, first of all, the worst-case scenario odds are remote,

---

16   Aeschylus, *Seven Against Thebes*, trans. Anthony Hecht and Helen Bacon, lines 457-907.

17   Ibid., lines 598-639.

18   Ibid., lines 465 and 503.

19   Ibid., lines 555-7.

and second of all, because the matchups, taken in aggregate, overwhelmingly favour his cause.

Adding to Eteocles' confidence is the invading force's state of disarray: poisoned by infighting, they have already dedicated locks of their hair as memorial tokens, such is their morale.[20] In contrast, Eteocles has rallied Thebes around him.[21] By the time he assigns a defender to the sixth gate, he feels all but assured of victory. Everything is going his way. But a paradox arises: every time a champion other than Eteocles and Polyneices goes to a gate, the odds of the worst-case scenario increase. When all the gates are still available (that is, at the first gate, before any assignations), the worst-case scenario odds are 1:49. When six gates are left, the worst-case odds rise to 1:36. Gate by gate, the odds continue to rise until the sixth gate. With four defenders left—if both brothers are still unassigned—the odds that they should meet at the highest gate have risen to 1:4. Eteocles' paradox is that the more confident he grows, the more he is at risk.

The foreseen surprise then catches Eteocles off guard when the scout announces that his brother mans the seventh gate. Eteocles, out of champions, suddenly realizes that the worst-case scenario has come to pass: he alone must confront Polyneices. Against 1:49 odds, the gods call him to die. Despite the propitious omens, Oedipus' curse calls him to die.[22] For all of the invaders' disarray, fate calls him to die.

---

20   Ibid., lines 68-70. See also lines 459-67 and 705-34.

21   Ibid., line 331 where Eteocles succeeds in calming the frantic chorus of Theban women.

22   The omens, nevertheless, are still propitious from the perspective of the city, which is spared.

Seeing the writing on the wall, he arms himself. By conceal-
ing the divine in the myriad of combinations and permutations possible with seven attackers, seven defenders, and
seven gates, Aeschylus confounds Eteocles' every expectation of success.

Fate and destiny can also be adapted in subtle ways for
modern, more skeptical audiences. Christine in *Mourning
Becomes Electra* has the perfect plan. Everyone knows that
her husband has a heart condition and that it is his first
night back after a lengthy absence. However, she has a heart-
stopping poison and plans to throw him into a rage. When
he reaches for his medicine to still the boiling blood, she will
give him poison instead. No one will be the wiser. Christine's
plan works. But, as her husband dies, their daughter unexpectedly walks into the bedroom. With his dying breath, he
points at Christine, who then faints, dropping the poison
in plain view for their daughter to see. And so, Christine
recounts the scene to her lover:

> I fainted before I could hide it! And I had planned
> it all so carefully. But how could I foresee that
> she would come in just at that moment! . . . I'd
> planned it so carefully—but something made
> things happen![23]

Strategy turns to tragedy as her reasonable expectations lie
in tatters. In skeptical ages, fate, destiny, and the gods enter
the theatre through the back door as a sense of foreboding

---

23   O'Neill, *The Hunted*, in *Three Plays*, p. 361.

and a feeling of unease. Euripides' direct attack becomes O'Neill's "something that makes things happen."

THE LIMITS OF KNOWLEDGE

Dramatists also derail heroes by putting them in situations where knowledge is wanting. When heroes must act and react where the uncertainty is impenetrable, their best-laid plans easily come to naught. Faustus and Tamburlaine, despite their ample intelligence and ability, find their plans upset when they wager too much where they know too little.

Faustus sells his soul "to practise more than heavenly power permits."[24] As he gambles against God, Faustus believes the odds are with him. Having mastered both the classics and theology, he entertains reasonable doubt over God's existence. Part of him inclines to the Pythagorean belief of metempsychosis or to the philosophies of the pre-Socratics, over whom hell has no power:

> FAUSTUS. This word "damnation" terrifies not him
> For he confounds hell in Elysium.
> His ghost be with the old philosophers![25]

To him, hell is just an empty threat:

> FAUSTUS. Come, I think hell's a fable.

---

24   Marlowe, *Doctor Faustus*, epilogue line 8.
25   Ibid., 1.3.60–2.

MEPHISTOPHELES. Ay, think so still, till experience
  change thy mind.

FAUSTUS. Why, think'st thou then that Faustus shall
  be damned?

MEPHISTOPHELES. Ay, of necessity, for here's the scroll
In which thou hast given thy soul to Lucifer.

FAUSTUS. Ay, and body too. But what of that?
Think'st thou that Faustus is so fond
To imagine that after this life there is any pain?
Tush, these are trifles and mere old wives' tales.[26]

Faustus' knowledge has a blind spot, and his losses are grievous since he has wagered too much where he knows too little.

To know all things is impossible. Metaphysical things—
heaven, hell, the substance of the soul, the purpose of existence, and the nature of God—*cannot* be known for certain, at
least not from the corruptible side of reality. In *Tamburlaine*,
Marlowe again turns to metaphysics to upset expectations.
A shepherd in former times accustomed to watch over his
flock, Tamburlaine disdains gods who turn a blind eye on
their own. Having conquered the world, he begins to assert
his justice on the gods:

TAMBURLAINE. Now, Casane, where's the
  Turkish Alcoran,

---

26   Ibid., 2.1.130–8.

And all the heaps of superstitious books
Found in the temples of that Mahomet
Whom I have thought a god? They shall be burnt.

USUMCASANE. Here they are, my lord.

TAMBURLAINE. Well said! Let there be a
    fire presently.
(*They light a fire.*)
In vain, I see, men worship Mahomet.
My sword hath sent millions of Turks to hell,
Slew all his priests, his kinsmen, and his friends,
And yet I live untouch'd by Mahomet.
There is a God, full of revenging wrath,
From whom the thunder and the lightning breaks,
Whose scourge I am, and him will I obey.
So Casane; fling them in the fire.
(*They burn the books.*)
Now, Mahomet, if thou have any power,
Come down thyself and work a miracle.
Thou art not worthy to be worshipped
That suffers flames of fire to burn the writ
Wherein the sum of thy religion rests.
Why send'st thou not a furious whirlwind down,
To blow thy Alcoran up to thy throne,
Where men report thou sitt'st by God himself?
Or vengeance on the head of Tamburlaine
That shakes his sword against thy majesty,
And spurns the abstracts of thy foolish laws?
Well, soldiers, Mahomet remains in hell;

He cannot hear the voice of Tamburlaine.
Seek out another godhead to adore:
The God that sits in heaven, if any god,
For he is God alone, and none but he.[27]

"I feel myself distemper'd suddenly," announces Tamburlaine as the Alcoran burns.[28] He takes ill and dies. Tamburlaine has run into the "more things" in Hamlet's "there are more things in heaven and earth," and, by running into "more things," his expectations come to naught.[29]

ERRORS OF INDUCTION

Here is the story of a turkey that had grown to trust the hand that feeds. But when Thanksgiving Day came, it found itself, contrary to expectation, on the dining table. Induction is the process of inferring a law from past instances. Induction works most of the time. It does not work, however, when things turn out differently. By using inductive reasoning, tragic characters such as Egmont, the Furies, and Macbeth—like turkeys—can be setting themselves up for a Thanksgiving Day surprise.

In Goethe's *Egmont*, Egmont belongs to an ancient knighthood known as the Order of the Golden Fleece. From its first days, the order guaranteed immunity to its members, save a trial by the Grand Master with the assembled chapter

---

27 Marlowe, *Tamburlaine*, pt. 2, 5.2.171–200.

28 Ibid., pt. 2, 5.2.216.

29 Shakespeare, *Hamlet*, 1.5.166.

of knights.[30] Trusting in the ancient prerogative of the order, Egmont answers Alba's summons. But this time is different; contrary to expectation, Alba dispenses with ceremony and takes Egmont's head.

Even older than the privileges accorded to the holy order of knights are those of the Furies: their prerogative to punish the shedding of kindred blood begins with the creation of the cosmos. When the Furies in Aeschylus' *Eumenides* arrive at the court of Athena in pursuit of the matricide Orestes, they have every expectation of winning the guilty verdict—the entire history of the universe inclines in their favour. But when Athena casts the deciding ballot in favour of Orestes, they lose.[31] What is more, beyond all expectation, the Furies are transformed into the Eumenides, the "Kindly Ones." Over the long run, even the Fates meet the fate of the turkey.

Consider also Macbeth, who hears the witches prophesy with a skeptic's ears:

MACBETH. The thane of Cawdor lives
A prosperous gentleman; and to be king
Stands not within the prospect of belief,
No more than to be Cawdor.[32]

When it all comes to pass, Macbeth, relying on induction, listens to their second prophecy with a believer's ears:

---

30   Goethe, *Egmont* pp. 41-2.
31   Aeschylus, *The Eumenides*, in *The Oresteian Trilogy*, trans. Philip Vellacott, p. 172.
32   Shakespeare, *Macbeth*, 1.3.72-5.

MACBETH. Bring me no more reports, let them
    fly all.
Till Birnam wood remove to Dunsinane
I cannot taint with fear. What's that boy Malcolm?
Was he not born of woman? The spirits that know
All mortal consequences have pronounc'd me thus:
"Fear not, Macbeth; no man that's born of woman
Shall e'er have power upon thee." Then fly,
    false thanes
And mingle with the English epicures!
The mind I sway by, and the heart I bear,
Shall never sag with doubt, nor shake with fear.[33]

Macbeth's confidence skyrockets, leaving him open to the unexpected: troops advancing under the cloak of Birnam Wood and an encounter with Macduff, who is "from his mother's womb untimely ripp'd."[34] When heroes reason, tragedy prefers them, like turkeys, to draw proofs by inductive methods.

NOT SO FAST . . . (HEURISTIC SHORTCUTS)

Heroes often feel that they have a New York minute—otherwise defined as "the time it takes for the light in front of you to turn green and the guy behind you to honk his horn"—to assess the situation and come up with a course of

---

33   Ibid., 5.3.1-10.
34   Ibid., 5.8.15.

action.[35] As such, they navigate through complex situations with the aid of heuristic shortcuts and commit before checking all of the facts. The Fall of Singapore during the Second World War illustrates how hasty decisions can produce surprising results. For seven days, the Japanese blitzed British Lieutenant-General Percival's unconquerable fortress with everything that they had. Though outnumbered three to one, the Japanese made three times the din. They made so much sound and fury that, when they offered Percival a chance to surrender immediately and unconditionally, Percival acquiesced. If only he would have held on for another day, he would have exposed their bluff: the initial blitz had stretched the Japanese lines so thin that they had run out of ammunition. And so, because Percival used heuristic shortcuts to calculate the enemy's strength, the Fall of Singapore, "the Gibraltar of the East," took place, one of the all-time great military disasters.

Othello, a general like Percival, also encounters the unexpected by acting before checking the facts. Iago frames Desdemona and Cassio for adultery. To rile Othello, he plants Desdemona's handkerchief, spotted with strawberries, in Cassio's room.[36] Othello, seeing Cassio with the handkerchief, jumps to the conclusion that his wife and Cassio are having an affair. Falling into a rage, he makes Desdemona pay with her life. By the time he examines the evidence, she is already dead. By acting on snap judgments, Othello runs face to face into an unexpected outcome.

---

35   Johnny Carson, qtd. in Safire, "On Language; In a New York Minute," *New York Times*, October 19, 1986.

36   Shakespeare, *Othello*, 3.3.321.

Like Othello, Shakespeare's Romeo also makes snap judgments. Seeing that Juliet has perished, he suicides without inquiring into the circumstances of her death. He never finds out that her death was a ruse staged by Friar Lawrence and Juliet for bringing the lovers together.[37] By jumping to conclusions, Romeo upsets their best-laid plans. Because the smallest details often have the largest implications and the smallest errors carry the gravest consequences, heroes who engage in heuristic shortcuts often find their expectations dashed.

THE MAGINOT LINE MENTALITY

The Maginot Line mentality offers another source of surprise in tragedy. When a hero expects an adversary to choose from two possible options, expectations fail if the enemy elects option three. This mentality arises because behaviour is based on probability, not certainty. Heroes who excel at anticipating others' moves are particularly susceptible to the Maginot Line mentality. Confidence encourages them to devise elaborate schemes around probabilities that only have the seeming of certainty. *Don Carlos* illustrates the Maginot Line mentality in action. Posa returns to Spain to usher out the Inquisition and usher in Enlightenment. He has travelled throughout Europe, court by court, enlisting secret friends hateful to Philip, tyranny, and intolerance. Revolution is in the air. Posa succeeds because he is good at second-guessing others. By using this skill, he insinuates himself into the royal court: "By God," marvels the reticent King Philip, "he reaches

---

37   Shakespeare, *Romeo and Juliet*, 4.1.90-120.

to my soul!"[38] With this skill, he can divine Eboli's intentions even before she can. So too, when he upsets his friend and co-conspirator Carlos, he works through the situation by putting himself into Carlos' shoes:

> POSA. Can it be true that I do not yet know him?
> Not properly! Can I have failed to notice
> Such a forbidding shadow on his spirit?
> Yet it is true—he doubts his greatest friend.
> No! I am thinking like his enemy;
> What evil has he ever done to me,
> That I should think him shallow and distrustful?
> I would behave like him, I can believe
> That he would feel excluded.[39]

Posa's ability to walk a mile in another's shoes makes him an effective and cunning strategist. But it also makes him susceptible to the Maginot Line mentality, the error of thinking, "I would behave like him [were I to be him]." The problem is, of course, that he is not him.

To kick-start the revolution, Posa initiates a power play: he martyrs himself, exposes Eboli, deceives the king, and hands off the torch to Carlos. The plan seems sound: Carlos, as crown prince, can carry the revolution further than Posa, a marquis, could. The waiting carriage will take Carlos to Flanders, where secret friends await. All Carlos has to do is get in. If Posa were Carlos, he would have boarded the

---

38   Schiller, *Don* Carlos, in *Don Carlos and Mary Stuart*, trans. Hilary Collier Sy-Quia and Peter Oswald, 3.10.616.

39   Ibid., 4.6.269-77.

waiting carriage. But the heel of the Maginot Line mentality lies in the fact that Posa is not Carlos. If Posa were Carlos, he would have thought more with his mind. But Carlos, thinking more with his heart, lets Philip in on the plan. As a result, Posa's plans come to naught:

> POSA. No!
> This I did not foresee. How could I know
> That you, led on by generosity,
> Would be more sly and subtle in your schemes
> Than I by thinking? I forgot your heart,
> And all my clever structures fall to nothing.[40]

Shakespeare's Caesar, like Posa, also falls prey to the Maginot Line mentality. His dying question, *"Et tu, Brute?"* conveys surprise: he had not expected Brutus to join the conspirators.[41] That Brutus did, however, created unexpected implications for Caesar. Caesar had reckoned that the days of the Republic were over; even if he were to die, the dysfunctional Republic had run its course. Those mired in debt might hope for a self-serving revolution, but for the majority, the cost of removing him outweighed the benefits. Because Caesar arrived at that conclusion after long deliberation, he thought that Brutus would have done the same. But Brutus, like Carlos, reasoned more with his heart and sided with the dying Republic. Within the Maginot Line mentality lies something of the vanity of genius, which believes the beauty

---

40   Ibid., 5.1.33-8.
41   Shakespeare, *Julius Caesar*, 3.1.77.

of its own conclusions to be self-evident to all. Because the Maginot Line mentality feeds off of the intelligence of heroes—and tragedy is full of clever heroes—it serves tragedy well.

FEEDBACK

Tragedy also turns to *feedback* to upset the best-laid plans. Feedback is defined in technical terms as the modification of a system by its internal dynamics. Feedback paves the way for the unexpected because its effects are nonlinear and acausal. In nonlinear systems, the outcome is a product of the dynamics between all its moving parts, rather than the sum of the function of each of its discrete elements. Nonlinear systems include angry mobs, schooling fish, or the flight of starlings. The behaviour of a mob is the product of the interaction between a multitude of individuals; it is not the behaviour of one individual multiplied many times. So too, the behaviour of schooling fish cannot be modeled by observing individual members of the species because its behaviour is a result of the interactions between the fish. Nonlinearity therefore represents a problem for heroes whose strategies involve straight-line expectations and predictions. If the system is nonlinear, logical projections must fall short. Consider the flight of starlings. Logical projections of where each starling will land based on its original position and trajectory will fail every time: because the flight of starlings is nonlinear, their endpoints are not based on their initial positions and trajectories. Feedback renders projections futile, and, by doing so, upsets the best-laid plans.

Feedback further complicates heroes' plans because, not only are its effects nonlinear, they are also acausal. In acausal systems, the chain of causality binding the initial state with the end state breaks. When causality breaks, it is hard to tell where things will go—without causality, how can predictions be made? Stock market booms and busts, for example, illustrate acausality. During a boom, a company reports disappointing earnings—its stock shoots up. During a bust, a company lowers its debt—its stock plummets. Acausal fear and greed are driving the market. Because stock prices decouple from the bottom line, even prudent investors mindful of balance sheets lose their shirts. In the same way, heroes who rely on all the pieces falling into place according to causal principles are in for a surprise when feedback rams into causality like a twelve-thousand-pound wrecking ball.

Feedback works well in the parallel-motion play, a form of tragedy with multiple protagonists: the more characters, the more interactions, and, the more interactions, the more feedback. Cascading misunderstandings in parallel-motion tragedy throw the linear and causal stream of action into disarray. As the outcome decouples from the initial state of affairs, the situation grows rife with uncertainty. In *Cinna*, for example, a quartet of main characters interacts: Augustus, Cinna, Emilia, and Maximus. In the course of their interactions, misunderstandings arise. As their misunderstandings feed back on one another, linearity yields to nonlinearity, and causality gives way to acausality. As a result, the outcome and the initial state of affairs decouple. The final state of affairs is the result of feedback within the quartet, not the culmination of some logical progression from the initial state.

Let us consider the four characters individually. Augustus thinks that, by adopting and heaping gifts on Emilia, she will forgive him. He is mistaken: she retains Cinna to avenge her father. Augustus believes that his wife loves him for his crown. He is mistaken, and, as a result, fails to take her good counsel. Augustus believes that, by heaping honours on his most trusted lieutenants, he secures their loyalty. He is mistaken: Cinna and Maximus plot his death. That he brings himself to the cusp of doom is the unintended consequence of his actions.

Cinna thinks that he can trust Maximus, his friend and fellow conspirator. He is mistaken: when Maximus discovers Cinna is romancing Emilia, he betrays the conspiracy to do away with him. Cinna thinks that Augustus is a tyrant who has swept away republican freedoms. He is mistaken: Augustus asks him whether he should restore the Republic. Cinna thinks that Emilia loves him for who he is. He is mistaken: when he voices second thoughts about the assassination, she shows him the door. After Augustus learns of the conspiracy, Cinna thinks that he can martyr himself in the name of the Republic. He is mistaken: Emilia informs everyone that he had acted only to win her hand, not from some moral enterprise. The unintended consequence of his actions is that he loses all he holds dear in the pursuit of all he holds dear.

Maximus believes that Cinna has rallied the conspirators in the name of liberty. He is mistaken: Cinna does so to win Emilia. Maximus believes that, with Cinna out of the way, he can win over Emilia. He is wrong: Emilia prefers to die with honour than to live in shame. That he reveals himself to be a jealous imbecile is the unintended consequence of his actions.

Emilia has every reason to think that Augustus will condemn her when the conspiracy comes to light. He had condemned her father for less. Moreover, Augustus stands ready to execute Cinna and Maximus for treachery, and Emilia is as culpable as they are. But she is mistaken. That Augustus restores Maximus, gives Cinna the consulship, and blesses Emilia and Cinna's marriage are the unintended consequences of Emilia's actions. As misunderstandings feed back on one another throughout Corneille's play, they decouple the outcome from the play's opening assumptions that mercy equals weakness and severity demonstrates strength. A newer, unexpected portrait of empire emerges in which the ruler appears as vulnerable as he is powerful. Power is to be projected through clemency. Do your enemies try to kill you? Then strengthen them with ties of marriage, make them governors, hand them consulships, and revenge them by kindness.

Feedback therefore upsets expectations by changing the course of the play midstream. Tragedies based on feedback differ from tragedies of fate, such as *Oedipus rex*. As *Oedipus rex* begins, the outcome has already been predetermined. The shepherd, Tiresias, and, towards the end, Jocasta can all foresee the outcome. In *Cinna*, no one—not Augustus, Emilia, nor the host of attendants and slaves—knows what will happen in the end.

TIGHT COUPLING

A tree planter once planted saplings as close together as matches in a matchbook. Decades later, lightning struck that part of the woods where he once worked. The entire forest burned. His story illustrates what I call *tight coupling*, another device whereby dramatists may upset the best-laid plans of mice and men. Coupling refers to the interdependency between different parts of a plan. Tightly coupled plans are characterized by a lack of redundancy, inflexible scripts, and time sensitivity. They dismay heroes because when one part of the plan goes down, the whole plan goes down. Like a densely planted wood, the gaps between the trees are insufficient.

Friar Lawrence's plan in *Romeo and Juliet*, for example, is tightly coupled. To unite the lovers, he proposes the following scheme to Juliet:

> FRIAR LAWRENCE. Hold, then. Go home, be merry, give consent
> To marry Paris. We'n'sday is to-morrow;
> To-morrow night look that thou lie alone,
> Let not thy nurse lie with thee in thy chamber.
> Take thou this vial, being then in bed,
> And this distilled liquor drink thou off,
> When presently through all thy veins shall run
> A cold and drowsy humour; for no pulse
> Shall keep his native progress, but surcease;
> No warmth, no [breath] shall testify thou livest;
> The roses in thy lips and cheeks shall fade
> To [wanny] ashes, thy eyes' windows fall,

Like death when he shuts up the day of life;
Each part, depriv'd of supple government,
Shall, stiff and stark and cold, appear like death,
And in this borrowed likeness of shrunk death
Thou shalt continue two and forty hours,
And then awake as from a pleasant sleep.
Now when the bridegroom in the morning comes
To rouse thee from thy bed, there art thou dead.
Then, as the manner of our country is,
[In] thy best robes, uncovered, on the bier,
Thou shalt be borne to that same ancient vault
Where all the kindred of the Capulets lie.
In the mean time, against thou shalt awake,
Shall Romeo by my letters know our drift,
And hither shall he come, an' he and I
Will watch thy [waking], and that very night
Shall Romeo bear thee hence to Mantua.[42]

Insofar as only two people are aware of the plan—one of whom will be unconscious—the plan lacks redundancy. Should anything happen to Friar Lawrence, there is no plan B. Inflexibility also contributes to the tightness of the script's coupling. Because the script relies on all the ducks lining up—the potion working, Juliet being unattended, Romeo receiving the letters, and the Capulet vault being unguarded—there are many paths leading to failure, but only one path to success. In addition, time sensitivity tightens the coupling. Each milestone must take place precisely

---

42   Shakespeare, *Romeo and Juliet*, 4.1.89-117.

as scheduled. Conceived Tuesday afternoon, the plan calls for Juliet to awake on Friday. From Verona to Mantua and back again totals a journey of 120 kilometers. Time-sensitive letters must travel back and forth between the towns. Romeo himself must return on Friday. The window of opportunity for the plan to work slips away like the minutes between connecting flights at Chicago O'Hare Airport.

Lack of redundancy, inflexible scripts, and time sensitivity couple together normally unrelated events. Friar Laurence posts a letter to Romeo. The letter carrier stops by a sick house. Suspecting the plague, the health authority seals the house. Although the letter never makes it to Romeo, the news of Juliet's death does.[43] Romeo procures poison. Arriving at the Capulet vault, he finds Juliet in deep sleep. Thinking her dead, Romeo suicides. Expectations fall apart: instead of a wedding, two funerals occur. Tragedy is always just around the corner when the plan is tightly coupled.

CHANCE AND THE UNEXPECTED THROUGH THE AGES

Mortals and immortals at cross purposes, epistemological uncertainty, errors of induction, heuristic errors, Maginot Line mentalities, feedback, and tight coupling: why does tragedy employ so many and such a variety of strategies to overturn heroes' best-laid plans? To answer this, we will look at the relationship between the unexpected and games of chance. Long before there was tragedy, games of chance

---

43   Ibid., 5.2.1-16.

thrilled gamblers with their unpredictable outcomes.[44] Seeing how the unpredictable outcomes in dice games would often confound gamblers' expectations, when tragedy gave form to the unexpected, it borrowed the idea of uncertainty from the gambling world, couching the unexpected in gambling metaphors. It will be remembered that Aeschylus, one of the pioneers of tragedy, used the game of dice as a visual analogy of the unexpected when he said that "the chances of battle are as dice in the hands of Ares."[45] Because ancient Greeks believed that a divine hand influenced the outcome of lots, dice, and other games of chance, ancient playwrights assigned the unexpected outcome to the will of the gods. One of the unintended consequences of expressing the unexpected through the gambling metaphor was that the idea of the unexpected in tragedy became associated with the sort of randomness and unpredictability found in games of chance. As a result, when popular concepts of how randomness works in games of chance grew more sophisticated, two things happened. First: heroes' schemes became more sophisticated, elaborate, and foolproof. Heroes, after all, are no dummies. They keep up with the times and play to win. Second: tragedy developed increasingly sophisticated strategies to stay ahead of the hero. The wealth of strategies

---

44   Based on evidence from painting, sculpture, and archaeology, David, *Games, Gods and Gambling*, 2-7, speculates that knucklebones—the heel of a running animal—may have been used as randomizers in games of chance from prehistoric times, and, most certainly by the First Dynasty in Egypt (c. 3500 BC) when game playing had already become a highly developed art.

45   Aeschylus, *Seven Against Thebes*, trans. Anthony Hecht and Helen Bacon, line 511.

tragedy employs to upset heroes' best-laid plans, therefore, evolves with the development of how randomness, chance, and probability is perceived and understood. In conclusion, we will draw a short history of how tragedy has adapted to popular concepts of randomness from the ancient to the modern world.

In the ancient world, unexpected outcomes were not considered random, but came, rather, at the direction of the gods. During Patroclus' funeral games in the *Iliad*, two accidents occur which appear random. First, during the chariot race, the whip falls from Diomedes' hand, and, second, during the foot race, Oelian Ajax slips in dung. On closer inspection, however, these accidents only seem random because the hand of god moves invisibly. To those in the know, Apollo is responsible for Diomedes' misfortune:

> And now he might have passed him or run to a
> doubtful decision,
> had not Phoibos Apollo been angry with Diomedes,
> Tydeus' son, and dashed the shining whip from his
> hands, so
> that tears began to stream from his eyes, for
> his anger
> as he watched how the mares of Eumelos drew far
> ahead of him
> while his own horses ran without the whip and
> were slowed.[46]

---

46   Homer, *Iliad*, trans. Richmond Lattimore, 23.382-7.

So too, Oelian Ajax has not so much slipped as he has been tripped up by Athena:

> Now as they were for making their final sprint for
>   the trophy,
> there Aias slipped in his running, for Athene unbal-
>   anced him,
> where dung was scattered on the ground from the
>   bellowing oxen slaughtered
> by swift-footed Achilleus, those he slew to
>   honour Patroklos;
> and his mouth and nose were filled with the cow
>   dung, so that Odysseus
> the great and much enduring took off the mixing-
>   bowl, seeing
> he had passed him and come in first, and the ox
>   went to glorious Aias.[47]

Games of chance, similarly, only seem to play out ran-domly: to those in the know, rolling 1, 3, 4, and 6 on four knucklebones was a propitious sign from the goddess, and, for that reason, came to be known as the "Venus throw."[48] Ancient tragedy took its cue from popular conceptions of chance and made the gods responsible for the unexpected. Euripides, for example, ends many of his tragedies with a short refrain attributing the unexpected to the action of the gods:

---

47   Ibid., 23.773-9.

48   See note 6.

CHORUS LEADER. Zeus on Olympus has many things in his treasure house, and many are the things the gods accomplish against our expectation. What men look for is not brought to pass, but a god finds a way to achieve the unexpected. Such is the outcome of this story.[49]

In the Middle Ages, the unexpected took up Lady Fortune's guise. "Watch out," interjects the Monk while reciting Hercules' tragedy, "when Fortune wants to play a trick, / She bides her time before she overthrows / Her victims in a way they least expect."[50] Although Fortune has replaced fate and the gods as the engineer of chance, the brute-force tactics remained the same. The idea of the unexpected had not changed much from fifth century Greece; but then, neither had the theory of probability. Ideas of probability would remain static until the Renaissance.

In the 1500s, Cardano and Tartaglia began scrutinizing games of chance with combinatorial analysis to lay down the mathematical basis for a theory of probability.[51] Was there an

---

49   Euripides, *Medea*, in *Cyclops, Alcestis, Medea*, trans. David Kovacs, lines 1415-9. See also the closing lines of Euripides' *Bacchae, Helen*, and *Andromache*.

50   Chaucer, *Canterbury Tales*, trans. David Wright, p. 182.

51   Cardano discusses probability in his book *Liber de Ludo Aleae* (*The Book on Games and Chance*) written 1525, revised in 1565, and not printed until 1663, see David, *Games, Gods and Gambling*, 43. In his 1556 work *General Trattato di Numeri et Misure* (*General Treatise on Number and Measure*), Tartaglia provides solutions to a variety of gambling problems, such as the possible number of ways *n* dice might turn up and the problem of how to share the stack of

underlying order behind the erratic roll? Could a consistent law govern the arbitrary toss? How many throws were possible with two dice? With three dice? Thus they chained wayward Fortune to probability theory by recording the results of many throws. The unknown *quality* of randomness gave way to a known *quantity*: the chance of any particular throw came to be understood as the ratio of that throw to the aggregate number of possible throws. Odds of the "Venus throw" could now be expressed as a ratio of 1:256. When a particular throw would come up was, of course, unknown, but now indirection could be used to find direction. That the indirection inherent in odds and probabilities could be used to make long-term forecasts and predictions lay at the heart of probability theory.

Flash forward to the Elizabethan era, the first great age of tragedy in the era of probability theory. Because risk had become a known quantity, gambling was now a game of skill. In other words, when tragic heroes "stand the hazard of the die" and set their "life upon a cast" (as Richard does in Shakespeare's *Richard III*) or when they find their "lives upon the cast" (as do De Flores and Beatrice in Middleton and Rowley's *The Changeling*) they are able to calculate and thereby comprehend the hazard—it is no longer a blind crapshoot.[52] When the odds change, they adjust the stakes

winnings if players end a game before its conclusion, see ibid., 37-8, 61-2. For a history of the emergence of probability theory in the Renaissance, see Bernstein, *Against the Gods: The Remarkable Story of Risk*, 39-56.

52   Shakespeare, *Richard III*, 5.4.9-10. Middleton and Rowley, *The Changeling*, 2.2.139.

accordingly. Such a shift implies that the hero now takes responsibility should the unexpected happen. Fate is no longer required. The barbaric relic of the deus ex machina is no longer required. Out rolls Fortune's wheel, and in comes the notion of individual culpability. The individual is now in control. As probability theory changed popular conceptions of chance, the art of tragedy—to maintain the gambling analogy—had to adapt to these changes in turn.

Tragedy needed a new guise for the unexpected, which it found in the blind spot of knowledge. "Our greatest ills we least mistrust, my lord," warns Lorenzo in *The Spanish Tragedy*, "And inexpected harms do hurt us most."[53] According to Horatio, "mischance on plots and errors" happens because "men's minds are wild."[54] Just as the Renaissance geometry of linear perspective changed the way architectural space had previously been represented by ancient and medieval artists by boldly bringing together two parallel lines at a vanishing point, probability theory also boldly changed the representation of unexpectation. According to my theory of risk theatre, the tragedy of accidental judgment thus evolved to align theatre with the studies of Cardano and Tartaglia. So claims Horatio as he surveys the carnage as *Hamlet* comes to an end:

> And let me speak to [th'] yet unknowing world
> How these things came about. So shall you hear
> Of carnal, bloody, and unnatural acts,

---

53 Kyd, *The Spanish Tragedy*, 3.4.4–5.
54 Shakespeare, *Hamlet*, 5.2.394-5.

Of accidental judgments, casual slaughters,
Of deaths put on by cunning and [forc'd] cause,
And in the upshot, purposes mistook
Fall'n on th' inventors' heads: all this can I
Truly deliver.[55]

In this age, the unexpected outcome arises more from "accidental judgments" than divine interference.

From the seventeenth to the eighteenth century, Pascal, Fermat, Laplace, and Bernoulli each took turns applying probability to theology, the natural sciences, economics, psychology, and jurisprudence.[56] They rendered the storm at sea into an actuarial table, and they calculated who would live and who would die in annuities.[57] By the numbers they con-

---

55   Ibid., 5.2.379-86.

56   Pascal came up with Pascal's Wager in which he put the existence of God on a probabilistic footing by arguing for God's existence based on the expected value of the belief in God. Pascal also, working alongside Fermat, developed a way to solve combinatorial problems with "Pascal's Triangle." Their work laid down the basis of the modern insurance and risk management industries. Laplace in his 1814 volume, *A Philosophical Essay of Probabilities*, demonstrated the usefulness of probability in interpreting scientific data and predicting natural events. In his 1713 *The Art of Conjecturing*, Jakob Bernoulli proved the "Law of Large Numbers," a cornerstone in today's finance and insurance industries.

57   In 1696, Edward Lloyd (the founder of the insurance market Lloyd's of London) began issuing the "Lloyd's List," detailing, among other things, the conditions at sea, accidents, and sinkings. The information in the "Lloyd's List" would, in time, allow underwriters to model the risks to merchant vessels of storms and other predictable weather patterns on an actuarial basis. See Bernstein, *Against the Gods: The*

quered cholera, and by the numbers they returned guilty verdicts.[58] As probability theory grew more robust, tragic heroes also became more confident. In antiquity, Ares rolled the bloody dice; man was thrall to chance. By 1788, the tables had turned, and now Egmont grasps the dice Ares once held. Like Ares in the old days, Egmont plays with destiny:

> I have never disdained, even for small stakes, to
> throw the bloody dice with my good comrades; and
> shall I hesitate now, when all the free worth of life
> is at issue?[59]

Schiller's Posa does the same—when he gambles, he becomes heaven's equal:

Remarkable Story of Risk, 88-96. Edmond Halley of Halley's comet fame determined in 1693 that life expectancy could be statistically inferred from age, a seminal moment for the pricing of annuities. See Hacking, *The Emergence of Probability: A Philosophical Study of Early Ideas About Probability Induction and Statistical Inference*, 111-21. On Bayes and Nicholas Bernoulli's contributions to legal probability, see Kaplan and Kaplan, *Chances Are... Adventures in Probability*, 176-206.

58   During one of the worst cholera outbreaks in London's history, Dr. John Snow used statistical inference and plotted the addresses of the deceased on a map to isolate the source of contamination to a water pump on the corner of Broad and Cambridge Streets. His discovery is all the more amazing seeing that it was thought at that time that cholera was transmitted through bad smells. See ibid., 136-7.

59   Goethe, *Egmont*, trans. Anna Swanwick, p. 31.

But who was it but I that chose this way,
Risking so much on such a doubtful throw?
Thinking to deal on equal terms with heaven?[60]

Posa has made the roll with the full knowledge that the indeterminacy in the die is elusive to man and God alike. He also knows, however, that the indeterminacy of the die is bound by the laws of probability and that those who know the probabilities are, at least at the gaming tables, equals.

In the nineteenth and twentieth centuries, probability theory continued to waylay the unknown. Seismicity fell under its dominion when Gutenberg and Richter showed that earthquakes plotted by magnitude obey a logical distribution.[61] Hurricanes came under its dominion when computers made Monte Carlo simulations possible, allowing insurers to model possible losses by stochastically generating thousands of hypothetical path maps based on historical data.[62]

---

60   Schiller, *Don Carlos*, in *Don Carlos and Mary Stuart*, trans. Hilary Collier Sy-Quia and Peter Oswald, 4.20.824-6.

61   While the timing of earthquakes cannot be predicted, the Gutenberg-Richter Law states that the frequency of a given sized earthquake is predictable and follows a power law. See Buchanan, *Ubiquity: Why Catastrophes Happen*, 45:

> In terms of energy, it turns out that the Gutenberg-Richter law boils down to one very simple rule: If earthquakes of type A release twice the energy of those of type B, then type A quakes happen four times less frequently. Double the energy, that is, and an earthquake becomes four times as rare. This simple pattern—a power law—holds for quakes over a tremendous range of energies.

62   On the contributions of probability theory to understanding and predicting chaotic weather systems, see Kaplan and Kaplan, *Chances*

Probability theory gave to its practitioners Aeolus' bag of winds and Neptune's trident. Man could do the work of gods. As probability theory gathered strength, so too did the next generation of tragic protagonists. The Heddas and Ninas of the nineteenth and twentieth centuries would no longer be knave to Fortune. "For once in my life," says Hedda, "I want to feel that I control a human destiny."[63] Like Hedda, Nina also directs destiny: "You've got to give up owning people," protests Darrell, "meddling in their lives as if you were God and had created them!"[64] No longer subject to Fortune, these women have become Fortune. However, even though they act like gods, the unexpected still catches them off guard.

As probability theory grew by leaps and bounds, tragedy needed an increasingly sophisticated apparatus to bring about the unexpected. In an enlightened age, the deus ex machina device would not cut it. Tragedies of accidental judgment—these are the tragedies where epistemological uncertainty, errors of induction, or heuristic errors catch the hero unawares—represented an advance, but something even more complex was required. Starting with the French neoclassicists and continuing through the Weimar classicists up to the present day, dramatists cranked up complexity. They incorporated more characters and filled their dramas with more moving parts. They tightened the coupling and increased the psychological depth. The genius of the tragedy of feedback lies in how its outcome is completely indeterminate: the ending is the product of the interactions rather than

---

Are... Adventures in Probability, 207-37.

63   Ibsen, *Hedda Gabler*, in *Four Major Plays*, trans. Jens Arup, p. 226.

64   O'Neill, *Strange Interlude*, in *Three Plays*, p. 226.

the intentions of all the characters acting at cross purposes. The enlightened Heddas and Ninas had assumed the role previously held by ancient gods in tragedy; feedback brought the new idols back to earth.

Risk theatre dramatizes the ancient tug-of-war between the wildness of the die and the mind's ingenuity; on its stage, heroes test their determinate strategies against the indeterminate die. Because risk theatre is a show, and the show needs to entertain, whether the toss comes up heads or tails, the unexpected always prevails. The unexpected can arise through the machinations of fate, destiny, and the gods (e.g., *Oedipus rex*). It can creep in through a blind spot in knowledge (e.g., *Tamburlaine*). Sometimes it represents an error of induction: this time *is* different (e.g., *Egmont*). Other times heuristic shortcuts backfire (e.g., *Othello*). Maginot Line mentalities may be engaged to illustrate the pitfalls of second-guessing (e.g., *Don Carlos*). Finally, in tragedies of feedback (e.g., *Cinna*) and tight coupling (e.g., *Romeo and Juliet*), complexity upsets even the most carefully made plans. I therefore propose that, although heroes in every age attempt to rationalize, contain, mitigate, and eliminate the unexpected with the most enlightened strategies available to them, the wildness of the unexpected in tragedy increases in tandem with their abilities. At different time periods the unexpected assumed different guises, but it always effected the complete disproportion of *improbable* loss in the face of the *probable* risks that heroes took.

PART IV
BEYOND
TRAGEDY
RISK THEATRE IN RELATION
TO OTHER GENRES
AND THE ROLE OF RISK
THEATRE IN MODERNITY

8 US AND THEM

How do we define ourselves? If we drink beer, for example, we may define ourselves as "beer drinkers." This sort of definition affirms a group's shared traits and characteristics. However, by making use of an "us and them" perspective, we may also define ourselves, if the case may be, as "not wine drinkers." This sort of definition is polarizing and calls attention to the existence of an "other" out there which differentiates "us" from "them."

Up until this point, I have defined tragedy for what it is: the dramatization of a gambling act which plays out at distinct tempi, has certain forms, arises from the myth of the price you pay, demonstrates the value of existence, and ends contrary to expectation. I have proposed an affirmative definition by enumerating tragedy's shared features. But there is a secondary and negative way of defining tragedy. Just as beer drinkers can identify themselves either as "the ones who drink beer" or "the ones who do not drink wine," we may also define tragedy through polarity: tragedy *is* what it is because it is *not* something else. I will now refine the definition of tragedy by contrasting its traits and characteristics with those of competing genres.

The "us and them" definition of tragedy will reveal two sets of features that distinguish the arts from one another. First, what I call *ex-ante arts* look forward to what will happen, while *ex-post arts* look back at what has already happened. Second, I deem that some arts presuppose that the world is an *open system* with unlimited resources, while other arts presuppose that the world is a *closed system* where resources are scarce. But, before examining these distinguishing features, let us take a look at how, in the first place, an "us and them" attitude divides the arts.

THE QUARREL BETWEEN PHILOSOPHY, COMEDY, HISTORY, AND TRAGEDY

Philosophy, comedy, history, and tragedy define themselves, in part, by rejecting each other. Look at the scorn tragedy heaps on the others: "Philosophy is odious and obscure," says Faustus.[1] "Comedies are fit for common wits," says Hieronimo in *The Spanish Tragedy*.[2] "Will no example out of history help?" asks Tasso.[3] Since Tasso appears in a tragedy, the question may as well be rhetorical.

How do you slight someone in a tragedy? Call him a historian. "You should be a historian; he who acts must provide for the immediate moment," scolds the Regent.[4] What does tragedy think of reason, the philosophers' grail? "I learnt that

---

1   Marlowe, *Doctor Faustus*, 1.1.108.

2   Kyd, *The Spanish Tragedy*, 4.1.151.

3   Goethe, *Torquato Tasso*, in *Plays*, trans. Charles E. Passage, p. 240.

4   Goethe, *Egmont*, in *Plays*, trans. Anna Swanwick, p. 10.

reason is a wild misleading mood," says Mortimer in Schiller's *Mary Stuart*.[5] Romeo likewise scoffs at philosophy:

> FRIAR LAWRENCE. I'll give thee armor to keep off
>   that word:
> Adversity's sweet milk, philosophy,
> To comfort thee though thou art banished.

> ROMEO. Yet "banished"? Hang up philosophy!
> Unless philosophy can make a Juliet,
> Displant a town, reverse a prince's doom,
> It helps not, it prevails not. Talk no more.[6]

How does philosophy view the others? "We seem to have in Philosophy," writes Hegel, "a process diametrically opposed to the historiographer."[7] According to Hegel, the only way history could be rehabilitated is if it were to be written by philosophers instead of historians. Otherwise the only lesson history teaches is that people learn nothing from history.[8] Ouch.

Philosophy also looks askance at comedy and tragedy. Plato considered comedy to be so degraded that he forbade citizens from learning it: only degenerates could stage it.[9] For

---

5   Schiller, *Mary Stuart*, in *Don Carlos and Mary Stuart*, trans. Hilary
     Collier Sy-Quia and Peter Oswald, 1.6.440-1.
6   Shakespeare, *Romeo and Juliet*, 3.3.54–60.
7   Hegel, *The Philosophy of History*, trans. J. Sibree, 9.
8   Ibid., 6, where Hegel writes: "But what experience and history teach
     is this—that peoples and governments never have learned anything
     from history, or acted on principles deduced from it."
9   Plato, *Laws*, in *Complete Works*, trans. Trevor J. Saunders, 816e-817a.

Plato, the only thing worse than comedy was tragedy: he bans tragedy altogether from both his proposed republic and from his "second-best" city-state of Magnesia.[10] Tragedy corrupts to such an extent that even degenerates were not allowed to stage it. Of all the amusements dangerous to philosophical life, Pascal singled out one: "None is more to be feared than the theatre."[11] Boethius agrees: when the tragic Muses make a guest appearance in his dialogue, they are promptly rebuked by Lady Philosophy as "hysterical sluts" and shown the door.[12] According to philosophers, audiences of tragedy are just as bad as the performance itself. When the tragic poet Agathon appears in Plato's *Symposium*, for example, he is made to admit that his audience can only amount to a "senseless crowd."[13]

How does history view the other genres? There is no love lost between history and philosophy. "You are like dogs," says Machiavelli's man of history to the philosopher, "who are always hanging around those who can feed them best."[14] Those who do things scorn those who think about doing

---

10   Ibid., 817a-e. Plato, *Republic*, in *Complete Works*, trans. G. M. A. Grube, rev. C. D. C. Reeve, 607b. In the *Laws*, the ideal state, which is inhabited by "gods or a number of the children of gods," reflects Plato's conceptual rift between the perfect heavens and the imperfect earth (739d). Although Magnesia is described as "second-best," it represents the peak of perfection on a terrestrial level.

11   Pascal, *Pensées*, trans. A. J. Krailsheimer, 232.

12   Boethius, *The Consolation of Philosophy*, trans. V. E. Watts, 1.1.

13   Plato, *Symposium*, in *Complete Works*, trans. Alexander Nehamas and Paul Woodruff, 194b.

14   Machiavelli, *The Life of Castruccio Castracani of Lucca*, in *The History of Florence and Other Selections*, trans. Judith Rawson, 50.

things; the active life and the contemplative life are at odds. To Spengler, nothing captures the highest sense of life so much as history. What did he think about the other arts? "The rest is mere philosophy," he claims.[15] History also views tragedy with suspicion. "The aim of tragedy," says Polybius, "is by no means the same as history, but rather the opposite."[16] In Polybius' view, history excels because it delivers the truth, while tragedy only charms audiences with temporary thrills.

How does comedy view the other arts? In Aristophanes' *Clouds*, Strepsiades, aping Socrates, mocks philosophers as those who "walk upon the air and look down upon the sun from a superior standpoint."[17] Philosophers and their high-brow interests form natural targets for comedians whose humour involves logical fallacies and bodily functions. The anonymous Renaissance drama *A Warning for Fair Women* opens with Comedy, History, and Tragedy competing for the right to perform. After History bows out, Tragedy and Comedy fight it out:

> TRAGEDY. I must have passions that must move
>   the soul;
> Make the heart heave and throb within the bosom,
> Extorting tears out of the strictest eyes,
> To rack a thought and strain it to its form,
> Until I rap the senses from their course.

15   Spengler, *The Decline of the West*, trans. Charles Francis Atkinson, 358–9.

16   Polybius, *The Rise of the Roman Empire*, trans. Ian Scott-Kilvert, 2.56.

17   Aristophanes, *Clouds*, in *Four Plays by Aristophanes*, trans. William Arrowsmith, p. 39.

This is my office.

> COMEDY. How some damned tyrant to obtain
>   a crown,
> Stabs, hangs, empoisons, smothers, cutteth throats:
> And then a Chorus, too, comes howling in,
> And tells us of the worrying of a cat:
> Then of a filthy whining ghost,
> Lapped in some foul sheet, or a leather pilch,
> Comes screaming like a pig half sticked,
> And cries—"*Vindicta!* Revenge, revenge!"
> With that a little rosin flasheth forth,
> Like smoke out of a tobacco-pipe, or a boy's squib,
> Then comes in two or three, like [un]to drovers,
> With tailors' bodkins stabbing one another:
> Is this trim? Is not here goodly things,
> That you should be so much accounted of? I would
>   not else—[18]

This caricature between Comedy, History, and Tragedy is possible because common opinion holds that the arts view reality from contrasting standpoints. What are these standpoints?

COMEDY AND TRAGEDY VS. HISTORY AND PHILOSOPHY: EX-ANTE VS. EX-POST ARTS

I suggest that the disagreement between philosophy, comedy, history, and tragedy arises, in part, because some of these arts

---

18   Anonymous, *A Warning for Fair Women*, *Induction* lines 38-58.

look at the world from an ex-ante perspective while others look at the world from an ex-post perspective. Ex-ante arts look forward towards the future. Because the future is indeterminate, neither the characters nor the audiences of ex-ante arts know the outcome. Ex-ante art is dramatic. The action progresses from forecasts, projections, and best guesses. Because audiences and the characters do not know the outcome, chance, luck, fate, and unknown unknowns lie in wait. The defining characteristic of ex-ante arts is that the unexpected happens ten times out of ten. No one knows where the pit lies or who holds the winning lottery ticket until someone either steps into the pit or hears the winning numbers announced.

Tragedy and comedy are both ex-ante arts. In tragedy, though the odds are a million to one against, Birnam Wood comes to high Dunsinane Hill *every time*. In Greek Old Comedy, the women bring about an end to the Peloponnesian War against all expectation by staging a sex strike.[19] In Greek New Comedy and its Roman emulators, the miser always recovers the stolen gold, kidnapped children are reunited with their families against all odds, and young lovers marry in spite of cantankerous patriarchs, onerous marriage laws, and an onslaught of economic and social prejudices.[20]

---

19 Aristophanes, *Lysistrata*, in *Four Plays by Aristophanes*, trans. Douglass Parker.

20 In Plautus, *The Pot of Gold*, in *The Comedy of Asses, The Pot of Gold, The Two Bacchises, The Captives*, trans. Wolfgang de Melo, Euclio, the miser recovers the stolen gold. Families torn apart by kidnappings are reunited in Plautus, *The Captives*, in *Amphitryon, The Comedy of Asses, The Pot of Gold, The Two Bacchises, The Captives*, trans. Wolfgang de Melo; Plautus, *The Two Menaechmuses* and

History and philosophy, on the other hand, are ex-post arts. By nature, ex-post arts reminisce and look to the past. The historian looks backwards: the "history of the future" is a nonsensical contradiction in terms. Philosophy also looks to the past: "Life must be understood backwards," says the philosopher.[21] Philosophy, like history, follows the crisis: Aurelius, in *Meditations*, reflects on Roman hegemony *after* its decline; Socrates, in Plato's *Crito* and *Phaedo*, ruminates on virtue *after* being condemned; Boethius, in *The Consolation of Philosophy*, recalls Neoplatonic precepts *after* being sentenced.[22] If Macbeth had lived, he *would have* become a philosopher; but he could not have become a philosopher until *after* the queen dies.

Readers expect explanations from ex-post arts. Like code breakers going through transmissions or astronomers tuning in radio telescopes, ex-post artists watch for patterns. Patterns remove the influence of chance and luck on the outcome, which is predicated on the pattern, not on some random

Curculio, in *Casina, The Casket Comedy, Curculio, Epidicus, The Two Menaechmuses*, trans. Wolfgang de Melo; Plautus *The Little Carthaginian* and *The Rope*, in *The Little Carthaginian, Pseudolus, The Rope*, trans. Wolfgang de Melo; Terence, *The Eunuch*, in *The Comedies*, trans. Betty Radice. Young lovers overcoming economic and social prejudices are ubiquitous in Greek New Comedy and Latin Comedy, see, for example Menander, *Old Cantankerous*, in *Plays and Fragments*, trans. Norma Miller and Terence, *The Brothers*, trans. Betty Radice.

21 Kierkegaard, *Papers and Journals: A Selection*, trans. Alastair Hannay, 161.

22 See Aurelius, *Meditations with Selected Correspondence*, trans. Robin Hard; Plato, *Crito* and *Phaedo*, in *Complete Works*, trans. G. M. A. Grube; Boethius, *The Consolation of Philosophy*, trans. V. E. Watts.

event. Historians and philosophers, as ex-post artists, tame chance. In ex-post art, everyone already knows the winning and losing lotto numbers.

Historians plait the eternal strand of events into patterns sensible to the mind. Sometimes, the patterns are linear, as in the case of Saint Augustine, Marx, or Fukuyama. For Saint Augustine, the struggle and eventual triumph of the "City of God" over the "Earthly City" shapes history.[23] Marx and Engels replace "City of God" with "proletariat" and "Earthly City" with "bourgeoisie."[24] Fukuyama, on the other hand, argues that the rise of democratic capitalist societies signals history's end.[25]

Other times, the patterns are cyclical, as in the case of Polybius, 1 and 2 Kings, and Herodotus. In Polybius' *anacyclosis* doctrine, forms of governance wash, rinse, and repeat from monarchy to tyranny and from tyranny to aristocracy; aristocracy gives way to oligarchy, which, in turn, yields to democracy. When democracy degenerates into ochlocracy, a monarch rises up to reboot the cycle.[26] In 1 and 2 Kings, a

---

23   In Augustine, *The City of God*, trans. Marcus Dods.

24   On the eventual triumph of the proletariat in the eternal class struggle, see Marx and Engels, *The Communist Manifesto*, trans. Samuel Moore, p. 341:

> The development of Modern Industry, therefore, cuts from under its feet the very foundation on which the bourgeoisie produces and appropriates products. What the bourgeoisie, therefore, produces, above all, is its own grave-diggers. Its fall and the victory of the proletariat are equally inevitable.

25   In Fukuyama, *The End of History and the Last Man*.

26   Polybius, *The Rise of the Roman Empire*, trans. Ian Scott-Kilvert, 6.2-10. Aristotle and Plato hold similar cyclical outlooks, where

binary cycle repeats. The legacy of kings is whether they "do evil" or "do right" in the sight of the Lord. Those who "do evil" imperil the Holy Land; those who "do right" preserve the throne.[27] In Herodotus' *hubris-atē-nemesis* cycle, overconfidence (*hubris*) leads to recklessness (*atē*), which, in turn, provokes divine retribution *(nemesis)*.[28] Whether following linear or cyclical patterns, history, like philosophy, finds a signal buried in the randomness of time's events. History has meaning. Unexpected events in the short term yield to history's pattern in the long term.

As an ex-post art like history, philosophy rationalizes and systematically subtracts the wildness from reality. It makes reality comprehensible by dividing it into five branches: metaphysics (the essence of nature), epistemology (the theory of knowledge), ethics (the study of action), politics (the use of force), and aesthetics (the role of art). To set each branch in order, competing doctrines arose: materialism (primacy of matter), idealism (mind over matter), empiricism (senses), rationalism (logic), nominalism (particulars), realism (universals), naturalism (natural laws), and theism (divine

imperfections in each form of government engender another in a perpetual cycle. See Plato, *Republic* 543c-569c and Aristotle, *Politics* 1301a-1316b.

27 For example, because Solomon does evil, the Lord punishes him by cleaving the Holy Land into two entities: the Kingdom of Israel and the Kingdom of Judah (1 Kings 11:6-11). On the other hand, because Hezekiah does right, the Lord adds fifteen years to his life, allows all his enterprises to prosper, and removes the Assyrian yoke from the Kingdom of Judah (2 Kings 18:1-20:21).

28 As exemplified in his stories of Croesus and Xerxes, see Herodotus, *The Histories*, trans. Aubrey de Sélincourt, 1.6-92 and 7.2-9.113

laws). Various schools exist within each of the doctrines. For example, Plato and Kant both champion idealism while Lucretius and Quine both draw from naturalism. Doctrine by doctrine, philosophers categorize thought and experience and apply their learning to philosophy's five branches in a monumental effort to reconstruct reality into the language of the mind. Philosophy creates meaning by cataloguing, arranging, and rearranging knowledge by school, doctrine, and branch. In categorizing knowledge, philosophy creates meaning and removes uncertainty. Philosophers may discuss the unexpected—as Taleb does in *Fooled by Randomness*—but nothing unexpected arises in their arguments, which follow one another step by step, and nothing unforeseen happens in their conclusions, which represent the logical culmination of their arguments.[29]

In summary:

Ex-post Arts (History & Philosophy)
- look backwards
- find patterns
- celebrate knowledge
- postulate causes and effects
- Promethean: know the outcome ahead of time
- rationalize
- increase our understanding
- tame risk
- based on the constants of human nature or reason

---

29   Taleb, *Fooled by Randomness: The Hidden Role of Chance in Life and in the Markets.*

- narrative
- increase certainty
- explain

Ex-ante Arts (Comedy & Tragedy)

- look forwards
- find black swans
- reveal the blind spot of knowledge
- highlight the role of chance, fortune, and fate
- Epimethean: understand too late
- obfuscate
- increase our sense of wonder
- are wild
- based on the swerve of unintended consequences and unexpected outcomes
- dramatic
- generate suspense
- mystify: "I never will speak word," says Iago when questioned (Shakespeare, *Othello*, 5.2.304)

In defining tragedy, it is helpful to realize that its ex-ante perspective aligns it with comedy but differentiates it from history and philosophy, both of which are ex-post arts. Tragedy defines itself in its antagonism with history and philosophy. Tragedy is not history or philosophy because of the polarity between the ex-ante and ex-post perspectives.

COMEDY VS. TRAGEDY:
OPEN VS. CLOSED SYSTEMS

If comedy and tragedy both embody ex-ante arts, how do the dramatic genres define themselves against one another? By examining whether comedy and tragedy take place within an open or a closed system allows an "us and them" distinction to be drawn between them. Open systems have access to and are replenished by fresh resources. The ocean is an open system whose cycles are driven and maintained by a constant influx of solar and geothermal energies. Closed systems, on the other hand, cannot access fresh resources by which they may be renewed. A fish tank in isolation is a closed system: its ability to sustain life eventually runs down. A fish tank with pumps and lights, however, is an open system: it sees an influx of energy and resources. The mines of Laurium, whose reserves of silver are finite, constitute a closed system. Once the silver has been mined, the mine shuts down. Life and social interactions may also be thought of as taking place within a closed system. In a memorable episode from the *Iliad*, Sarpedon exhorts Glaucus to enter the fray. It is memorable for how Sarpedon elects to see the battlefield as a closed system:

> "Man, supposing you and I, escaping this battle,
> would be able to live on forever, ageless, immortal,
> so neither would I myself go on fighting in
>   the foremost
> nor would I urge you into the fighting where men
>   win glory.

But now, seeing that the spirits of death stand close
about us
in their thousands, no man can turn aside nor
escape them,
let us go on and win glory for ourselves, or yield it
to others."[30]

First of all, Sarpedon conceives of life as a scarce resource because it takes place in time, and time, as we know, marches ever onwards, but never backwards. Only if he were "able to live on forever, ageless, immortal" would he think otherwise. Now, because he is mortal and his time is limited, he conceives of the exchange of honour as taking place in the closed system of the battlefield. On Sarpedon's battlefield, warriors either gain glory by killing, or relinquish their glory by being killed. One gains glory at another's expense. Like the silver at the Laurium mines, which, whether it lies beneath the ground or has been fashioned into coins above ground, is of a finite quantity, the total quantity of glory available on Sarpedon's battlefield, no matter how many times it changes hands, is conserved. Because the total quantity is conserved, the exchange of glory can be thought of as taking place in a closed system. Because Sarpedon chooses to conceive of life and glory as pursuits taking place within a closed system, his exhortation is memorable for its pathos: their exercise at Troy is a zero-sum game.

While comedy and tragedy both embody ex-ante arts, comedy differs from tragedy because comedy presupposes

---

30   Homer, *Iliad*, trans. Richmond Lattimore, 12.322-8

that the world is an open system, a world of plenty where fresh resources can flow in. Conversely, tragedy differs from comedy because tragedy presupposes that the world is a closed system, a world of privation.

Because tragedy operates in a closed system, one gains honour only by stripping it from another: Don Rodrigo, for example, can only recover his father's honour by wresting it back from the Count. How?—by killing him.[31] To wear the crown, Macbeth must remove it from Duncan's head. To assert his rights, Polyneices must deny his brother's rights.[32] Everything is in short supply. In the closed system of tragedy, dog eats dog. It is different, however, in comedy's open system. No dowry? A pot of gold turns up.[33] No citizenship? A green card appears out of nowhere.[34] Spendthrift freeloading sons thrive:

---

31   Corneille, *The Cid*, in *The Cid, Cinna, The Theatrical Illusion*, trans. John Cairncross, lines 397-442.

32   Aeschylus, *Seven Against Thebes*, trans. Anthony Hecht and Helen Bacon, lines 784-815.

33   Euclio unexpectedly discovers, loses, and recovers a pot of gold which he eventually gives to his daughter as a dowry in Plautus, *The Pot of Gold*, in *Amphitryon, The Comedy of Asses, The Pot of Gold, The Two Bacchises, The Captives*, trans. Wolfgang de Melo.

34   Citizenship is a prized asset in Greek as well as Roman comedy (which is set in Greece), as ancient Athenian law forbids marriage between citizens and foreigners, see *Oxford Classical Dictionary*, 3rd ed., s.v. "marriage law." A stock character in comedy is the girl of citizen birth who, because she has been kidnapped or abandoned, is unaware of her status. She falls in love with a citizen, whom she is unable to marry until a recognition scene takes place wherein she is reunited with the body politic. See note 20.

MICIO. He dines and wines and reeks of scent: I pay
for it all. He keeps a mistress: I shall pay up as long
as it suits me, and when it doesn't, maybe she will
shut her door on him. He has broken a door-lock;
I'll have it mended. He has torn someone's clothes;
they can be repaired.[35]

In tragedy's closed system, the only way to fix a broken
door would be to replace it by taking someone else's door.
Similarly, the only way to make good torn clothes in tragedy
would be to take the shirt off someone else's back. Tragedy
presents a world of perpetual shortages and rolling blackouts;
the world of comedy, in contrast, flows with milk and honey.

Natural selection in the dog-eat-dog world of tragedy
favours alpha-type personalities and produces tragic heroes
who have the strength of Hercules, the charisma of Richard,
and the endurance of Rasputin. Comedy, on the other hand,
fosters incompetence. Its heroes are the sort who live after
midnight and sleep till noon. It is a topsy-turvy place where
moochers find a meal, irresponsible libertines flourish, and
clever slaves bail out dimwitted masters. Such is how life
adapts to a world of plenty.

Tragedy and the Second Law of Thermodynamics

Closed systems in nature, regulated by the Second Law of
Thermodynamics, begin in an organized state, full of potential and vigour, but suffer, in the end, a heat death, a state

---

35   Terence, *The Brothers*, trans. Betty Radice, in *The Comedies*, p. 344.

in which their once productive sources of energy have dissipated into a formless and uniform distribution of spent heat energy, the tired byproduct of work. Though the total amount of energy in the system is conserved and remains the same, the system is said to suffer a heat death because, in a state of uniform energy distribution, mechanical work, production, creation, organization, and anything requiring the vital spark is impossible. Because the system is closed, it lacks the means to replenish its initial vitality. Coal, for example, is a fuel source full of potential. Put it into a steam locomotive's engine, fire it up, and it will drive the locomotive. As it propels the locomotive, however, its energy is transformed into heat. Once its energies have dissipated into heat, it loses its ability to perform any further work. If the locomotive is operating in a closed system, that is to say, in a system without access to fueling stations, once the stockpile of coal is exhausted, the locomotive will come to a standstill. The way in which we experience the world makes it possible to grasp the rudiments of the Second Law with ease. We see that Second Law at work when we make coffee: it starts off hot and cools down because heat flows from hot to cold, not vice versa. We see the law at work when we shuffle a deck of cards arranged by suit and number: order yields to disorder, not vice versa. Despite the straightforwardness of the Second Law, however, its stipulation that the entropy or disorder of closed systems continually increases has far-reaching implications. One implication is that time's arrow cannot be reversed. Time, to the Second Law, flows forwards because it measures the diminishing potential for work to be done as energy is transformed into heat. To reverse time's arrow would be to defy the Second Law. Another implication with tragic implications is the death of the universe and with it, all human achievement: the universe, being a closed system, will eventually succumb to a heat death, bringing everything to a standstill. The simple, yet profound implications of the Second Law prompted the great astrophysicist Eddington to declare:

> The law that entropy always increases—the
> second law of thermodynamics—holds, I think,
> the supreme position among the laws of Nature.
> If someone points out to you that your pet theory
> of the universe is in disagreement with Maxwell's
> equations—then so much the worse for Maxwell's
> equations. If it is found to be contradicted by
> observation—well, these experimentalists do bungle
> things sometimes. But if your theory is found to
> be against the second law of thermodynamics I
> can give you no hope; there is nothing for it but
> to collapse in deepest humiliation. This exaltation
> of the second law is not unreasonable. There are
> other laws which we have strong reason to believe
> in, and we feel that a hypothesis which violates
> them is highly improbable; but the improbability
> is vague and does not confront us as a paralyzing
> array of figures, whereas the chance against a breach
> of the second law (i.e. against a decrease of the
> random element) can be stated in figures which
> are overwhelming.[36]

36   Eddington, *The Nature of the Physical World*, 74-5.

If we apply the theory of thermodynamics to tragedy, we notice that by analogy, tragedy obeys the Second Law. Tragedy may be viewed of as a fiery engine that consumes ambition, purpose, and desire. Into the maw of its furnace, heroes are cast like lumps of flashing coal. They set afire tragedy's engine for a moment and then are no more. Tragedy, as if it were a closed thermodynamic system, ends up in a lower state of potential, whether by the death of a Tamburlaine or a Caesar, the exile of Oedipus, or the loss of a Joan of Arc or a master builder. Fuel, once spent, loses its potential; likewise, the energy of the human will, purpose, endeavour, and the fire of the human imagination go cold. Time, in tragedy, measures the rising entropy, or disorder, of the dramatic world. By an immutable law, as it were, as the minutes give way to hours, and the hours give way to days, kingdoms collapse, heroes perish, and order gives way to disorder.

Comedy and the Spontaneous Generation of Order from Chaos

As an open system, however, the world of comedy ends up in a higher state of potential: slaves become freedmen, refugees become citizens, cantankerous misers rejoin the community, and children get married. Comedy saw the secret Achilles' heel of the Second Law, saw that nothing precludes a deck of playing cards, when shuffled many times, from inexplicably returning to its original sequence organized number by number and suit by suit and saw how symmetry can spontaneously emerge as snowflakes crystallize. Inspired by the possibility that order can spontaneously arise from chaos, comedy mocks the Second Law by dramatizing the spontaneous capacity of the random element in engendering higher structures. Though scientists have yet to define how order emerges from chaos, the effects of this process are visible all around in both the world of comedy and the natural world.[37] On a cosmic scale, nature structures random

---

37   For a discussion of the crystallization of snowflakes, the formation of galaxies, the emergence of life, and other examples where nature, in seeming defiance of the Second Law, spontaneously generates order from chaos, see Prigogine, *From Being to Becoming*. On the shortcomings of the Second Law in the face of nature's creativity, see also Davies, *The Cosmic Blueprint*, 139:

> The central issue ... is whether the surprising—one might even say unreasonable—propensity for matter and energy to self-organize 'against the odds' can be explained using the known laws of physics, or whether completely new fundamental principles are required. In practice, attempts to explain complexity and self-organization using the basic laws of physics have met with little success. In spite of the fact that the trend towards ever-greater organizational complexity is a conspicuous feature of the universe, the appearance of new levels of organization is frequently regarded as a puzzle, because it seems to go 'the wrong way' from a thermodynamic point of view. Novel forms of self-organization are therefore generally unexpected and prove to be something of a curiosity. When presented with organized systems, scientists are sometimes able to model them in an *ad hoc* way after the fact. There is always considerable difficulty, however, in understanding how they came to exist in the first place, or in predicting entirely new forms of complex organization. This is especially true in biology. The origin of life, the evolution of increasing biological complexity, and the development of the embryo from a single egg cell, all seem miraculous at first sight, and all remain largely unexplained.

atoms of hydrogen and helium into stars, solar systems, clusters, and the spiral arms of galaxies reaching far out into the void. On a terrestrial level, nature defies the Second Law, organizing inanimate atoms of carbon, hydrogen, oxygen, and nitrogen into amino acids, proteins, and forms of ever higher complexity until matter, at last, acquires life. From the inception of life, nature instils animals with sentience, and up each phyla from fish to mammal, increases the sentience of its creations until its crowning achievement: the human brain. As the most complex machine in the universe, the brain, though a product of nature, is capable of appreciating and solving all of nature's mysteries. It is as though there is a vanity of nature which animates matter with the purpose of creating an intelligence capable of being a looking glass unto itself. Comedy is the artistic analogue of this ability of nature to create complexity from simplicity. Comedy is order from chaos, biodiversity, evolution, and nature's laugh at the Second Law. It finds a way when tragedy says that it is impossible.

While comedy and tragedy both embody ex-ante arts, they differ from one another in terms of openness and closedness. When one presupposes that the world is a closed system and sees the iron rule of the Second Law inexorably drawing the heat death ever closer, one writes tragedy. When one presupposes that the world is, at bottom, an open system, full of diversity and the creative spirit, one writes comedy.

CATEGORIZING GENRES BY THEIR OPPOSING STANDPOINTS

The antagonistic "us and them" definition of tragedy finds that tragedy is itself because it is at odds with the genres of philosophy, history, and comedy. The world of philosophy is one in which sense, perception, experience, and phenomenon are internalized and translated into the mental constructs of logic, reason, language, and number. The philosopher tames the wild world, comprehends the evil that men do, and justifies the presence of suffering. Tragedy, however, is at odds with philosophy's view. Instead, tragedy upholds that mental constructs imperfectly reflect reality. What is more, in tragedy, the wildness of the world cannot be tamed. The evil that men do is beyond comprehension, and suffering cannot be justified, unless from an aesthetic perspective. Tragedy is itself in rejecting philosophy's standpoint that logic and reason can explain suffering and tame uncertainty.

The world of history is full of patterns and cycles. History is a heavy wheel hurtling into the future and charged with social and political momentum. Those who understand history can see where things are going. It is possible to fore-cast, adjust, and adapt. Tragedy, however, is at odds with history's view. Instead, tragedy upholds that patterns and cycles are deceptive: in tragedy, "this time is different," or better yet, "every time is different." There is no way of adjusting and adapting. Tragedy is itself in rejecting history's standpoint that patterns and cycles remove chance and uncertainty from the outcome.

In comedy, although things never go as expected, the world is alright. Despite looming uncertainties, God is on your side:

"Coincidence must really be a divinity," says Demeas, "She looks after many of the things we cannot see."[38] Benevolent powers guide human affairs. Tragedy, however, backed by the Second Law, refutes comedy's position. The world is not alright. God is not on your side. The unexpected outcome happens every time, and, in tragedy, it is always for the worse. Therefore, tragedy, by definition, rejects comedy.

Tragedy seems to offer little in the way of a consolation. Things never go as expected. Change is always for the worse. The world is incomprehensible. And wild. But, in tragedy, a common refrain can often be heard: "My lord, it is not upon you alone that these ills have come: you have lost a trusty wife, but so have many others."[39] Thus we return to the stock "not to you alone" consolation of tragedy, a beautiful device in its head-on affirmation of the existence of suffering. It asks no recompense for hardships nor does it feel the need to offer excuses for life's difficulties. Instead, it calls on the afflicted to commiserate with one another as human beings should and binds the suffering masses together in a living embrace. Is this not the most honest and compassionate of consolations? Who are we to complain, and where do we seek justice when suffering is a human constant, forwards, backwards, and for all eternity?

---

38   Menander, *The Girl from Samos*, trans. Norma Miller, in *Plays and Fragments*, lines 163-4.

39   Euripides, *Hippolytus*, in *Children of Heracles, Hippolytus, Andromache, Hecuba*, trans. David Kovacs, lines 834-5.

9 WHY RISK THEATRE TODAY?

How is it possible to redefine tragedy as risk theatre two and a half millennia after its inception? After all, the definitions of history, philosophy, and comedy crystallized long ago. The historian believes that the study of the past informs the present and anticipates the world to come. The philosopher believes that reason unlocks the world's secrets. The comedian believes that laughter makes merry. But what does the tragedian believe?

I believe that definitions are robust when they observe three conventions. First, a term is robust when it retains ties with its etymological roots. Second, harmony should exist between a term's technical and lay usages. Third, the term's meaning should remain stable through time. Tragedy fails on all three of these points. Its definition, as a result, has proved, for theorists of drama, to be fruitfully ambiguous. Due to this ambiguity, it has been possible for me to reinvent tragedy as risk theatre, and doubtless, it will be possible for others to reinvent tragedy again tomorrow.

Philosophy, *history*, *comedy*, and *tragedy* are all transliterations of Greek terms. *Philosophy* comes from Greek *philosophia* "love of knowledge."[1] Since philosophy is born out of a love of knowledge, the word retains ties with its etymological roots. Comedy (from *kōmos* "merrymaking") and history (from *historía* "inquiry") likewise retain memories of their etyma.[2] True to its namesake, comedy engages in revelry and satire, while history inquires into the root cause of an event. Etymology is important, as it anchors both the term and its derivatives: *philosophy, to philosophize,* or *philosopher* denote faculties, actions, and occupations revolving around a love of knowledge. Going back to its roots, tragedy is a "goat song" (from *trágos* "goat" and *ōidē* "song").[3] That makes a tragedian a "writer of goat songs." But this, to us, is unhelpful. The term has lost anchor and drifts.

A term's robustness also stems from the harmony between its lay and technical meanings. When both meanings coincide, ideas flow freely between specialists and non-specialists. When the street philosopher says, "My philosophy is that no matter what happens, enjoy yourself because life is short," his use of *philosophy* is not far removed from the philosophy of a professional Epicurean: to both of them *philosophy* means a personal guiding theory of behaviour. Therefore, *philosophy*'s lay and technical definitions harmonize. The same, however, does not hold true for *tragedy*, which projects a multitude of formal definitions. It could signify a pitiful and fearful show.[4]

---

1   *Oxford English Dictionary*, 3rd ed., s.v. "philosophy."

2   Ibid., s.vv. "comedy" and "history."

3   Ibid., s.v. "tragedy."

4   See Aristotle, *Poetics*, in *Poetics, On the Sublime, On Style*, trans. Stephen Halliwell, 1453a.

It could be a stage where wisdom is won through suffering.[5] Or it could be the dramatization of how, as the Bible puts it, "pride goeth before the fall."[6] Others say that *tragedy* is a

---

5   Such an interpretation arose from the *parodos* (the chorus' entrance song) in Aeschylus, *Agamemnon*, in *The Oresteian Trilogy*, trans. Philip Vellacott, p. 48:

> Zeus, whose will has marked for man
> The sole way where wisdom lies;
> Ordered one eternal plan:
> *Man must suffer to be wise.*
> Head-winds heavy with past ill
> Stray his course and stay his heart:
> Sorrow takes the blind soul's part—
> Man grows wise against his will.
> For powers who rule from thrones above
> By ruthlessness commend their love.

6   Lamentations 16:18 (King James Version). Chaucer's collection of tragedies certainly invites the notion that "pride goeth before the fall." See Croesus' tragedy in Chaucer, *Canterbury Tales*, trans. David Wright, p. 199:

> The wealthy Croesus, King of Lydia once,
> Of whom the Persian Cyrus stood in awe,
> Was taken in his pride and arrogance
> And led away to be burned in the fire.

The idea that "pride goeth before the fall" in classical tragedies can be traced back to interpretations of Aristotle which, first of all, associate *hamartia* with a "tragic flaw," and next, associate this "tragic flaw" with pride. See Aristotle's *Poetics*, in *Poetics, On the Sublime, On Style*, trans. Stephen Halliwell, 1453a7-11 where Aristotle describes tragedy's ideal protagonist:

> Such a person is someone not preeminent in virtue and justice, and one who falls into adversity not through evil and depravity, but through some kind of error [*hamartia*]; and one belonging to the class of those who enjoy great

story of the fall of kings.[7] It could also be the venue in which Apollo and Dionysus' ancient enmity plays out.[8] The formal descriptions of tragedy are, for the most part, at odds with its lay usage that signifies "a disaster" or "a sad story." A term becomes fragile when its lay and technical meanings fail to harmonize. The term feels broken.

A persistence of sense grounds a term by aligning its usage in the past, present, and future. The term *philosophy*, for example, communicates philosophy's essence because its meaning is stable. From Plato's Theory of Ideas and Leibniz' Monads to Kant's Absolute Idea and Wittgenstein's

---

renown and prosperity, such as Oedipus, Thyestes, and eminent men from such lineages.

On such interpretations of Aristotle, see Kaufmann, *Tragedy & Philosophy*, 2.15:

> The popular notion that the central theme of Greek tragedy is that pride comes before a fall is very wrong and depends on projecting Christian values where they have no place. For Aristotle and the tragic poets, pride was no sin but an essential ingredient of heroism.

7   See, for example, Boethius, *The Consolation of Philosophy*, trans. V. E. Watts, 2.2, where Philosophy asks Boethius: "Isn't this what tragedy commemorates with its tears and tumult—the overthrow of happy realms by the random strokes of Fortune?"

8   See Nietzsche, *The Birth of Tragedy*, trans. Walter Kaufmann, section 1:

> We shall have gained much for the science of aesthetics, once we perceive not merely by logical inference, but with the immediate certainty of vision, that the continuous development of art is bound up with the *Apollinian* and *Dionysian* duality—just as procreation depends on the duality of the sexes, involving perpetual strife with only periodically intervening reconciliations.

Tractatus, philosophy is and has been a reductionist attempt to map reality into the language of the mind. While the term *philosophy* (as well as the terms *history* and *comedy*) can be interchanged between modern English and ancient Greek without confusion, the same cannot be said of *tragedy.* Events that moderns understand to constitute tragedy (in the vernacular sense of "the Challenger tragedy," "the Chernobyl tragedy," or "the AIDS tragedy") were never so called by the ancients. The reason may lie in the fact that many ancient tragedies—including Euripides' *Iphigenia in Tauris,* one of Aristotle's favourite tragedies—had happy endings.[9] The Greeks used a different term to signify *tragedy* in the sense of "the Challenger tragedy": *sumphorá.*[10] The Sicilian Expedition that irrevocably broke Athenian hegemony is described as a *sumphorá.*[11] The Battle of Salamis (one of two watershed losses that shifted the balance of power to the West for a millennium) is, from a Persian perspective, a *sumphorá.*[12] Also

9   See Aristotle, *Poetics,* in *Poetics, On the Sublime, On Style,* trans. Stephen Halliwell, 1454a.

10   The Liddell-Scott-Jones *Greek-English Lexicon,* 1996 ed., s.v. "sumphorá" translates the term as a "mishap" or "misfortune."

11   Plutarch, *Nicias,* in *The Rise and Fall of Athens,* trans. Ian Scott-Kilvert, 30.1:

> When the terrible story [sumphorá] first reached Athens, it is said that the people could not believe it, especially because of the messenger who first broke the news.

12   Aeschylus, *Persians,* in *Suppliant Maidens, Persians, Prometheus, Seven Against Thebes,* trans. Herbert Weir Smyth, line 435-7:

> MESSENGER. Be well assured of this, the disaster is not as yet half told. So dire an affliction [sumphorá] of calamity fell upon them as to outweigh these ills, aye twice over.

telling is Tiresias' proleptic words foretelling Oedipus' doom in Sophocles' tragedy:

> TIRESIAS. Listen to me closely:
> the man you've sought so long, proclaiming,
> cursing up and down, the murderer of Laius—
> he is here. A stranger,
> you may think, who lives among you,
> he soon will be revealed a native Theban
> but he will take no joy in the revelation [*sumphorá*].
> Blind who now has eyes, beggar who now is rich,
> he will grope his way toward a foreign soil,
> a stick tapping before him step by step.
> Revealed at last, brother and father both
> to the children he embraces, to his mother
> son and husband both—he sowed the loins
> his father sowed, he spilled his father's blood![13]

In this passage, Tiresias categorizes Oedipus' imminent moment of tragic recognition as a *sumphorá*.[14]

Like the Greeks from whose language the loanwords were derived, the Romans used a constellation of terms to describe the art form of tragedy: *tragoedia* for the play, *tragoedus* the

---

13   Sophocles, *Oedipus the King*, trans. Robert Fagles, lines 510-23.

14   See Calame, *Masks of Authority*, trans. Peter M. Burk, 110n.13:
       This transformation is described by Tiresias as a *sumphorá*
       (454), a reversal of fortune; reversal is a formative element
       of the tragic plot according to Aristotle (*Poetics* 1452a22-
       29), who cites the *Oedipus Tyrannus* precisely in connec-
       tion with this issue.

actor, and *tragicus* either for the performance (style of dec-
lamation, staging, etc.,) or for "actor" or "playwright."[15] Like
the Greeks, the Romans failed to connect the constellation
of terms describing the art form of tragedy with real-life
tragedy. Instead, the Romans used the term *clades* to refer
to *tragedy* in the sense of "the Chernobyl tragedy." Suetonius
calls the Great Fire of Rome that raged six days and seven
nights a *clades* and adds that Nero, enjoying the spectacle,
"put on his tragedian's costume and sang *The Sack of Ilium*
from beginning to end."[16] Livy uses the same word to describe
the tragedy at Lake Trasimene and the rout at the Battle of
Cannae that imperiled Rome.[17] The affinity between *clades*
and the modern term *tragedy* can further be demonstrated by
quoting Watts' translation of Boethius:

---

15   *Oxford Latin Dictionary*, 1st ed., s.vv. *tragoedia, tragoedus*, and *tragicus*.

16   Suetonius, *Nero*, in *The Twelve Caesars*, trans. Robert Graves, rev.
      Michael Grant, 38.2: "This terror [*clades*] lasted for six days and
      seven nights, causing many people to take shelter in monuments
      and tombs."

17   Livy, *History of Rome*, trans. B. O. Foster, 22.7:
          Such was the famous battle of Trasumennus, a disaster
          [*clades*] memorable as few others have been in Roman
          history. Fifteen thousand Romans were killed on the field;
          ten thousand, scattered in flight over all Etruria, made their
          way by different roads to the City.
      See also ibid., 22.50:
          Such was the battle of Cannae, a calamity [*clades*] as
          memorable as that suffered at the Allia, and though less
          grave in its results—because the enemy failed to follow up
          his victory—yet for the slaughter of the army even more
          grievous and disgraceful.

But even if you do not know the stories of the foreign philosophers, how Anaxagoras was banished from Athens, how Socrates was put to death by poisoning, and how Zeno was tortured, you do know of Romans like Canius, Seneca and Soranus, whose memory is still fresh and celebrated. The sole cause of their tragic sufferings [*clades*] was their obvious and complete contempt of the pursuits of immoral men which my teaching had instilled in them.[18]

Thus, ancient Greek and Latin employed different words to distinguish between events of great destruction and tragic drama, both of which are rendered in English by the same word *tragedy*. This is a major and seldom recognized distinction that lends tremendous fluidity to the term.

By the beginning of the Christian era, public productions of Greek and Roman tragedies were on the wane.[19] By the seventh century, as classical antiquity drew to a close, the theatre as the ancient world knew it had also ceased to exist.[20] Because the ancient term *tragedy* and its cognates refer back to the art form of tragedy, when tragedy ceased to be a living art form, the term lost its footings. It would not regain a lexical foundation until the resurgence of tragedy

---

18   Boethius, *The Consolation of Philosophy*, trans. V. E. Watts, 1.3.

19   Kelly, *Ideas and Forms of Tragedy*, 16 argues that, in the first century AD, public productions of tragedies gave way to public recitations and private readings.

20   Ibid., 36-50, where Kelly interprets the jumbled interpretations of classical theatre that Isidore and his contemporaries came up with as a sign that the theatrical activity of the ancient world had ceased.

in the English Renaissance. Between the close of classical antiquity and the English Renaissance, the term *tragedy* would become more and more polyvalent. To Boethius in the sixth century, tragedy commemorates the unexpected overthrow of happy realms by random fortune.[21] Averroës in the twelfth century translates *tragedy* as "eulogy," and understands that it is a poem of praise.[22] To Albert the Great in the thirteenth century, tragedy amounts to a recitation of degenerate deeds.[23] In the fourteenth century, Dante understands tragedy to be a poem on "Safety, Love, and Virtue."[24] That the term *tragedy* could take on so many and such contradictory meanings testifies to its lexical instability during the millennia spanning the Middle Ages.

Only within the last four hundred years, according to the *Oxford English Dictionary*, has the lay definition of *tragedy* stabilized to denote "an unhappy or fatal event" in

---

21   Boethius, *The Consolation of Philosophy*, trans. V. E. Watts, 2.2.

22   Instead of transliterating the Greek *tragōidia* into Arabic, Averroës translates it as *madīḥ* "eulogy." See Averroës, *Averroes' Middle Commentary*, trans. Charles E. Butterworth, 13n.10.

23   Albert the Great, *De generatione et corruptione* 1.1.8:

   Tragoediae autem carmina sunt vituperationis quibus Antiquorum vituperia simpliciter inter villanos cantantur, dicta a tragos quod est hircus: quia foeda cantantes foetidum animal hircum in remuneration accipiebant.

   Tragedies, however, are songs of censure in which the degenerate deeds of the ancients are candidly sung amongst villagers. They are so-called from the Greek word *trágos*, which is a goat. The reason for this is that those singing of unclean deeds received in remuneration a goat, which is an unclean animal (my translation).

24   Dante, *De vulgari eloquentia*, trans. A. G. Howell, p. 57.

the modern sense of the term.[25] We can see the present day meaning emerging in Kyd's *Spanish Tragedy*, which appeared towards the end of the sixteenth century. When Hieronimo says: "When in Toledo there I studied, / It was my chance to write a tragedy," the term refers, of course, to the art form of tragedy.[26] And when Lorenzo threatens Pedringano that "This very sword whereon thou took'st thine oath / Shall be the worker of thy tragedy" or when Revenge promises Andrea that his foes will suffer an "endless tragedy" the term points to "an unhappy or fatal event."[27] Around the same time, the tragedies of Marlowe and Shakespeare began exploring the social consequences of a hero's fall. The suicides of Romeo and Juliet diminish the Montague and Capulet houses. The Danish throne passes into Norwegian hands on the death of Hamlet. The halls no longer ring out with *sic probo* ("I prove it thus") after Faustus perishes.[28] Without Tamburlaine, the world seems an emptier place. By considering the aftermath of a hero's fall, Marlowe and Shakespeare make way for the lay definition of *tragedy* to denote an unexpected event with a high human cost as in the modern sense of "the Chernobyl tragedy." We owe the modern understanding of the term *tragedy* in large part to Marlowe and Shakespeare. When the

---

25   *Oxford English Dictionary*, 3ʳᵈ ed., s.v. "tragedy" notes that the term's use to signify "an unhappy or fatal event or series of events **in real life** [emphasis added]" dates no earlier than the sixteenth century.

26   Kyd, *The Spanish Tragedy*, in *Six Renaissance Tragedies*, 4.1.75-6.

27   Ibid. 2.1.92-3 and 4.5.48.

28   Marlowe, *Doctor Faustus*, 1.2.2. As the commentary, ad. loc. notes, the phrase *sic probo* expresses a "triumphant conclusion in scholastic debate."

day eventually comes for their influence to wane, it is likely that the meaning of *tragedy* will shift once again.

Unlike the terms *philosophy*, *comedy*, and *history*, the term *tragedy* is polyvalent and impersistent. Its technical and lay usages vary widely to the point where they contradict one another, and it has lost its connection with its etymological roots. When a term has lost everything, it can then mean anything. In fact, after two and a half millennia, *tragedy* is still a term in search of a definition. Because, as an orphaned term, it refuses to commit to a single, concise definition, theories of tragedy at all times were easily swayed by popular sentiment.

Aristotle lived in an age interested in hearing teleological explanations and studying the final causes of natural or human activities. Unsurprisingly, in the *Poetics*, he would famously define tragedy according to its final effect on audiences by claiming that the purpose of tragedy was to accomplish, through pity and fear, the catharsis of such emotions.[29]

Cardinal Richelieu and the founders of the French Academy lived in seventeenth century France, an age fraught with religious unrest and civil wars. Accordingly, they sought stability and respite from troubles by instituting rule, law, and structure everywhere they could.[30] The French Academy thus imparted stable forms upon tragedy, and bound it to the stricture of the unities of action, time, and place. Plays

---

29   Aristotle, *Poetics*, in *Poetics, On the Sublime, On Style*, trans. Stephen Halliwell, 1449b.

30   From the sixteenth to the mid-seventeenth century, France endured the assassinations of Henry III (1589) and Henry IV (1610) as well as the Wars of Religion (1562-1598) which pitted Huguenots against Catholics.

would conform to a five-act structure and characters would obey the laws of decorum. In short, tragedy encapsulated the neoclassical ideals they craved in life but could not have.

Hegel set down his thoughts on tragedy against the backdrop of the Newtonian cosmos, a mechanical and clockwork universe filled with equal and opposing forces set in motion by the freshly minted laws of motion.[31] Is there not something mechanical in the way in which he defines the tragic as the collision between innocence and duty (*Hamlet*), the "two highest moral powers" (*Antigone*), "the antagonism of brothers" (*Seven Against Thebes*), or subjective and objective freedom (Socrates)?[32] It were as though Hegel conceived of tragedy's players as billiard balls caroming on the green felt of theatre's deterministic stage. And, what is more, when he describes these collisions as "actions" and "reactions" between "opposing forces" that "disturb the unity of that which is opposed to it," is it any longer possible *not* to see the influence of Newton?[33] Newton's First Law of Motion, after

31 Newton's *Principia* was published in 1687, some eighty-three years before Hegel's birth. As with quantum theory or the theory of relativity in the twentieth century, these sea changes in conceiving how reality is fundamentally structured take a century, or longer, to percolate through the imaginations of the scientists, artists, and the laypeople.

32 Hegel's scattered writings on tragedy have been assembled into a convenient edition for English readers; see Hegel, *Hegel on Tragedy*, eds. Anne and Henry Paolucci. On *Hamlet*, see p. 83; on *Seven Against Thebes*, see p. 117; on *Antigone*, see p. 325; on Socrates, see p. 364.

33 Ibid., 128:

   Inasmuch as, however, the action which is based on this collision disturbs the unity of that which is opposed to

all, states that "every body continues in its state of rest, or of uniform motion in a right line, unless it is compelled to change that state by forces impressed upon it," and his Third Law also contains language similar to Hegel's when it states that "to every action (force) there is always opposed an equal reaction."[34] Hegel's theory of tragedy, like the others, is for all time, but is also curiously time-bound.

Nietzsche lived in the late nineteenth century, an age coming to terms with a burgeoning awareness that the enlightened and rational mind is but a dam, and a small dam, holding back the profuse flood of a thousand unconscious and irrational thoughts. In 1846, Dostoyevsky called attention to the unconscious mind in his novel *The Double*, in which he maintains the suspense by hinting, but never letting on, whether Mr. Golyadkin's doppelgänger is a walking, talking, and actual double, or a mental double, the figment of the brain's irrational anxieties and fears.[35] Though *The Double* failed to achieve success or acclaim in Dostoyevsky's lifetime, its publication signaled the arrival of psychology and the mental life into, if not the mainstream, at

---

it, it calls into being by its antagonism the opposing force of that which it confronts, and consequently the *action* is immediately associated with the *reaction*. With this analysis of the forces rendered necessary by dramatic action, we have at length arrived at the notion of the Ideal as a fully defined process.

34 Newton, *Mathematical Principles of Natural Philosophy*, in *The World of Physics*, vol. 1, 499.

35 Dostoyevsky, *The Double*, in *Notes from Underground, The Double*, trans. Jessie Coulson.

least the fringes of the mainstream.[36] Forty-four years later, however, psychology had entered and become entrenched in the mainstream. When Hamsun's *Hunger* was published in 1890, a work similar to *The Double* in that it was, in the author's words, "an attempt to describe the strange, peculiar life of the mind, the mysteries of the nerves in a starving body," it turned Hamsun into an overnight sensation.[37] Is it a surprise then, that Nietzsche's theory of tragedy, which was published in 1872, grounds tragedy in the phenomenon of what he terms the Apollinian and the Dionysian, conflicting states of mind where either the "ego" and the will prevails or where the rational mind is overcome by intoxication, dance, and ecstasy?[38] Nietzsche defines tragedy neither by its final effect—as Aristotle did—nor by its internal structures—as the French Academy did. Like Hegel, he finds a conflict within tragedy, but whereas Hegel's conflict involved colliding masses, Nietzsche's conflict between the Apollinian and the Dionysian has become massless, for the Apollinian and the Dionysian represent artistic "phenomena" or "impulses."[39] Tragedy to Nietzsche has become a "psychological question,"

---

36 On the reception to *The Double*, see Coulson, introduction to *Notes from Underground, The Double*, by Fyodor Dostoyevsky, 7-9.

37 Hamsun, *Hunger*, trans. Sverre Lyngstad. On the reception to *Hunger*, see Lyngstad, introduction to *Hunger*, by Knut Hamsun, vii-viii.

38 On the definitions of the "Apollinian" and the "Dionysian," see Nietzsche, *The Birth of Tragedy*, trans. Walter Kaufmann, sections 1-5.

39 On the Apollonian and Dionysian as "phenomena," see ibid., section 1; as "impulses" see section 4.

a mental image of the mind at conflict with itself.[40] When a term has lost everything, it looks for meaning everywhere, and often grounds itself to the genius of its age.

My theory of risk theatre is a product of the present age, a time fascinated with uncertainty and risk. In the beginning of the twentieth century, Planck, Heisenberg, Schrödinger, and the founders of quantum theory shook the foundations of the clockwork Newtonian cosmos by postulating that uncertainty is an integral, ubiquitous, and irreducible aspect of reality. Their claims prompted Einstein, Bohr, and Hawking to debate not only whether "God plays dice" or "God does not play dice," but also *where* the dice are thrown.[41] This age has seen the deterministic universe where Laplace's demon

---

40   On tragedy as a "psychological question" or "a question for psychiatrists," see ibid., "Attempt at Self-Criticism," section 4.

41   In a letter to Max Born, in *The Born-Einstein Letters*, trans. Irene Born, September 7, 1944 Einstein writes:

> We have become Antipodean in our scientific expectations. You believe in the God who plays dice, and I in complete law and order in a world which objectively exists, and which I, in a wildly speculative way, am trying to capture. I firmly believe, but I hope that someone will discover a more realistic way, or rather a more tangible basis than it has been my lot to find. Even the great initial success of the quantum theory does not make me believe in the fundamental dice-game, although I am well aware that our younger colleagues interpret this as a consequence of senility. No doubt the day will come when we will see whose instinctive attitude was the correct one.

See also Einstein, qtd. in Hermanns, *Einstein and the Poet*, 58: "As I have said so many times, God doesn't play dice with the world." Hawking, "Does God Play Dice?" (lecture, n.p., 1999) suggests that God is an "inveterate gambler" and continues by saying that "not

could use classical mechanics to calculate the precise location and momentum for every particle in the universe forwards and backwards indefinitely give way to Heisenberg's uncertainty principle and the principle of wave-particle duality.[42]

The proliferation of technology in the twentieth century also proliferated risks greater than those the world has ever confronted. In the search for the perfect weapon, scientists have created bombs capable of destroying civilization many times over. In the search for perfect power, engineers have built nuclear reactors without containment buildings, along fault lines, in tsunami prone districts, and sometimes, as though to

only does God definitely play dice, but He sometimes confuses us by throwing them where they can't be seen."

42   By demonstrating the indeterminate structure of reality at the atomic and subatomic levels, the Heisenberg Uncertainty Principle and the principle of wave-particle duality rule out the possibility that Laplace's demon could use classical mechanics to work out a universal chain of causation. "Laplace's demon" is the name given to the all-knowing entity in Laplace's thought experiment which attempts to show that, given sufficient processing power, both the distant past and future could be extrapolated from a perfect understanding of the present. See Laplace, *A Philosophical Essay on Probabilities*, trans. F. W. Truscott and F. L. Emory, 4:

We ought then to regard the present state of the universe as the effect of its anterior state and as the cause of the one which is to follow. Given for one instant an intelligence which could comprehend all the forces by which nature is animated and the respective situation of the beings who compose it—an intelligence sufficiently vast to submit these data to analysis—it would embrace in the same formula the movements of the greatest bodies of the universe and those of the lightest atom; for it, nothing would be uncertain and the future, as the past, would be present to its eyes.

dare God, along fault lines in tsunami prone areas.[43] In the search for perfect wealth, hedge funds have leveraged their assets 100:1 to pick up, as one observer remarked, "nickels in front of bulldozers."[44] In 1998, the blowup of the Long-Term Capital Management hedge fund—run by not less than two Nobel Prize winners—threatened to bring down the entire global financial system.[45] In the search for the perfect crop, bioengineers have developed genetically modified organisms which can either eradicate famine by increasing yields or create famine by short-circuiting the food supply. Because of advancements in technology, yesterday's *local* risks are today's *global* risks. Heretofore, the casualties of war were local; today a nuclear winter looms over all seven continents. Heretofore, the consequences of earthquakes and tsunamis were local;

---

43   The Diablo Canyon Power Plant in California is situated on the shores of the Pacific Ocean and encircled by the Hosgri, Los Osos, Shoreline, and San Luis Bay faults. See Baker, "Nuclear Power's Last Stand in California: Will Diablo Canyon Die?" *San Francisco Chronicle*, November 14, 2015. The Metsamor Nuclear Power Plant in Armenia lacks a containment building and is considered one of the world's most dangerous, see Lavelle and Garthwaite, "Is Armenia's Nuclear Power Plant the World's Most Dangerous?" *National Geographic*, April 14, 2011.

44   Lowenstein, *When Genius Failed: The Rise and Fall of Long-Term Capital Management*, 102. In the attempt to increase returns, hedge funds would often leverage their assets, using borrowed money to make investments. The downside of leverage is that losses become more damaging, since the borrowed money must still be repaid.

45   Robert Merton and Myron Scholes, two of the founding partners, ironically won the Nobel Memorial Prize in Economic Science in 1997 just as the first cracks in their trading strategies were appearing. See ibid., 96-120.

Fukushima demonstrates how global the risks are today. Heretofore, financial losses were local; today a miscalculation in the offices of a Greenwich, Connecticut hedge fund can rock the world. Heretofore, blights impacted villages; today the risks and rewards of using genetically modified crops impacts the world at large. Today is a risk age because the scale of technology to do good or to do evil has increased, and continues to increase, by powers of ten.[46] As the inhabitants of the risk age and as the custodians of future ages, it is our moral obligation to understand upside risk and downside risk, the value and ruin of risk, the forms the unexpected takes, and the impact of unintended consequences. Risk theatre is tragic theory for today's risk age because the stories of Macbeth, Eteocles, and Oedipus force us to examine the meaning of risk, the likelihood of the unexpected, and the impact of unintended consequences. Like Nietzsche's psychological theory of tragedy or Hegel's mechanistic theory, risk theatre emerges today—if not by my hand, then I would think by another's hand—because its time is now.

Though the idea of risk theatre developed out of twentieth and twenty-first century themes, I believe that it will stand the test of time. From Aeschylus onwards, images of dice and references to gambling have been common in tragic drama. Tragedy has shown interest in uncertainty from day one.

Risk theatre's other major claim is that the stage is the place where audiences go to see how much honour is worth, what the price of friendship is, and how much they will pay

---

46   For an interesting statistic, see Goldin and Kutarna, *Age of Discovery*, 4: "Scientists alive today outnumber all scientists who ever lived up to 1980."

for power and glory. As the Duchess' parable of the salmon and the dogfish attests, my claim that tragedy values life by risking life is likewise grounded in the text:

> DUCHESS. I prithee who is greatest, can you tell?
> Sad tales befit my woe: I'll tell you one.
> A salmon, as she swam unto the sea
> Met with a dog-fish who encounters her
> With this rough language: "Why art thou so bold
> To mix thyself with our high state of floods,
> Being no eminent courtier, but one
> That for the calmest and fresh time o'th'year
> Dost live in shallow rivers, rank'st thyself
> With silly smelts and shrimps? And darest thou
> Pass by our dog-ship without reverence?"
> "O," quoth the salmon, "sister be at peace:
> Thank Jupiter we both have passed the net,
> Our value never can be truly known
> Till in the fisher's basket we be shown.
> I'th' market my price may be the higher,
> Even when I am nearest to the cook, and fire."
> So, to great men, the moral may be stretched:
> "Men oft are valued high, when th'are
>   most wretched."[47]

Risk theatre may be a new term, but tragedy, from its beginnings through to the present day, has always been, in its own way, an eternal theatre of risk.

---

47   Webster, *The Duchess of Malfi*, 3.5.119–37.

If the historian believes in inquiry, the philosopher in reason, and the comedian in laughter, what does the tragedian believe? Here is what my idea of what a twenty-first century tragedian would say:

> Tragedy is risk theatre. Risk theatre reveals the value of the all-too-human by inviting heroes to play at the no-limit table.

> Each act of risk theatre represents an act of gambling. The hero's temptation leads to the wager. The wager in turn leads to the cast. If the cycle plays out once, it is a standalone tragedy. If the cycle occurs in succession, it is a perpetual-motion tragedy. If many cycles play out concurrently, then parallel-motion tragedy results.

> Depending on how the troika of temptation, wager, and cast are set within the play, tragedy plays out at different tempi. Gradual tragedies proceed like clockwork. Backloaded tragedies end at a frenetic pace. Frontloaded tragedies begin with a bang and end in reflection.

> The myth of the price you pay forms my foundation myth. There are many heads, but only one crown. To gain the crown involves placing something of equal value at risk. Life, the soul, honour, dignity, love, friendship, and family can be offered in pledge to roll the dice. Price discovery takes place

as the bets are placed. The bet forms an equal sign between what is staked and what is at stake.

The seven commonplaces of tragedy furnish the spectacle of risk theatre and motivate heroes to go big or go home. When the heroes go big, audiences flock to see my show.

To ensure that the price is paid, I waylay heroes with the unexpected. Heroes are like sports cars— fancy red sports cars. The unexpected is a brick wall. The unexpected fills audiences with awe and wonder: awe at the collision and wonder at how it could have happened despite all of the precautions.

In tragedy, life is elevated by sacrifice; life finds its value through sacrifice. Instead of being commod- itized, life is aestheticized. Tragedy gets at the very essence of human experience by binding sufferers together. When audiences desire to see the greatest show on earth, they go to see risk theatre.

In this book, I have laid out a model of tragedy. Models are important because they help us understand. If we wish to understand the motions of planets, we build models of the solar system. If we wish to understand global warming, we build climate change models. If we wish to understand economics, we draw models of supply and demand. Then we test these models to see if they get it right. If the geocentric, or earth-centred model explains the motions of planets, then great. If not, to achieve a higher understanding, we replace it with a heliocentric, or sun-centred model. When a model gets it right, our understanding increases.

Just as the motions of Mercury, Mars, and Venus are to the heliocentric model, so are the works of Aeschylus, Shakespeare, and O'Neill to the risk theatre model. By observing the dramatic trajectories of Eteocles, Macbeth, and Lavinia, we can see whether risk theatre gets it right. If it can be demonstrated that each dramatic act is also a gambling act that triggers highly improbable events, then it may be said that risk theatre adds to our understanding of drama.

It is not, however, just our understanding of the dramatic process that is at stake. In closing, I wish to impress upon you that, just as risk theatre is a model of tragedy, *tragedy itself is a model of life*. Tragedy is a tool where we model life to arrive at a higher understanding of life. But we only arrive at a higher understanding if tragedy gets it right. How do we know if tragedy gets it right?—we can find out by identifying and verifying its presuppositions.

Just as the heliocentric model presupposes that the solar system is sun-centred and proceeds from this assumption, the tragic model likewise proceeds from a set of presuppositions. First, it presupposes that, in life, more things can happen than what we project, predict, and forecast will happen. Second, it presupposes that the "more things that happen" happen more frequently than we expect. And third, it presupposes that grievous harm for individuals and communities result when these "more things" happen.

To bring us to a higher understanding, tragedy simu-lates these presuppositions on the stage. It dramatizes the temptation, wager, and cast to show how gambling acts can trigger risk events. It aestheticizes opportunity cost and the debt to nature to reveal the value of all the human assets laid in pledge. It pits the best and the brightest against fate, chance, black swans, and unknown unknowns to demonstrate the absolute fragility of human endeavour. And, to show how the "more things that happen" can happen more often than we expect, it brings about the unexpected, low-probability outcome, *every time*. When you least expect it, Birnam Wood comes to Dunsinane Hill.

But, how useful are tragedy's dramatizations? Is tragedy that art that draws us higher, brings us to a more perfect understanding of life? That depends, in part, on whether it gets its initial presuppositions right. Just as we can test the heliocentric model by observing the path of the planets, we can test tragedy's presuppositions by observing life, which is, in the end, art's crucible.

How can we test the tragic model against life? First, we narrow down the great expanse of life to see whether tragedy's presuppositions ring true. The stock market, with its multitude of participants and wealth of data makes for a useful proxy of life. The stock market is a microcosm of life because, on the trading floors and computer terminals, many individuals and organizations come together to act and react with one another. By looking at the stock market, we can test tragedy's presuppositions, one by one.

First, we ask whether more things happen in the stock market than what the experts project, predict, and forecast will happen. The South Sea Bubble, the Great Depression, Black Monday, the Dot-Com Bust, and the Great Recession provide memorable examples of "more things that happen." Did Newton not say after being blindsided by the South Sea Bubble that: "I can calculate the movement of the stars but not the madness of men"?[48] In the days leading up to the Great Depression, did celebrity Yale economist Irving Fisher not say that stock prices have reached "what looks like a permanently high plateau"?[49] In the days leading up to the Dot-Com Bust, did experts not say that the "new economy" justified the extreme valuations of tech stocks? Did anyone foresee that on Black Monday, August 19, 1987, the Dow would fall 29.2 percent? And, did Federal Reserve Chairman Ben Bernanke not say, as the Great Recession began to unfold, that the subprime mortgage collapse was "likely to be contained"?[50] These examples collectively illustrate how more things can happen than what we think will happen.

Next, we ask whether the "more things that happen" happen more frequently than we expect. Here, the stock market, with its wealth of data, provides a clear answer. According to standard financial models, the odds of a 6.8 percent decline in the stock market in one day are one in twenty million. The odds of a 7.7 percent decline in one day are one in fifty billion. The odds of three separate declines in one month of 3.5 percent or greater are one in five-hundred billion. And finally, the odds of a 29.2 percent decline in one

---

48   Newton, quoted in Thies, *Global Economics*, 187.

49   Fisher, "Fisher Sees Stocks Permanently High," *New York Times*, October 16, 1929.

50   The Economic Outlook: Hearing Before the Joint Economic Committee, U.S. Congress, March 28, 2007 (statement of Chairman Ben S. Bernanke).

day are a one in 10^{50} event. The odds are so improbable that it would be amazing to witness one such fall in a millennium, let alone all of them in a generation.

But what do the actual stock market records reveal? On August 31, 1998, the Dow fell 6.8 percent. According to standard financial models, such a decline should happen once every 80,000 or so years. On October 27, 1997, it fell 7.7 percent. A decline of this magnitude should happen once every 200 million years. The month of August 1998 witnessed three separate declines: 3.5 percent, 4.4 percent, and then 6.8 percent: this is a one in 2 billion year event. And then, on Black Monday, it fell 29.2 percent. Such a fall is so improbable that it lies outside the realm of belief. These examples collectively illustrate how the "more things that happen" happen more frequently—much more frequently—than we expect.[51]

Finally, we ask whether grievous losses result when more things happen than what we expect will happen. Perhaps the South Sea Bubble of 1720 has been all but forgotten, and the Great Depression is but a distant memory. But some of us, I think, recall the mayhem of Black Monday, and most of us know someone who has lost a bundle in the Dot-Com Bust or the Great Recession. Even if some of these collapses seem far away, they collectively illustrate how, and for a long time, when more things happen than what we think will happen, individuals and communities alike suffer grievous losses.

---

51   The odds of stock market declines based on the standard Gaussian model are taken from Mandelbrot and Hudson, *The (mis)Behavior of Markets*, 3-4 and 279n.4.

The stock market shows us how the most improbable and devastating events happen with much greater frequency than we expect. If we allow that the stock market is a microcosm of life, then it is with rising confidence that we can say that the tragic model reflects reality. After all, tragedy is also full of improbable, unforeseeable, and catastrophic events. The implication of this is important, as it means that tragedy, by forever dramatizing risk, adds to our understanding of risk. And I think that tragedy, because it adds to our understanding of such a captivating and elusive concept, has a claim of being the greatest show on earth.

BIBLIOGRAPHY

Aeschylus. *Agamemnon, Libation-Bearers, Eumenides, Fragments*. Translated by Herbert Weir Smyth. Loeb Classical Library 146. Cambridge, MA: Harvard University Press, 1999.

———. *The Oresteian Trilogy*. Translated by Philip Vellacott. Baltimore: Penguin, 1959.

———. *Prometheus Bound and Other Plays*. Translated by Philip Vellacott. London: Penguin, 1961.

———. *Seven Against Thebes*. Translated by Anthony Hecht and Helen Bacon. New York: Oxford University Press, 1973.

———. *Suppliant Maidens, Persians, Prometheus, Seven Against Thebes*. Translated by Herbert Weir Smyth. Loeb Classical Library 145. Cambridge, MA: Harvard University Press, 1999.

Abel, Lionel. *Metatheatre: A New View of Dramatic Form*. New York: Hill and Wang, 1963.

Albert the Great. *De generatione et corruptione*. In *Opera omnia*. Vol. 4. Edited by Auguste Borgnet. Paris: Vivès, 1890.

Anonymous. *A Warning for Fair Women*. Edited by A. F. Hopkinson. London: M. E. Sims & Co., 1904.

Apollodorus. *The Library of Greek Mythology*. Translated by Robin Hard. Oxford: Oxford University Press, 1997.

Apuleius. *The Golden Ass*. Translated by Jack Lindsay. Bloomington: Indiana University Press, 1962.

Aristophanes. *Four Plays by Aristophanes*. Translated by William Arrowsmith, Richmond Lattimore, and Douglass Parker. New York: Meridian, 1994.

Aristotle, *On the Heavens*. Translated by W. K. C. Guthrie. Loeb Classical Library 338. Cambridge, MA: Harvard University Press, 1939.

———. Longinus, Demetrius. *Poetics, On the Sublime, On Style*. Translated by Stephen Halliwell, W. H. Fyfe, Doreen C. Innes, W. Rhys Roberts. Revised by Donald Russell. Loeb Classical Library 199. Cambridge, MA: Harvard University Press, 1995.

———. *Politics*. Translated by H. Rackham. Loeb Classical Library 264. Cambridge, MA: Harvard University Press, 1932.

Athenaeus. *The Deipnosophists*. Translated by C. B. Gulick. Loeb Classical Library 224. Cambridge, MA: Harvard University Press, 1929.

Atkinson, Brooks J. Review of *Strange Interlude* by Eugene O'Neill. Directed by Philip Moeller. John Golden Theatre, New York. *New York Times*, January 31, 1928.

———. Review of *Strange Interlude* by Eugene O'Neill. Directed by Philip Moeller. John Golden Theatre, New York. *New York Times*, May 13, 1928.

Augustine. *The City of God*. Translated by Marcus Dods. New York: Random House, 2000.

Aurelius. *Meditations with Selected Correspondence*. Translated by Robin Hard. Oxford: Oxford University Press, 2011.

Averroës. *Averroes' Middle Commentary on Aristotle's Poetics*. Translated by Charles E. Butterworth. Princeton: Princeton University Press, 1986.

Baker, David R. "Nuclear Power's Last Stand in California: Will Diablo Canyon Die?" *San Francisco Chronicle*. November 14, 2015.

Barrett, W. S. *Euripides, Hippolytos*. Oxford: Clarendon Press, 1964.

Benjamin, Walter. *The Origin of German Tragic Drama*. Translated by John Osborne. London: Verso, 1998.

Bernstein, Peter L. *Against the Gods: The Remarkable Story of Risk*. New York: John Wiley & Sons, 1996.

Boethius. *The Consolation of Philosophy*. Translated by V. E. Watts. Harmondsworth: Penguin, 1969.

Bolt, Robert. *A Man for All Seasons*. New York: Random House, 1960.

Born, Hedwig, Max Born, and Albert Einstein. *The Born-Einstein Letters: The Correspondence Between Albert Einstein and Max and Hedwig Born 1916-1955*. Translated by Irene Born. New York: Walker, 1971.

Brecht, Bertold. "A Short Organum for the Theatre." In *Brecht on Theatre: The Development of an Aesthetic*, translated by John Willett, 179-205. New York: Hill and Wang, 1964.

Buchanan, Mark. *Ubiquity: Why Catastrophes Happen*. New York: Three Rivers Press, 2000.

Burns, Robert. *The Complete Illustrated Poems, Songs & Ballads*. London: Chancellor Press, 1990. First Published 1965 by J. M. Dent & Co.

Calame, Claude. *Masks of Authority: Fiction and Pragmatics in Ancient Greek Poetics*. Translated by Peter M. Burk. Ithaca: Cornell University Press, 2005.

Chaucer, *Canterbury Tales*. Translated by David Wright. Oxford: Oxford University Press, 1998.

Cicero. *Cicero on the Emotions: Tusculan Disputations 3 and 4*. Translated by Margaret Graver. Chicago: University of Chicago Press, 2002.

———. *On Old Age, On Friendship, On Divination*. Translated by W. A. Falconer. Loeb Classical Library 154. Cambridge, MA: Harvard University Press, 1923.

Corneille, Pierre. *The Cid, Cinna, The Theatrical Illusion*. Translated by John Cairncross. London: Penguin, 1975.

———. "Discourse on Tragedy and of the Methods of Treating It, According to Probability and Necessity." In *Dramatic Essays of the Neoclassic Age*, edited by Henry Hitch Adams and Baxter Hathaway, 2-34. New York: Benjamin Blom, 1965. First Published 1947 by Columbia University Press.

———. "Of the Three Unities of Action, Time, and Place." In *The Continental Model: Selected French Critical Essays of the Seventeenth Century in English Translation*, edited by Scott Elledge and Donald Schier, translated by Donald Schier, 101-15. Rev. ed. Ithaca, NY: Cornell University Press, 1970.

———. "On the Uses and Elements of Dramatic Poetry." In *European Theories of the Drama*, edited by Barrett

H. Clark and Henry Popkin, translated by Beatrice Stewart MacClintock, 100-10. Rev. ed. New York: Crown, 1965.

Coulson, Jessie. Introduction to *Notes from Underground, The Double*, by Fyodor Dostoyevsky, 7-12. Translated by Jessie Coulson. London: Penguin, 1972.

Dante. *De vulgari eloquentia*. Translated by A. G. Howell. London: Rebel Press, 1973.

David, F. N. *Games, Gods and Gambling: The Origins and History of Probability and Statistical Ideas from the Earliest Times to the Newtonian Era*. New York: Hafner, 1962.

Davies, Paul. *The Cosmic Blueprint: New Discoveries in Nature's Creative Ability to Order the Universe*. Philadelphia: Templeton Foundation, 2004. First published 1988 by Simon and Schuster.

Dostoyevsky, Fyodor. *Notes from Underground, The Double*. Translated by Jessie Coulson. London: Penguin, 1972.

Dyson, Freeman. *The Scientist as Rebel*. New York: New York Review of Books, 2006.

Eddington, Arthur. *The Nature of the Physical World*, Ann Arbor: University of Michigan Press, 1958. First published 1928 by Cambridge University Press.

Eliot, T. S. *Murder in the Cathedral*. 4th ed. San Diego: Harcourt, 1963.

Esslin, Martin. *Brecht: The Man and His Work*. Rev. ed. Garden City, NY: Doubleday, 1971.

———. *The Theatre of the Absurd*. Garden City, NY: Doubleday, 1961.

Euripides. *Bacchae, Iphigenia at Aulis, Rhesus*. Edited and Translated by David Kovacs. Loeb Classical Library 495. Cambridge, MA: Harvard University Press, 2002.

———. *Children of Heracles, Hippolytus, Andromache, Hecuba*. Edited and Translated by David Kovacs. Loeb Classical Library 484. Cambridge, MA: Harvard University Press, 1995.

———. *Cyclops, Alcestis, Medea*. Edited and Translated by David Kovacs. Loeb Classical Library 12. Cambridge, MA: Harvard University Press, 2001.

Fisher, Irving. "Fisher Sees Stocks Permanently High." *New York Times*. October 16, 1929.

Ford, John. *'Tis Pity She's a Whore*. In *Six Renaissance Tragedies*. Edited by Colin Gibson. New York: Palgrave, 1997.

Fukuyama, Francis. *The End of History and the Last Man*. New York: Avon Books, 1993. First published 1992 by Free Press.

Geiringer, Karl. *Haydn: A Creative Life in Music*. 2nd ed. Berkeley: University of California Press, 1968.

Goethe, Johann Wolfgang von. *Faust: Part One*. Translated by Philip Wayne. London: Penguin, 1949.

———. *Plays: Egmont, Iphigenia in Tauris, Torquato Tasso*. Edited by Frank G. Ryder. Translated by Anna Swanwick, Frank G. Ryder, and Charles E. Passage. The German Library 20. New York: Continuum, 2006.

Goldin, Ian and Chris Kutarna. *Age of Discovery: Navigating the Risks and Rewards of Our New Renaissance*. New York: St. Martin's Press, 2016.

Hacking, Ian. *The Emergence of Probability: A Philosophical Study of Early Ideas About Probability Induction and*

Statistical Inference. 2nd ed. Cambridge: Cambridge University Press, 2006.

Hawking, Stephen. "Does God Play Dice?" Public lecture. n.p., 1999. Stephen Hawking's official website, accessed September 23, 2017, http://www.hawking.org.uk/does-god-play-dice.html

Hayman, Ronald. *Brecht: A Biography.* New York: Oxford University Press, 1983.

Haydn, Franz Joseph. *The Creation.* Tölz Boys' Choir and the Tafelmusik Baroque Orchestra. Bruno Weil. With Ann Monoyios, Jörg Hering, and Harry Van der Kamp. Recorded 1993. Sony S2K 57965, 1994, 2 compact discs.

Hegel, Georg Wilhelm Friedrich. *Hegel on Tragedy.* Edited by Anne and Henry Paolucci. 2001 ed. Smyrna, DE: Griffon House, 2001. First published 1962 by Doubleday.

———. *The Philosophy of History.* Rev. ed. Translated by J. Sibree. New York: Wiley Book, 1944.

Hermann, Fritz-Gregor. "Eteocles' Decision in Aeschylus' *Seven against Thebes.*" In *Tragedy and Archaic Greek Thought,* edited by Douglas Cairns, 39-80. Swansea: Classical Press of Wales, 2013.

Hermanns, William. *Einstein and the Poet: In Search of the Cosmic Man.* Brookline Village, MA: Branden Press, 1983.

Herodotus. *The Histories.* Translated by Aubrey de Sélincourt. Rev. ed. London: Penguin, 1996.

Hesiod. *Theogony, Works and Days, Shield.* Translated by Apostolos N. Athanassakis. 2nd ed. Baltimore: Johns Hopkins University Press, 2004.

Homer. *The Iliad of Homer.* Translated by Richmond Lattimore. Chicago: University of Chicago Press, 1951.

———. *The Odyssey of Homer.* Translated by Richmond Lattimore. New York: HarperCollins, 1999. First published 1967 by Harper & Row.

(Homer). *The Homeric Hymns: A Verse Translation.* Translated by Thelma Sargent. New York: W. W. Norton & Company, 1975.

Horace. *The Complete Works of Horace.* Translated by Charles E. Passage. New York: Frederick Ungar, 1983.

Ibsen, Henrik. *Four Major Plays.* Translated by James McFarlane and Jens Arup. Oxford: Oxford University Press, 1998.

Isidore of Seville. *The Etymologies of Isidore of Seville.* Translated by Stephen A. Barney, W. J. Lewis, J. A. Beach, and Oliver Berghof. Cambridge: Cambridge University Press, 2006.

Jessup, Richard. *The Cincinnati Kid.* Boston: Little, Brown, 1963

Kaplan, Michael and Ellen Kaplan. *Chances Are… Adventures in Probability.* New York: Penguin, 2006.

Kaufmann, Walter. *Tragedy and Philosophy.* Garden City, NY: Anchor Books, 1969. First published 1968 by Doubleday.

Keller, Helen. *Peace at Eventide.* London: Methuen & Co., 1932.

Kelly, Henry Ansgar. *Ideas and Forms of Tragedy from Aristotle to the Middle Ages.* Cambridge Studies in Medieval Literature 18. Cambridge: Cambridge University Press, 1993.

Kierkegaard, Søren. *Papers and Journals: A Selection.* Translated by Alastair Hannay. London: Penguin, 1996.

Kyd, Thomas. *The Spanish Tragedy.* In *Six Renaissance Tragedies.* Edited by Colin Gibson. New York: Palgrave, 1997.

Laplace, Pierre Simon. *A Philosophical Essay on Probabilities.* Translated by F. W. Truscott and F. L. Emory. New York: Dover, 1951.

Lavelle, Marianne and Josie Garthwaite. "Is Armenia's Nuclear Plant the World's Most Dangerous?" *National Geographic.* April 14, 2011.

Littlewood, J. E. *Littlewood's Miscellany.* Edited by Béla Bollobás. Cambridge: Cambridge University Press, 1986. First published 1953 as *A Mathematician's Miscellany* by Methuen & Co.

Livy. *History of Rome: Books 21-22.* Translated by B. O. Foster. Loeb Classical Library 233. Cambridge, MA: Harvard University Press, 1929.

Lowe, Melanie. "Creating Chaos in Haydn's *Creation.*" *Online Journal of the Haydn Society of North America* 3.1 (Spring 2013): 1-35. https://www.rit.edu/affiliate/haydn/creating-chaos-haydns-creation

Lowenstein, Roger. *When Genius Failed: The Rise and Fall of Long-Term Capital Management.* Rev. ed. New York: Random House, 2011.

Machiavelli, Niccolò. *The History of Florence and Other Selections.* Edited by Myron P. Gilmore. Translated by Judith A. Rawson. New York: Washington Square Press, 1970.

Malamud, Bruce D., Gleb Morein, and Donald L. Turcotte. "Forest Fires: An Example of Self-Organized Critical Behavior." *Science* 281, issue 5384 (18 September 1998): 1840-2. doi:10.1126/science.281.5384.1840.

Mandelbrot, Benoit and Richard L. Hudson. *The (mis) Behavior of Markets: A Fractal View of Financial Turbulence.* New York: Basic, 2004.

Marlowe, Christopher. *The Complete Plays.* Edited by J. B. Steane. London: Penguin, 1969.

———. *Doctor Faustus: A- and B-texts (1604, 1616).* Edited by David Bevington and Eric Rasmussen. The Revels Plays. Manchester: Manchester University Press, 1993.

Marx, Karl and Friedrich Engels. *The Communist Manifesto.* Translated by Samuel Moore. London: Penguin, 2002.

Menander. *Plays and Fragments.* Translated by Norma Miller. London: Penguin, 1987.

Middleton, Thomas. *The Revenger's Tragedy.* In *Six Renaissance Tragedies.* Edited by Colin Gibson. New York: Palgrave, 1997.

Middleton, Thomas and William Rowley. *The Changeling.* In *Six Renaissance Tragedies.* Edited by Colin Gibson. New York: Palgrave, 1997.

Miller, Arthur. *Death of a Salesman.* Jubilee ed. New York: Penguin, 1999.

———. "Tragedy and the Common Man." In *The Theater Essays of Arthur Miller,* edited by Robert A. Martin, 3-7. New York: Viking Press, 1978.

Milton, John. *Samson Agonistes*. Edited by A. W. Verity. Cambridge: Cambridge University Press, 1925.

Minnich, Richard A. "Fire Mosaics in Southern California and Northern Baja California." *Science* 219, issue 4590 (18 March 1983): 1287-94. doi:10.1126/science.219.4590.1287.

Murray, Oswyn. "Life and Society in Classical Greece." In *The Oxford History of Greece and the Hellenistic World*, edited by John Boardman, Jasper Griffin, and Oswyn Murray, 240-76. Oxford: Oxford University Press, 1986.

Mussato. *Ecerinis*. In *Humanist Tragedies*, translated by Gary R. Grund, The I Tatti Renaissance Library 45, 2-47. Cambridge, Massachusetts: Harvard University Press, 2011.

Newton, Isaac. *Mathematical Principles of Natural Philosophy*. In *The World of Physics: A Small Library of the Literature of Physics from Antiquity to the Present*. Vol. 1. Edited by Jefferson Hane Weaver, Lloyd Motz, and Dale McAdoo. New York: Simon and Schuster, 1987.

Nietzsche, Friedrich. *The Birth of Tragedy and The Case of Wagner*. Translated by Walter Kaufmann. New York: Vintage, 1967.

Norton, Thomas and Thomas Sackville. *Gorboduc*. In *The Minor Elizabethan Drama: Pre-Shakespearean Tragedies*. Vol. 1. Everyman's Library 491. London: J. M. Dent and Sons, 1949. First published 1910 by J. M. Dent and Sons.

O'Neill, Eugene. *Long Day's Journey Into Night*. 2nd ed. New Haven: Yale University Press, 1989.

————. *Three Plays.* New York: Vintage, 1995.

O'Neill, Patrick. *James O'Neill.* History of San Francisco Theater. Vol. 20. San Francisco: Writers' Program of the Works Projects Administration in Northern California, 1942.

Ovid. *The Art of Love, and Other Poems.* 2nd ed. Translated by J. H. Mozley. Loeb Classical Library 232. Cambridge, Massachusetts: Harvard University Press, 1979.

Pascal, Blaise. *Pensées.* Translated by A. J. Krailsheimer. Rev. ed. London: Penguin, 1995.

Plato. *Complete Works.* Edited by John Cooper. Indianapolis: Hackett Publishing Company, 1997.

Plautus. *Amphitryon, The Comedy of Asses, The Pot of Gold, The Two Bacchises, The Captives.* Edited and translated by Wolfgang de Melo. Loeb Classical Library 60. Cambridge, MA: Harvard University Press, 2011.

————. *Casina, The Casket Comedy, Curculio, Epidicus, The Two Menaechmusus.* Edited and translated by Wolfgang de Melo. Loeb Classical Library 61. Cambridge, MA: Harvard University Press, 2011.

————. *The Little Carthaginian, Pseudolus, The Rope.* Edited and translated by Wolfgang de Melo. Loeb Classical Library 260. Cambridge, MA: Harvard University Press, 2012.

Plutarch. *The Rise and Fall of Athens: Nine Greek Lives.* Translated by Ian Scott-Kilvert. London: Penguin, 1960.

Polybius. *The Rise of the Roman Empire.* Abridged ed. Translated by Ian Scott-Kilvert. London: Penguin, 1979.

Prigogine, Ilya. *From Being to Becoming: Time and Complexity in the Physical Sciences.* San Francisco: W. H. Freeman and Company, 1980.

Pushkin, Alexander. *The Queen of Spades.* In *The Greatest Gambling Stories Ever Told,* edited by Paul Lyons, translated by Ethel O. Bronstein, 113-36. Guilford: Lyons Press, 2002.

Racine, Jean. *Iphigenia, Phaedra, Athaliah.* Translated by John Cairncross. London: Penguin, 1970.

Rebel, Jean-Féry. *Les élémens.* The Academy of Ancient Music. Christopher Hogwood. Recorded June 1978. L'Oiseau-Lyre 001002702, 2007, compact disc.

Rembrandt. *Judas Returning the Thirty Silver Pieces.* 1629. Oil on Oak Panel, 79 x 102.3 cm. Mulgrave Castle, Lythe, North Yorkshire, England. Accessed on July 12, 2017. https://commons.wikimedia.org/wiki/File:Judas_Returning_the_Thirty_Silver_Pieces_-_Rembrandt.jpg.

Rodin, Auguste. *Rodin on Art and Artists: Conversations with Paul Gsell.* Translated by Romilly Fedden. New York: Dover, 1983.

Roisman, Hanna M. "The Messenger and Eteocles in the *Seven Against Thebes.*" *L'antiquité classique* 59 (1990) 17-36.

Safire, William. "On Language; In a New York Minute." *New York Times.* October 19, 1986.

Sahr, Robert. "Inflation Conversion Factors for Years 1774 to Estimated 2027." Accessed July 12, 2017. http://liberalarts.oregonstate.edu/spp/polisci/faculty-staff/robert-sahr/inflation-conversion-factors-years-1774-estimated-2024-dollars-recent-years/individual-year-conversion-factor-table-0.

Sambursky, Shmuel. "On the Possible and the Probable in Ancient Greece." *Osiris* 12 (1956) 35-48. doi: 10.1086/368595.

Schein, Seth. *The Mortal Hero: An Introduction to Homer's Iliad*. Berkeley: University of California Press, 1984.

Schiller, Friedrich. *Don Carlos and Mary Stuart*. Edited by Hilary Collier Sy-Quia. Translated by Hilary Collier Sy-Quia and Peter Oswald. Oxford: Oxford University Press, 1996.

———. *The Robbers and Wallenstein*. Translated by F. J. Lamport. London: Penguin, 1979.

Seneca. *Thyestes*. In *Oedipus, Agamemnon, Thyestes, Hercules on Oeta, Octavia*. Translated by John G. Fitch. Loeb Classical Library 78. Cambridge, MA: Harvard University Press, 2004.

Shakespeare. *Macbeth*. Directed by Rupert Goold. Arlington, VA: PBS Home Video, 2011. DVD, 158 min.

———. *The Riverside Shakespeare*. Edited by G. Blakemore Evans. Boston: Houghton Mifflin Company, 1974.

Smith, Adam. *The Wealth of Nations: Books I-III*. Edited by Andrew Skinner. London: Penguin, 1999.

Sophocles. *Electra and Other Plays*. Translated by E. F. Watling. London: Penguin, 1953.

———. *Oedipus rex*. Translated and adapted by William Butler Yeats. Directed by Tyrone Guthrie. Chatsworth, CA: Image, 1957. DVD, 88 min.

———. *The Three Theban Plays*. Translated by Robert Fagles. New York: Penguin, 1984.

Spengler, Oswald. *The Decline of the West.* Abridged ed. Edited by Arthur Helps and Helmut Werner. Translated by Charles Francis Atkinson. New York: Vintage, 2006.

Strindberg, August. *Miss Julie.* In *Miss Julie and Other Plays.* Translated by Michael Robinson. Oxford: Oxford University Press, 1998.

Suetonius. *The Twelve Caesars.* Translated by Robert Graves. Revised by Michael Grant. Rev. ed. London: Penguin, 2003.

Taleb, Nicholas Nassim. *Fooled by Randomness: The Hidden Role of Chance in Life and in the Markets.* 2nd ed. New York: Random House, 2005. First Published 2004 by Thomson/Texere.

Terence. *The Comedies.* Translated by Betty Radice. London: Penguin, 1976.

Tevis, Walter. *The Hustler.* New York: Harper & Brothers, 1959.

Thies, Clifford F. *Global Economics: A Holistic Approach.* Lanham: Lexington, 2018

Thomson, George. *Aeschylus and Athens: A Study in the Social Origins of Drama.* London: Lawrence & Wishart, 1916.

Thucydides. *History of the Peloponnesian War.* Rev. ed. Translated by Rex Warner. New York: Penguin, 1972.

Tierno, Michael. *Aristotle's Poetics for Screenwriters.* New York: Hyperion, 2002.

Webster, John. *The Duchess of Malfi.* Edited by Brian Gibbons. New Mermaids. 5th ed. London: Bloomsbury, 2014.

INDEX

Please note that the italicized "n" after a page reference refers to a footnote on that page.

N

ABOUT THE TYPE

This book was set in Berling. Designed in 1951 by Karl Erik Forsberg for the Typefoundry Berlingska Stilgjuteri AB in Lund, Sweden, it was released the same year in foundry type by H. Berthold AG. A classic old-face design, its generous proportions and inclined serifs make it highly legible.